Lecture Notes in Computer Science   **9585**

Commenced Publication in 1973
Founding and Former Series Editors:
Gerhard Goos, Juris Hartmanis, and Jan van Leeuwen

Marco Gavanelli · John Reppy (Eds.)

Practical Aspects of Declarative Languages

18th International Symposium, PADL 2016
St. Petersburg, FL, USA, January 18−19, 2016
Proceedings

 Springer

Editors
Marco Gavanelli
Dipartimento di Ingegneria
Università di Ferrara
Ferrara
Italy

John Reppy
University of Chicago
Chicago
USA

ISSN 0302-9743   ISSN 1611-3349   (electronic)
Lecture Notes in Computer Science
ISBN 978-3-319-28227-5   ISBN 978-3-319-28228-2   (eBook)
DOI 10.1007/978-3-319-28228-2

Library of Congress Control Number: 2015939925

LNCS Sublibrary: SL2 – Programming and Software Engineering

Printed on acid-free paper

This Springer imprint is published by SpringerNature
The registered company is Springer International Publishing AG Switzerland

Preface

Declarative languages build on sound theoretical bases to provide attractive frameworks for application development. These languages have been successfully applied to many different real-world situations, ranging from database management to active networks to software engineering to decision support systems.

New developments in theory and implementation have opened up new application areas. At the same time, applications of declarative languages to novel problems raise numerous interesting research issues. Well-known questions include designing for scalability, language extensions for application deployment, and programming environments. Thus, applications drive the progress in the theory and implementation of declarative systems, and benefit from this progress as well.

PADL is a forum for researchers and practitioners to present original work emphasizing novel applications and implementation techniques for all forms of declarative concepts, including, functional, logic, constraints, etc.

This book collects the contributions accepted for publication at the 18th International Symposium on Practical Aspects of Declarative Languages (PADL 2016), held in St. Petersburg, Florida, USA, during January 18–19, 2016.

Originally established as a workshop (PADL 1999 in San Antonio, Texas), the PADL series developed into a regular annual symposium; the preceding editions took place in San Antonio, Texas (1999), Boston, Massachusetts (2000), Las Vegas, Nevada (2001), Portland, Oregon (2002), New Orleans, Louisiana (2003), Dallas, Texas (2004), Long Beach, California (2005), Charleston, South Carolina (2006), Nice, France (2007), San Francisco, California (2008), Savannah, Georgia (2009), Madrid, Spain (2010), Austin, Texas (2012), Rome, Italy (2013), San Diego, California (2014), and Portland, Oregon (2015).

PADL 2016 was organized by the Association for Logic Programming (ALP), in collaboration with the Organizing Committees of the co-located events at the Symposium on Principles of Programming Languages (POPL 2016), the Department of Engineering at the University of Ferrara (Italy), and the Department of Computer Science at the University of Chicago (USA).

The conference received 17 submissions. Each paper was carefully reviewed by at least three members of the Program Committee. In all, 11 papers were selected and are presented in these proceedings.

The chairs wish to thank the reviewers for their careful work in selecting the best papers, the ALP and ACM for the support, and Gopal Gupta for his help with the organization.

January 2016

Marco Gavanelli
John Reppy

Organization

PADL 2016 was organized by the ALP (Association for Logic Programming).

Program Committee

Mario Alviano	University of Calabria, Italy
Lars Bergstrom	Mozilla Research, USA
Edwin Brady	University of St. Andrews, UK
Mats Carlsson	SICS, Sweden
Manuel Carro	Technical University of Madrid (UPM) and IMDEA Software Institute, Spain
Thomas Eiter	Vienna University of Technology, Austria
Thom Fruehwirth	University of Ulm, Germany
Marco Gavanelli	University of Ferrara, Italy
Geoffrey Mainland	Drexel University, USA
Enrico Pontelli	New Mexico State University, USA
John Reppy	University of Chicago, USA
Ricardo Rocha	University of Porto, Portugal
Torsten Schaub	University of Potsdam, Germany
Tom Schrijvers	KU Leuven, Belgium
Paul Tarau	University of North Texas, USA
Niki Vazou	University of California, San Diego, USA
Dimitrios Vytiniotis	Microsoft Research, UK
Daniel Winograd-Cort	Yale University, USA
Neng-Fa Zhou	CUNY Brooklyn College and Graduate Center, USA
Lukasz Ziarek	SUNY Buffalo, USA

Additional Reviewers

Beck, Harald	Reis, Rogério
Dao-Tran, Minh	Romero, Javier
Gebser, Martin	Saad, Aya
Karachalias, Georgios	Sharaf, Nada
Mantadelis, Theofrastos	Weinzierl, Antonius
Mariño, Julio	Zaki, Amira

Sponsoring Institutions

Association for Logic Programming
Università di Ferrara, Ferrara, Italy
University of Chicago, Chicago, USA

Contents

Constraint and Logic Programming

Using Constraint Logic Programming to Schedule Solar Array Operations
on the International Space Station 3
    Jan Jelínek and Roman Barták

The KB Paradigm and its Application to Interactive Configuration 13
    Van Hertum Pieter, Ingmar Dasseville, Gerda Janssens,
    and Marc Denecker

A GPU Implementation of the ASP Computation 30
    Agostino Dovier, Andrea Formisano, Enrico Pontelli, and Flavio Vella

The Picat-SAT Compiler 48
    Neng-Fa Zhou and Håkan Kjellerstrand

Functional Programming

Default Rules for Curry 65
    Sergio Antoy and Michael Hanus

Generic Matching of Tree Regular Expressions over Haskell Data Types 83
    Alejandro Serrano and Jurriaan Hage

A Size-Proportionate Bijective Encoding of Lambda Terms as Catalan
Objects Endowed with Arithmetic Operations 99
    Paul Tarau

Computing with Catalan Families, Generically 117
    Paul Tarau

Simplifying Probabilistic Programs Using Computer Algebra 135
    Jacques Carette and Chung-chieh Shan

Haskino: A Remote Monad for Programming the Arduino 153
    Mark Grebe and Andy Gill

From Monads to Effects and Back 169
    Niki Vazou and Daan Leijen

Author Index 187

Constraint and Logic Programming

Using Constraint Logic Programming to Schedule Solar Array Operations on the International Space Station

Jan Jelínek and Roman Barták[✉]

Faculty of Mathematics and Physics, Charles University in Prague,
Malostranské nám. 25, 118 00 Prague, Czech Republic
jelinek@ksi.mff.cuni.cz, bartak@ktiml.mff.cuni.cz

Abstract. Solar arrays are the main source of energy at the International Space Station (ISS). Most of the time they automatically track the sun, but some ISS operations impose additional constraints on the arrays and the arrays may need to be parked or even locked. These operations must be carefully planned to prevent thermal stresses, environmental contamination, and structural loads. This paper describes a novel approach to plan solar array operations on the ISS using constraint logic programming. Opposite to previous approaches, it assumes global optimization while still taking in account safety and operation constraints.

Keywords: Scheduling · Solar arrays · Space station · Constraints

1 Introduction

Space applications are demanding for complex operation and safety constraints and contain many objectives. This demand is even stronger for human space flight missions such as the International Space Station (ISS). In this paper we present a constraint-based planner for solar array operations on the ISS. Solar arrays at the ISS are designed to automatically track the sun, which is what they do most of the time. However, some ISS operations such as docking a spacecraft, extra vehicular activities, water dumps, thruster firings etc. impose additional constraints on solar array operations to prevent thermal stresses, environmental contamination, and structural loads. In such situations, solar arrays may need to be parked or even locked/latched, which must be planned in advance according to expected operations of the ISS.

Currently, the solar array planning problem is solved manually by a team of people known as PHALCONs (Power, Heating, and Lighting Controllers). It takes about four weeks to manually produce an ISS solar array operations plan for a typical four-week planning horizon. The Solar Array Constraint Engine (SACE), built on top of the AI planning system EUROPA [4], was proposed to automatically generate solar array operations plans subject to all operation constraints and user-configurable solution preferences [8]. The SACE uses an

© Springer International Publishing Switzerland 2016
M. Gavanelli and J. Reppy (Eds.): PADL 2016, LNCS 9585, pp. 3–12, 2016.
DOI: 10.1007/978-3-319-28228-2_1

approach similar to manual scheduling. It goes greedily from left to right and optimizes a given configuration according to fixed schedules of previous configurations. If it fails then it merges the current configuration with the previous one. The advantage is tractability of sub-problems solved, but in principle the schedule is suboptimal and may not be found at all even if a feasible plan exists.

To overcome the sub-optimality of SACE, we developed a novel constraint-based optimizer for scheduling solar array operations that does global optimization. In particular, we formulated the problem as a constraint satisfaction problem where the planning component is modeled using optional activities. Our approach and the SACE are the only two automated planners for this domain.

2   Problem Description

ISS solar array planning is a very complex problem with many constraints and objectives. In this section we briefly describe the core parts of the problem to illustrate this complexity. The problem formulation is taken mainly from the challenge domain at the International Competition on Knowledge Engineering for Planning and Scheduling 2012 [3]; more details can also be found in [8].

The ISS has eight solar arrays, each of which is mounted on a rotary joint called the Beta Gimbal Assembly (BGA). The solar arrays are split into two groups each of which consists of four solar arrays mounted via the Solar Array Rotary Joint (SARJ) to the station (Fig. 1). Thus each panel has two degrees of rotational freedom, though one degree of freedom is shared between the panels in the same group. Each rotary joint can be in exactly one mode: Autotrack, Park, or Lock (Latch for BGA), or the joint can turn between the modes. The state of each joint is also described by the angle of orientation (360 positions).

In the Autotrack mode, the onboard software automatically rotates the panel so its surface is pointing directly onto the sun to maximize energy generated – a known constant speed of rotation is assumed. The Autotrack mode must last at least 90 min. In the Park mode, a drive motor is engaged to maintain panel's current angle, while in the Lock and Latch modes, a physical barrier is used to

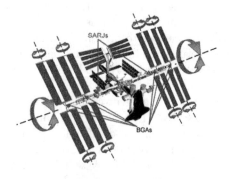

Fig. 1. Solar arrays connected via rotary joints to ISS (from [3]).

lock the panel in its current orientation. Transition into and out of Lock/Latch modes takes 20 min.

The input to the solar array planning problem consists of a sequence of configurations, where each configuration starts when the previous configuration finishes. This time may be flexible and in such a case the planner decides the appropriate time. This is the only situation when the groups of solar arrays interact; otherwise they can be scheduled independently. Each panel can be in exactly one mode in each configuration. The configuration also determines whether turning is disallowed (during docking, undocking, reboost, maneuver), allowed at the end of the configuration (approach, prop purge, water dump), or allowed both at the beginning and at the end (attitude hold). It also defines a maximum rotation speed for SARJs (it is fixed for BGAs) and a contingency mode when some constraints can be violated. Finally, there are other parameters of the configuration determining for a pair of BGA and SARJ a set of four soft constraints: Power Generation (P), Structural Load (L), Environmental Contamination (E), and Longeron Shadowing (S). Each of these constraints is expressed as a 360 ×360 table (Fig. 2) with three types of values: Green (preferred/best), Yellow (acceptable), and Red (infeasible in most situations/worst). The table is used as follows. If both BGA and SARJ are parked or locked/latched at some orientations then the value of the constraint is at the intersection of row and column corresponding to the orientations. If BGA (SARJ) is autotracking and SARJ (BGA) is parked or locked then the value of the constraint is the worst value in a row (column) defined by the orientation of SARJ (BGA). If both BGA and SARJ are autotracking then the value of the constraint is the worst value in the whole table. It is not allowed to use orientations with the red value for P, L, and S tables. Red value is allowed for the E table, but it is reflected in the quality of the plan. Turning of BGA can start only after turning of its SARJ finished and all BGAs (for a given SARJ) must start turning at the same time. Constraints imposed by the color tables are not assumed during turning.

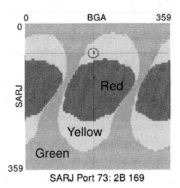

Fig. 2. A table with safety areas for orientation angles of SARJ and BGA (from [3]) (Color figure online).

The task is to determine for each joint in each configuration the following sequence of "activities":

- unlocking – transition out of lock/latch (optional)
- turning to the required orientation (optional)
- being in a selected mode
- turning to the next required orientation (optional)
- locking – transition into lock/latch (optional).

There might be some wait times between the "activities" (BGA turning waits until SARJ turning finishes). A joint can be in a selected mode in several consecutive configurations to satisfy the minimal duration constraint of the mode.

The plans are evaluated using four criteria. The most important criterion is color in the tables: table S first, then tables L and E, and finally table P (Fig. 5 shows the priority order). The second criterion is mode: Autotrack is preferred, followed by Park, and Lock/Latch to be last. Then, the number of changes in rotations should be minimized (the joint can rotate in positive and negative directions). Finally, the time spent in turning should be minimized. We are looking for a schedule such that no configuration can be scheduled better without worsening the schedule of another configuration.

3   Used Approach

It is possible to implement an ad-hoc algorithm to solve the problem. We used such an approach in another space-oriented project of planning Mars Express orbiter operations [5] and this project confirmed that ad-hoc approaches are not flexible and are hard to maintain. Solving approaches based on modeling the problem in some known solving formalism such as constraint satisfaction are much easier to maintain while keeping good runtime efficiency [6]. Therefore we propose to model the solar array operations planning problem as a constraint satisfaction problem. Based on our past experience we decided to use the `clpfd` library of SICStus Prolog [2] because the declarative character of Prolog makes modeling even more natural. Full technical details of the method are given in [1], we highlight here the critical ideas of the model and of the solving approach. First, we model the planning problem using optional activities. This transforms the planning problem (selection of activities) into a scheduling problem (time allocation of activities). Second, we use `table` and `case` constraints to encode the complex constraints. Finally, we use an iterative optimization approach.

3.1   The Core Model

The input of the problem consists of a sequence of configurations. Each configuration defines which constraints must be satisfied by the joints. In particular, color tables (Fig. 2) are specific for each configuration and for each joint and for example turning may be disallowed in some configurations. There are no time gaps between the configurations, but start times might be flexible and

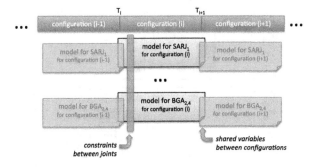

Fig. 3. The core structure of the constraint model.

then the planner decides also the exact start times. Of course the transitions between configurations must be consistent. In particular, the orientation of a panel at the end of configuration is identical to the orientation of the panel at the start of next configuration; if the joint is locked at one configuration then it remains locked until it is unlocked etc. These transition constraints are only between subsequent configurations. Hence we can model each configuration as a separate constraint satisfaction problem and the models of subsequent configurations share some variables. There are also constraints between the models of joints for the same configuration, for example, all BGAs must start turning at the same time. Figure 3 sketches the core structure of the complete constraint model. In the following sections, we will give some details of the model for a single joint in one configuration.

3.2 Variables

For each joint j on the side s in the configuration i we know that only the following activities (in this order) can be used: unlocking, initial (start) turning, being in a mode, final (end) turning, and locking. These activities follow each other with possible gaps between unlocking and turning at the start of configuration and between turning and locking at the end of configuration. Hence, it is enough to model the activities using their durations only as their start and completion times can easily be computed from the start of the configuration and from these durations. As some of these activities may not present, we use the idea of optional activities with possible zero durations. Figure 4 describes the schedule for a single configuration. Variables D represent durations of activities. The gaps between turning and locking/unlocking are modeled using variables D^S and D^F that indicate the duration between the start of configuration and the start of initial turning (D^S) and between the start of final turning and the end of configuration (D^F). In addition to duration variables, we also need variables indicating how much (in degrees) the joint rotates (variables R), what the actual orientation of the mode is (variable O; for the Autotrack mode it represents the orientation at the end), and what the mode in the configuration is (variable M). Variable T_i represents the start time of the configuration i.

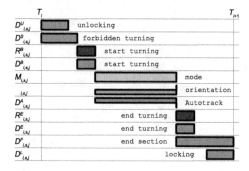

Fig. 4. Actions and variables modeling them in a single configuration for one joint.

3.3 Constraints

There are basically three types of constraints in the model. We need to model the allowed/preferred combinations of angles of BGA and its corresponding SARJ as described using color tables (Fig. 2). Then there are constraints related to particular modes for synchronizing activities within the configuration. Finally, there are constraints modeling the objectives via various cost functions.

Table Constraints. Recall that for each configuration, for each BGA and its corresponding SARJ there are four color tables indicating safety areas for rotation angles of each BGA and the corresponding SARJ. Color in these tables is the most important objective criterion and Fig. 5 defines the ordering of allowed (feasible) combinations of colors. We preprocess these tables by combing quadruples of 3-color tables into a single table with "colors" 0–23. More precisely, for each configuration i, for each pair of modes of BGA b and SARJ a on the side s and for possible combinations of orientation angles O we compute the combined color and we represent it using the color loss function $c_{i,s,b}(M_{i,s,a}, M_{i,s,b}, O_{i,s,a}, O_{i,s,b}) \rightarrow [0; 23]$. This function combines tables P, L, E, S (Fig. 2) with a given color preference order (Fig. 5). It is then represented as a `table` constraint [2] defining the quality of schedule. The `table` constraint represents the constraint using a set of consistent value-tuples and hence it is appropriate to model constraints given in extension (such as those represented by functions $c_{i,s,b}$).

Synchronization Constraints. The hard constraints from the problem description can be modeled using logical constraints usually in the form of implication. For example to describe that the Autotrack mode spans through several configurations (then we model its cumulative duration using variables D^C) we can use the following implication constraint:

$$(M_{i,s,j} = AUTOTRACK \wedge (D^U_{i,s,j} = 0 \wedge D^B_{i,s,j} = 0) \wedge (D^E_{i,s,j} = 0 \wedge D^L_{i,s,j} = 0))$$
$$\implies D^C_{i,s,j} = D^C_{i-1,s,j} + D^A_{i,s,j},$$

0	S	L	E	P		8	S	L	E	P		16	S	L		P
1	S	L	E	P			S	L	E	P		17	S	L		P
2	S	L		E	P		10	S	L		P		18	S	L	E	P
3	S	L	E	P		11	S	L		P		19	S	L	E	P
4	S	L		P		12	S	L	E	P		20	S	L	E	P
5	S	L		P		13	S	L	E	P		21	S	L	E	P
6	S	L	E	P		14	S	L	E	P		22	S	L		P
7	S	L	E	P		15	S	L	E	P		23	S	L		P

Fig. 5. Color preferences order.

To overcome weak propagation of logical constraints we suggest to combine them into `case` constraints with strong domain filtering. The `case` constraint represents the constraint in a compact way as a directed acyclic graph, where each vertex is annotated by a constrained variable and arcs going out of the vertex are annotated by sets of possible values for the corresponding variable and optionally by a formula describing some local constraint (see Fig. 6 for an example). Each path in the graph then describes a possible way to satisfy the `case` constraint and hence this constraint is appropriate to model a disjunction of constraints sharing some variables. Figure 6 shows the graph for the `case` constraint modeling the duration of the Autotrack mode (the above implication is represented by the branch at the bottom of the graph). Other constraints of the problem are modeled in a similar style (see [1]).

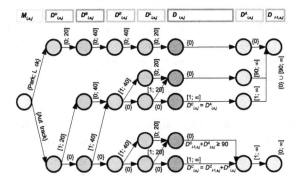

Fig. 6. The graph for the `case` constraint on the duration of the Autotrack mode.

Objective Functions. There is no single global objective function given, there are only partial objective functions $f_{i,s}$, one for each configuration i and side s. Each of these functions has four parts. The most important is the cost of colors:

$$f^C_{i,s} = \sum_b c_{i,s,b}(M_{i,s,a}, M_{i,s,b}, O_{i,s,a}, O_{i,s,b}).$$

The second cost function is the cost of the modes:

$$f^M_{i,s} = \sum_j m(M_{i,s,j}),$$

where m is the loss function for modes meeting the condition $m(AUTOTRACK)$ $< m(PARK) < m(LOCK)$. The third cost function is the number of changes of directions $f_{i,s}^D$ that depends on $M_{i-1,s,j}$, $R_{i-1,s,j}^E$, $R_{i,s,j}^B$, $M_{i,s,j}$ and $R_{i,s,j}^E$. The least important function is the cost of turning (measured by the turning angle):

$$f_{i,s}^L = \sum_j |R_{i,s,j}^B| + |R_{i,s,j}^E|.$$

3.4   Optimization Algorithm

The quality of plan for each configuration is evaluated by a vector of four values $(f_{i,s}^C, f_{i,s}^M, f_{i,s}^D, f_{i,s}^L)$, where smaller values (lexicographically) are preferred. Recall that these values are obtained via the equality constraints described in the previous section. To evaluate the quality of the whole plan we need to put together all these quadruples into a single vector while respecting the priorities within each quadruple. As no global objective was given in the problem specification we suggest to evaluate the quality of the whole plan via the global evaluation vector with the values $f_{i,s}^C$ for all configurations and sides first, then the values $f_{i,s}^M$ followed by $f_{i,s}^D$ and finally $f_{i,s}^L$. We have chosen this option, because the achievable color depends on the duration of turning nonlinearly and because a small change in the duration of turning can result in a significant difference in the achievable color. This approach should result in less stress on solar panels.

As mentioned above the multi-criteria optimization is realized via lexicographical ordering of individual criteria. We use the following approach to find a plan with the smallest evaluation vector. First, we find an optimal solution (assignment of variables) for the first criterion (objective function). Then we solve the problem again, but with an extra constraint binding the value of the first objective function to the computed optimum value and optimizing the second objective function etc. until all functions are optimized. Note that the plan obtained when optimizing a certain criterion also gives the values of all remaining criteria. Hence we can use such a value as the upper bound when optimizing the next criterion etc. Note also that for every extended problem at this level of abstraction there exists a solution, if the first search iteration was successful. Consequently it is possible to interrupt the algorithm at any time and get at least a partially optimized plan if it isn't enough time for full optimization.

Classical branch and bound method [7] is used to find an optimal solution for a single objective function. Various variable ordering heuristics and branching schemes can be used during variable labeling. As different strategies have different success rates and runtimes in different situations, we don't use one fixed strategy, but we exploit a set of strategies. The idea is running the optimizer with a given combination of variable ordering heuristics and branching schemes for a limited time and if it does not find a solution then trying a different combination. We do not use all combinations of variable ordering heuristics and branching schemes, because that is time consuming; we selected only a few pairs with the best results in initial experiments [1].

Table 1. Comparison of different approaches. Time is the total time in seconds to solve all 100 scenarios. Number of time outs is the number of plans out of 100 that a given approach does not consider as optimal because of insufficient time for the optimization. The greedy algorithm has no timeouts but it can claim a suboptimal solution as the optimal solution, because this algorithm can cut the branch with the optimal solution off at some stage of search. The average value in final plans shows the average value of the corresponding part of the objective function across all scenarios (smaller numbers are better).

Method	Time[s]	Number of time outs				Average value in final plans			
		$f_{i,s}^C$	$f_{i,s}^M$	$f_{i,s}^D$	$f_{i,s}^L$	$f_{i,s}^C$	$f_{i,s}^M$	$f_{i,s}^D$	$f_{i,s}^L$
Final	1075	0	10	7	19	1.02	3.24	0.01	36.61
Wider	19758	0	2	8	14	1.02	3.19	0.01	32.19
Perpendicular	1369	8	5	1	7	2.15	3.21	0.01	21.57
Greedy	725	–	–	–	–	1.71	3.68	0.00	87.24

4 Results and Conclusions

We have found the problem instances provided with the problem specification in [3] too easy (all solved optimally) and due to confidentiality, no real-life data could be provided by NASA. Based on data collected from ISS Live! (http://spacestationlive.nasa.gov/) during one month we noticed that joints are not in the Autotrack mode only for short periods of time. Hence rather than generating plans for the four-week horizon, the planning horizon used in experiments is only seven hours long, which corresponds to observed durations when planning is really necessary. Based on the most difficult instance from [3] we created 100 test cases with more complex color tables [1].

We compare the proposed algorithm "Final" with some alternative approaches. The variation "Wider" uses a full portfolio of variable ordering heuristics and branching schemes to show that we chose an appropriate subset of available heuristics. "Perpendicular" is the algorithm that optimizes plans in configurations, i.e., all objective functions of one configuration are optimized before any objective function of another configuration is optimized. It is similar to left-to-right scheduling of the SACE approach, but it isn't a greedy algorithm. "Greedy" is our implementation of the SACE approach based on [8], because their implementation is not publicly accessible. Testing was performed on the laptop with an Intel® Core™ i5-520M processor (2.40 GHz) and 8GB PC3-8500 DDR3 SDRAM. The results are summarized in Table 1. They demonstrate that the proposed global optimization approach gives results of much better quality than left-to-right scheduling with the runtime comparable to the greedy approach. The "Final" algorithm is only 1 % worse in the score of $f_{i,s}^M$ than "Wider", but each expansion of the portfolio of heuristics has a negative effect on the runtime. "Perpendicular" has about 41 % better score than "Final" in the least important part of the objective function at the expense of the most important part of the objective function, where it has about 111 % worse score.

So these plans put more strain on solar arrays. "Greedy" needs only about 33 % less time for optimization of all plans than "Final", but the average score is significantly worse in all parts of the objective function except $f^D_{i,s}$. So our approach is able to provide significantly better plans in a slightly longer time.

The major contribution is showing that off-the-shelf technology with some specialized optimization procedure overcomes left-to-right scheduling in terms of schedule quality while keeping time efficiency comparable.

Acknowledgement. The authors thank Jeremy Frank for information about the solar array operations at ISS and about the SACE approach. Roman Barták is supported by the Czech Science Foundation under the project P202/12/G061.

References

1. Jelínek, J., Barták, R.: A constraint-based optimizer for scheduling solar array operations on the international space station. In: Proceedings of the International Workshop on Planning and Scheduling for Space (IWPSS), pp. 53–61 (2015)
2. Carlsson, M., Ottosson, G., Carlsson, B.: An open-ended finite domain constraint solver. In: Hartel, Pieter H., Kuchen, Herbert (eds.) PLILP 1997. LNCS, vol. 1292. Springer, Heidelberg (1997)
3. Frank, J.: Planning solar array operations on the international space station. In: The International Competition on Knowledge Engineering for Planning and Scheduling (ICKEPS) (2012)
4. Frank, J., Jónsson, A.: Constraint-based attribute and interval planning. J. Constraints **8**(4), 339–364 (2003)
5. Kolombo, M., Pecka, M., Barták, R.: An ad-hoc planner for the mars express mission. In: Proceedings of the 5th International Workshop on Planning and Scheduling for Space (IWPSS) (2013)
6. Kolombo, M., Barták, R.: A constraint-based planner for mars express orbiter. In: Gelbukh, A., Espinoza, F.C., Galicia-Haro, S.N. (eds.) MICAI 2014, Part II. LNCS, vol. 8857, pp. 451–463. Springer, Heidelberg (2014)
7. Land, A.H., Doig, A.G.: An automatic method of solving discrete programming problems. Econometrica **28**(3), 497–520 (1960)
8. Reddy, S., Frank, J., Iatauro, M., Boyce, M., Kürklü, E., Ai-Chang, M., Jónsson, A.: Planning solar array operations for the international space station. ACM Trans. Intell. Syst. Technol. **2**(4), 41:1–41:24 (2011)

The KB Paradigm and its Application to Interactive Configuration

Van Hertum Pieter[(✉)], Ingmar Dasseville, Gerda Janssens, and Marc Denecker

Department of Computer Science, KU Leuven, Leuven, Belgium
{pieter.vanhertum,ingmar.dasseville,gerda.janssens,
marc.denecker}@cs.kuleuven.be

Abstract. The knowledge base paradigm aims to express domain knowledge in a rich formal language, and to use this domain knowledge as a knowledge base to solve various problems and tasks that arise in the domain by applying multiple forms of inference. As such, the paradigm applies a strict separation of concerns between information and problem solving. In this paper, we analyze the principles and feasibility of the knowledge base paradigm in the context of an important class of applications: interactive configuration problems. In interactive configuration problems, a configuration of interrelated objects under constraints is searched, where the system assists the user in reaching an intended configuration. It is widely recognized in industry that good software solutions for these problems are very difficult to develop. We investigate such problems from the perspective of the KB paradigm. We show that multiple functionalities in this domain can be achieved by applying different forms of logical inferences on a formal specification of the configuration domain. We report on a proof of concept of this approach in a real-life application with a banking company.

1 Introduction

In this paper, we investigate the application of knowledge representation and reasoning to the problem of *interactive configuration*. In the past decades enormous progress in many different areas of computational logic was obtained. This resulted in a complex landscape with many declarative paradigms, languages and communities. One issue that fragments computational logic is the reasoning/inference task. Computational logic is divided in different declarative paradigms, each with its own syntactical style, terminology and conceptuology, and designated form of inference (e.g., deductive logic, logic programming, abductive logic programming, databases (query inference), answer set programming (answer set generation), constraint programming, etc.). Yet, in all of them declarative propositions need to be expressed. Take, e.g., "each lecture takes place at some time slot". This proposition could be an expression to be deduced from a formal specification if the task was a verification problem, or to be queried in a database, or it could be a constraint for a scheduling problem. It is, in the first place, just a piece of information and we see no reason why depending on the

© Springer International Publishing Switzerland 2016
M. Gavanelli and J. Reppy (Eds.): PADL 2016, LNCS 9585, pp. 13–29, 2016.
DOI: 10.1007/978-3-319-28228-2_2

task to be solved, it should be expressed in a different formalism (classical logic, SQL, ASP, MiniZinc, etc.).

The Knowledge Base (KB) paradigm [8] was proposed as an answer to this. The KB paradigm applies a strict separation of concerns to information and problem solving. A KB system allows to store information in a knowledge base, and provides a range of inference methods. With these inference methods various types of problems and tasks can be solved using the *same knowledge base*. As such the knowledge base is neither a program nor a description of a problem, it cannot be executed or run. It is nothing but information. However, this information can be used to solve multiple sorts of problems. Stated differently, many declarative problem solving paradigms are mono-inferential: are based on one form of inference. Instead, the KB-paradigm is multi-inferential. We believe that this implements a more natural, pure view of what declarative logic is aimed to be. The FO($\cdot$) KB project [8] is a concrete project that runs now for a number of years. Its aim is to integrate different useful language constructs and forms of inference from different declarative paradigms in one rich declarative language and a KB system. So far, it has led to the KB language FO($\cdot$) and the KB system IDP which were used in the configuration experiment described in this paper.

An interactive configuration (IC) problem [9] is an interactive version of a constraint solving problem. One or more users search for a configuration of objects and relations between them that satisfies a set of constraints. Industry abounds with interactive configuration problems: configuring composite physical systems such as cars and computers, insurances, loans, schedules involving human interaction, webshops (where clients choose composite objects), etc. However, building such software is renown in industry as difficult and no broadly accepted solution methods are available [3]. Building software support using standard imperative programming is often a nightmare, due to the fact that (1) many functionalities need to be provided, (2) they are complex to implement, and (3) constraints on the configuration tend to spread out over the application, in the form of snippets of code performing some computation relative to the constraint (e.g., context dependent checks or propagations) often leading to an unacceptable maintenance cost. This makes interactive configuration an excellent domain to illustrate the advantages of declarative methods over standard imperative or object-oriented programming.

Our research question is: can we express the constraints of correct configurations in a declarative logic and provide the required functionalities by applying inference on this domain knowledge? This is a KRR question albeit a difficult one. In the first place, some of the domain knowledge may be complex. For an example in the context of a computer configuration problem, take the following constraint: *the total memory usage of different software processes that needs to be in main memory simultaneously, may not exceed the available RAM memory*. It takes an expressive knowledge representation language to (compactly and naturally) express such a constraint. Many interactive configuration problems include complex constraints: various sorts of quantification, aggregates (as illustrated above), definitions (sometimes inductive), etc. Moreover, an interactive configuration system needs to provide many functionalities: checking the validity of a fully specified configuration, correct and safe reasoning on a partially specified configuration (this involves reasoning on incomplete knowledge, sometimes with infinite or unknown domains), computing impossible values or forced values for attributes, generating sensible questions to the user, providing explanation why certain values are impossible, backtracking if the user regrets some choices, supporting the user by filling in his don't-cares potentially taking into account a cost function, etc.

That declarative methods are particularly suitable for solving this type of problem has been acknowledged before, and several systems and languages have been developed [9,17,21,23].

The first contribution of our work is the analysis of IC problems from a Knowledge Representation point of view. We show that multiple functionalities in this domain can be achieved by applying different forms of logical inferences on a formal specification of the configuration domain. We focus on a study of the different forms of inference, determining the forms of inference in terms of which the different functionalities can be supplied. The second contribution is vice versa: a study of the feasibility and usefulness of the KB paradigm in this important class of applications. The logic used in this experiment is the logic FO($\cdot$) [7], an extension of first-order logic (FO), and the system is the IDP system [6]. We discuss the complexity of (the decision problems of) the inference problems and why they are solvable, despite the high expressivity of the language and the complexity of inference. This research has its origin in an experimental IC system we developed in collaboration with industry.

2 The FO(.) KB Project

The Language. FO($\cdot$) refers to the class of extensions of first order logic (FO) as is common in logic, e.g. FO(LFP) stands for the extension of FO with a least fixpoint construction [11]. Currently, the language of the IDP system in the project is FO(T, ID, Agg, arit, PF) [7,14]: FO extended with types, definitions, aggregates, arithmetic and partial functions. In this project we will use the subset language FO(T, Agg, arit, PF). Abusing notation, we will use FO($\cdot$) as an abbreviation for this language. Below, we introduce the aspects of the logic and its syntax on which this paper relies.

A *vocabulary* is a set Σ of type, predicate and function symbols. Variables x, y, atoms A, FO-formulas φ are defined as usual. Aggregate terms are of the form $Agg(E)$, with Agg an aggregate function symbol and E an expression $\{(\overline{x}, F(\overline{x}))|\varphi(\overline{x})\}$, where φ can be any FO-formula, F a function symbol and $\overline{x}$ a tuple of variables. Examples are the cardinality, sum, product, maximum and minimum aggregate functions. For example $sum\{(x, F(x))|\varphi(x)\}$ is read as $\Sigma_{x \in \{y|\varphi(y)\}}F(x)$. A *term* in FO($\cdot$) can be an aggregate term or a term as defined in FO. A *theory* is a set of FO($\cdot$) formulas.

A partial set on domain D is a function from D to $\{\mathbf{t}, \mathbf{u}, \mathbf{f}\}$. A partial set is two-valued (or total) if $\mathbf{u}$ does not belong to its range. A *(partial) structure* $\mathcal{S}$

consists of a domain D_τ for all types τ in the vocabulary Σ and an assignment of a partial set $\sigma^\mathcal{S}$ to each symbol $\sigma \in \Sigma$, called the interpretation of σ in $\mathcal{S}$. The interpretation $P^\mathcal{S}$ of a predicate symbol P with type $[\tau_1, \ldots, \tau_n]$ in $\mathcal{S}$ is a partial set on domain $D_{\tau_1} \times \ldots \times D_{\tau_n}$. For a function F with type $[\tau_1, \ldots, \tau_n] \to \tau_{n+1}$, the interpretation $F^\mathcal{S}$ of F in $\mathcal{S}$ is a partial set on domain $D_{\tau_1} \times \ldots \times D_{\tau_n} \times D_{\tau_{n+1}}$. In case the interpretation of σ in $\mathcal{S}$ is a two-valued set, we abuse notation and use $\sigma^\mathcal{S}$ as shorthand for $\{\bar{d} | \sigma^\mathcal{S}(\bar{d}) = \mathbf{t}\}$. The precision-order on the truth values is given by $\mathbf{u} <_p \mathbf{f}$ and $\mathbf{u} <_p \mathbf{t}$. It can be extended pointwise to partial sets and partial structures, denoted $\mathcal{S} \leq_p \mathcal{S}'$. Notice that total structures are the maximally precise ones. We say that $\mathcal{S}'$ extends $\mathcal{S}$ if $\mathcal{S} \leq_p \mathcal{S}'$.

A total structure S is called *functionally consistent* if for each function F with type $[\tau_1, \ldots, \tau_n] \to \tau_{n+1}$, the interpretation F^S is the graph of a function $D_{\tau_1} \times \ldots \times D_{\tau_n} \mapsto D_{\tau_{n+1}}$. A partial structure $\mathcal{S}$ is functionally consistent if it has a functionally consistent two-valued extension. Unless stated otherwise, we will assume for the rest of this paper that all (partial) structures are functionally consistent.

A domain atom (domain term) is a tuple of a predicate symbol P (a function symbol F) and a tuple of domain elements $(d_1, \ldots, d_n)$. We will denote it as $P(d_1, \ldots, d_n)$ (respectively $F(d_1, \ldots, d_n)$). We say a domain term t of type τ is uninterpreted in $\mathcal{S}$ if $\{d | d \in D_\tau \land (t = d)^\mathcal{S} = \mathbf{u}\}$ is non-empty.

To define the satisfaction relation on theories, we extend the interpretation of symbols to arbitrary terms and formulas using the Kleene truth assignments [12]. For a theory T and a partial structure $\mathcal{S}$, we say that $\mathcal{S}$ is a model of T (or in symbols $\mathcal{S} \vDash T$) if $T^\mathcal{S} = \mathbf{t}$ and $\mathcal{S}$ is two-valued.

Inference Tasks. In the KB paradigm, a specification is a bag of information. This information can be used for solving various problems by applying a suitable form of inference on it.

FO is standardly associated with deduction inference: a deductive inference task takes as input a pair of theory T and sentence φ, and returns $\mathbf{t}$ if $T \models \varphi$ and $\mathbf{f}$ otherwise. This is well-known to be undecidable for FO, and by extension for FO$(\cdot)$. However, to provide the required functionality of an interactive configuration system we can use simpler forms of inference. Indeed, in many such domains a fixed finite domain is associated with each unknown configuration parameter.

A natural format in logic to describe these finite domains is by a partial structure with a finite domain. Also other data that are often available in such problems can be represented in that structure. As such various inference tasks are solvable by finite domain reasoning and become decidable. Below, we introduce base forms of inference and recall their complexity when using finite domain reasoning. We assume a fixed vocabulary Σ and theory T.

Modelcheck(T, S): input: a total structure S and theory T over the vocabulary interpreted by S; output is the boolean value $S \models T$. Complexity is in **P**.

Modelexpand$(T, \mathcal{S})$: input: theory T and partial structure $\mathcal{S}$; output: a model I of T such that $\mathcal{S} \leq_p I$ or *UNSAT* if there is no such I. Modelexpand [24] is a generalization for FO($\cdot$) theories of the modelexpansion task as defined in Mitchell et al. [13]. Complexity of deciding the existence of a modelexpansion is in **NP**.

Optimize($T, \mathcal{S}, t$): input: a theory T, a partial structure $\mathcal{S}$ and a term t of numerical type; output: a model $I \geq_p \mathcal{S}$ of T such that the value t^I of t is minimal. This is an extension to the modelexpand inference. The complexity of deciding that a certain t^I is minimal, is in $\boldsymbol{\Delta^P_2}$.

Propagate($T, \mathcal{S}$): input: theory T and partial structure $\mathcal{S}$; output: the most precise partial structure $\mathcal{S}_r$ such that for every model $I \geq_p \mathcal{S}$ of T it is true that $I \geq_p \mathcal{S}_r$. The complexity of deciding that a partial structure $\mathcal{S}'$ is $\mathcal{S}_r$ is in $\boldsymbol{\Delta^P_2}$. Note that we assume that all partial structures are functionally consistent, which implies that we also propagate functional constraints.

Query($\mathcal{S}, E$): input: a (partial) structure $\mathcal{S}$ and a set expression $E = \{\overline{x} \mid \varphi(\overline{x})\}$; output: the set $A_Q = \{\overline{x} \mid \varphi(\overline{x})^{\mathcal{S}} = \mathbf{t}\}$. Complexity of deciding that a set A is A_Q is in **P**.

Approximative versions exist for some of these inferences, with lower complexity [23]. More inferences exist, such as simulation of temporal theories in FO($\cdot$) [4], which were not used in the experiment.

3 Interactive Configuration

In an IC problem, one or more users search for a configuration of objects and relations between them that satisfies a set of constraints.

Typically, the user is not aware of all constraints. There may be too many of them to keep track of. Even if the human user can oversee all constraints that he needs to satisfy, he is not a perfect reasoner and cannot comprehend all consequences of his choices. This in its own right makes such problems hard to solve. The problems get worse if the user does not know about the relevant objects and relations or the constraints on them, or if the class of involved objects and relations is large, if the constraints get more complex and more "irregular" (e.g., exceptions), if more users are involved, etc. On top of that, the underlying constraints in such problems tend to evolve quickly. All these complexities occur frequently, making the problem complex for a human user. In such cases, computer assistance is needed: the human user chooses and the system assists by guiding him through the search space.

For a given IC problem, an IC system has information on that problem. There are a number of stringent rules to which a configuration should conform, and besides this there is a set of parameters. Parameters are the open fields in the configuration that need to be filled in by the user or decided by the system.

3.1 Running Example: Domain Knowledge

A simplified version of the application in Sect. 5.1 is used in Sect. 4 as running example. We introduce the domain knowledge of this example here.

Table 1. Example data

PriceOf		PreReq		MaxCost		IsOS
software	*int*	*software*	*software*	*employee*	*int*	*software*
Windows	60	Office	Windows	Secretary	100	Windows
Linux	20	LaTeX	Linux	Manager	150	Linux
LaTeX	10					
Office	30					
DualBoot	40					

Example 1. Software on a computer has to be configured for different employees. Available software includes operating systems, editors and text processors. Each software has a price. Some software is required for other software. If more than one OS is needed, a DualBoot System is required. The software, the requirements, the budgets of the employees and the prices of software can be seen in Table 1.

3.2   Subtasks of an Interactive Configuration System

Any system assisting a user in interactive configuration must be able to perform a set of subtasks. We look at important subtasks that an interactive configuration system should support.

Subtask 1: Acquiring Information From the User. The first task of an IC system is acquiring information from the user. The system needs to get a value for a number of parameters of the configuration from the user. There are several options: the system can ask questions to the user, it can make the user fill in a form containing open text fields, dropdown-menus, checkboxes, etc. Desirable aspects would be to give the user the possibility to choose the order in which he gives values for parameters and to omit filling in certain parameters (because he does not know or does not care). For example, in the running example a user might need a LaTeX-package, but he does not care about which OS he uses. In that case the system will decide in his place that a Linux system is required. Since a user is not fully aware of all constraints, it is possible that he inputs conflicting information. This needs to be handled or avoided.

Subtask 2: Generating Consistent Values for a Parameter. After a parameter is selected (by the user or the system) for which a value is needed, the system can assist the user in choosing these values. A possibility is that the system presents the user with a list of all possible values, given the values for other parameters and the constraints of the configuration problem. Limiting the user with this list makes that the user is unable to input inconsistent information.

Subtask 3: Propagation of Information. Assisting the user in choosing values for the parameters, a system can use the constraints to propagate the information that the user has communicated. This can be used in several ways. A system can communicate propagations through a GUI, for example by coloring certain fields red or graying out certain checkboxes. Another way is to give a user the possibility to explicitly ask "what if"-questions to the system. In Example 1, a user can ask the system what the consequences are if he was a secretary choosing an Office installation. The system answers that in this case a Windows installation is required, which results in a Linux installation becoming impossible (due to budget constraints) and as a consequence it also derives the impossibility of installing LaTeX.

Subtask 4: Checking the Consistency for a Value. When it is not possible/desirable to provide a list of possible values, the system checks that the value the user has provided is consistent with the known data and the constraints.

Subtask 5: Checking a Configuration. If a user makes manual changes to a configuration, the system provides him with the ability to check if his updated version of the configuration still conforms to all constraints.

Subtask 6: Autocompletion. If a user has finished communicating all his preferences, the system autocompletes the partial configuration to a full configuration. This can be done arbitrarily (a value for each parameter such that the constraints are satisfied) or the user can have some other parameters like a total cost, that have to be **optimized**.

Subtask 7: Explanation. If a supplied value for a parameter is not consistent with other parameters, the system can explain this inconsistency to the user. This can be done by showing minimal sets of parameters with their values that are inconsistent, or by showing (visualizations of) constraints that are violated. It can also explain to the user why certain automatic choices are made, or why certain choices are impossible.

Subtask 8: Backtracking. It is not unthinkable that a user makes a mistake, or changes his mind after seeing consequences of choices he made. Backtracking is an important subtask for a configuration system. Backtracking can be supported in numerous ways. The simplest way is a simple back button, where the last choice a user made is reverted. A more involved option is a system where a user can select any parameter and erase his value for that parameter. The user can then decide this parameter at a later timepoint. Even more complex is a system where a user can supply a value for a parameter and if it is not consistent with other parameters the system shows him which parameters are in conflict and proposes other values for these parameters such that consistency can be maintained.

4   Interactive Configuration in the KB Paradigm

To analyze the IC problem from the KB point of view, we aim at formalizing the subtasks of Sect. 3 as inferences. In this paper we do not deal with user interface aspects. For a given application, our knowledge base consists of a vocabulary Σ, a theory T expressing the configuration constraints and a partial structure $\mathcal{S}$. Initially, $\mathcal{S}_0$ is the Σ-partial structure that contains the domains of the types and the input data. During IC, $\mathcal{S}_0$ will become more and more precise partial structures $\mathcal{S}_i$ due to choices made by the user. For IC, the KB also contains $L_{\mathcal{S}_0}$, the set of all uninterpreted domain atoms/terms[1] in $\mathcal{S}_0$. These domain terms are the logical formalization of the parameters of the IC problem. Σ and T are fixed. As will be shown in this section, all subtasks can be formalized by (a combination of) inferences on this knowledge base consisting of $\Sigma, T, \mathcal{S}_0, L_{\mathcal{S}_0}$ and information gathered from the user.

Example 2. Continuing Example 1, use vocabulary Σ consisting of types: *software*, *employee* and *int* (integers), predicates *Install(software)*, *IsOS(software)* and *PreReq(software,software)*, functions *PriceOf(software):int*, *MaxCost (employee):int* and two constants *Requester: employee* and *Cost: int*. The initial partial structure $\mathcal{S}_0$ consists of $\{employee \rightarrow \{Secretary, Manager\}, software \rightarrow \{Windows, Linux, LaTeX, Office, DualBoot\}\}$ and interpretations for *MaxCost (employee):int, IsOs(software), PriceOf(software):int* and *PreReq(software, software)* as can be seen in Table 1. The set of parameters $L_{\mathcal{S}_0}$ is $\{Requester, Install(Windows), Install(Linux), Install(Office), Install(LaTeX), Install (DualBoot), Cost\}$. The theory T consists of the following constraints:

$\forall s1\, s2 : Install(s1) \wedge PreReq(s1, s2) \Rightarrow Install(s2).$
// The total cost is the sum of the prices of all installed software.
$Cost = sum\{(s, PriceOf(s)) | Install(s)\}.$
$Cost < MaxCost(Requester).$
$\exists s : Install(s) \wedge IsOS(s).$
$Install(Windows) \wedge Install(Linux) \Rightarrow Install(DualBoot).$

Subtask 1: Acquiring Information From the User. Key in IC is collecting information from the user on the parameters. During the run of the system, the set of parameters that are still open, changes. In our KB system, a combination of the inferences introduced in Sect. 2, which is called a derived inference, is used to calculate this set of parameters.

Definition 1. *Calculating Uninterpreted Terms. GetOpenTerms(T, S) is the derived inference with input a theory T, a partial structure $\mathcal{S} \geq_p \mathcal{S}_0$ and the set $L_{\mathcal{S}_0}$ of terms. Output is a set of terms such that for every term t in that set, there exist models I_1 and I_2 of T that expand $\mathcal{S}$ for which $t^{I_1} \neq t^{I_2}$. Or formally:*

$$\{l | l \in L_{\mathcal{S}_0} \wedge \{d | (l = d)^{\mathcal{S}'} = \mathbf{u}\} \neq \emptyset \wedge \mathcal{S}' = Propagate(T, \mathcal{S})\}$$

The complexity of deciding whether a given set of terms A is the set of uninterpreted terms is in $\mathbf{\Delta_2^P}$.

---

[1] In the rest of this paper, a domain atom is treated as a term that evaluates to true or false.

An IC system can use this set of terms in a number of ways. It can use a metric to select a specific term, which it can pose as a direct question to the user. It can also present a whole list of these terms at once and let the user pick one to supply a value for. In Sect. 5.1, we discuss two different approaches we implemented for this project.

Example 3. In Example 2, the parameters and domains are already given. Assume that the user has chosen the value *Manager* for *Requester*, true for *Install(Windows)* and false for *Install(Linux)*. The system will return *GetOpen-Terms*$(T, S) = \{Install(Office),\ Install(DualBoot),\ Cost\}$.

Subtask 2: Generating Consistent Values for a Parameter. A domain element d is a possible value for term t if there is a model $I \geq_p S$ such that $(t = d)^I = \mathbf{t}$

Definition 2. *Calculating Consistent Values*. *GetConsistentValues*$(T,$ $S, t)$ *is the derived inference with as input a theory T, a partial structure S and a term $t \in GetOpenTerms(T, S)$. Output is the set*

$$\{t^I \mid I \text{ is a model of } T \text{ expanding } S\}$$

The complexity of deciding that a set P is the set of consistent values for t is in $\mathbf{\Delta_2^P}$.

Example 4. The possible values in the initial partial structure S_0 are: $\{Secretary,\ Manager\}$ for *Requester*, the integers for *Cost* and $\{true,\ false\}$ for the others.

Subtask 3: Propagation of Information. It is informative for the user that he can see the consequences of assigning a particular value to a parameter.

Definition 3. *Calculating Consequences*. *PosConsequences*(T, S, t, a) *and **NegConsequences**(T, S, t, a) are derived inferences with input a theory T, a partial structure S, an uninterpreted term $t \in GetOpenTerms(T, S)$ and a domain element $a \in GetConsistentValues(T, S, t)$. As output it has a set C^+, respectively C^- of tuples (q, b) of uninterpreted terms and domain elements. $(q, b) \in C^+$, respectively C^- means that the choice a for t entails that q will be forced, respectively prohibited to be b. Formally,*

$$C^+ = \{(q, b) \mid (q = b)^{S'} = \mathbf{t} \wedge (q = b)^S = \mathbf{u}$$
$$\wedge\ S' = Propagate(T, S \cup \{t = a\})$$
$$\wedge\ q \in GetOpenTerms(T, S) \setminus \{t\}\ \}$$
$$C^- = \{(q, c) \mid (q = c)^{S'} = \mathbf{f} \wedge (q = c)^S = \mathbf{u}$$
$$\wedge\ S' = Propagate(T, S \cup \{t = a\})$$
$$\wedge\ q \in GetOpenTerms(T, S) \setminus \{t\}\ \}$$

The complexity of deciding whether a set P is C^+ or C^- is in $\mathbf{\Delta_2^P}$.

Example 5. Say the user has chosen *Requester* : *Secretary* and wants to know the consequences of making *Install(Windows)* true. The output in this case contains $(Install(LaTeX), \mathbf{f})$ in $PosConsequences(T, \mathcal{S}, t, a)$ and $(Install(LaTeX), \mathbf{t})$ in $NegConsequences(T, \mathcal{S}, t, a)$ since this combination is too expensive for a secretary. Note that there is not always such a correspondence between the positive and negative consequences. For example, when deriving a negative consequence for *Cost*, this does not necessarily imply a positive consequence.

Subtask 4: Checking the Consistency for a Value. A value d for a term t is consistent if there exists a model of T in which $t = d$ that extends the partial structure representing the current state.

**Definition 4. *Consistency Checking. CheckConsistency(T, $\mathcal{S}$, t, d)* *is the derived inference with as input a theory T, a partial structure $\mathcal{S}$, an uninterpreted term t and an domain element d. Output is a boolean b that represents if $\mathcal{S}$ extended with $t = d$ still satisfies T. Complexity of deciding if a value d is consistent for a term t is in* NP.*

Subtask 5: Checking a Configuration. Once the user has constructed a 2-valued structure S and makes manual changes to it, he may need to check if all constraints are still satisfied. A theory T is checked on a total structure S by calling $Modelcheck(T, S)$, with complexity in **P**.

Subtask 6: Autocompletion. If a user is ready communicating his preferences (Subtask 1) and there are undecided terms left which he does not know or care about, the user may want to get a full configuration (i.e. a total structure). This is computed by modelexpand. In particular:

$$I = Modelexpand(T, \mathcal{S})$$

In many of those situations the user wants to have a total structure with a minimal cost (given some term representing the cost t). This is computed by optimize:

$$I = Optimize(T, \mathcal{S}, t).$$

Example 6. Assume the user is a secretary and all he knows is that he needs Office. He chooses *Secretary* for *Requester* and true for *Install(Office)* and calls autocompletion. A possible output is a structure S where for the remaining parameters, a choice is made that satisfies all constraints, e.g., $Install(Windows)^S = \mathbf{t}$, $Install(DualBoot)^S = \mathbf{t}$ and the other *Install* atoms false. This is not a cheapest solution (lowest cost). By calling optimize using cost-term *Cost*, the DualBoot is dropped.

Subtask 7: Explanation. It is clear that a whole variety of options can be developed to provide different kinds of explanations to a user. If a user supplies an inconsistent value for a parameter, options can range from calculating a minimal inconsistent subset of the theory T as in [18,20,25], to giving a proof of inconsistency as in [15], to calculating a minimally precise partial configuration that has this inconsistency. We look at a derived logical inference for this last option.

Definition 5. *Calculating Minimal Inconsistent Structures. UnsaStructure$(T, \mathcal{S})$ is a derived inference with as input a theory T and a partial structure $\mathcal{S}$ that cannot be extended to a model of T and as output all minimal (partial) structures $\mathcal{S}' \leq_p \mathcal{S}$ such that $\mathcal{S}'$ cannot be extended to a model I of T. Formally[2], we return:*

$$min_{\leq_p}\{\mathcal{S}'|\mathcal{S}' \leq_p \mathcal{S} \wedge \neg(\exists I \geq_p \mathcal{S}' \wedge I \vDash T)\}$$

Complexity of deciding if a set is the set of minimal inconsistent structures is Δ_2^p.

Example 7. Say a secretary wants to install all software. This is not possible, so he asks for an explanation. Running *UnsatStructure* on the theory of Example 2 and that structure extended with *Requester = Secretary* and *Install(software)* true for all software will return a set with among others a structure in which *Requester = Secretary*, *Install(Windows)* and *Install(Linux)* are true, since a secretary does not have the budget to install two operating systems.

Subask 8: Backtracking. If a value for a parameter is not consistent, the user has to choose a new value for this parameter, or backtrack to revise a value for another parameter. In Sect. 3.2 we discussed three options of increasing complexity for implementing backtracking functionality. Erasing a value for a parameter is easy to provide in our KB system, and since this is a generalization of a back button (erasing the last value) we have a formalization of the first two options. Erasing a value d for parameter t in a partial structure $\mathcal{S}$ is simply modifying $\mathcal{S}$ such that $(t = d)^{\mathcal{S}} = \mathbf{u}$. As with explanation, a number of more complex options can be developed. We look at one possibility. Given a partial configuration $\mathcal{S}$, a parameter p and a value d that is inconsistent for that parameter, calculate a minimal set of previous choices that need to be undone such that this value is possible for this parameter. We can use Definition 5 and calculate *UnsatStructure$(T \wedge (t = d), \mathcal{S})$*. This inference calculates a set of minimal sets of previous choices that need to be undone. Backtracking over one of the sets in this set results in a maximal partial subconfiguration $\mathcal{S}'$ of $\mathcal{S}$ such that d is a possible value for t in $\mathcal{S}'$.

5   Proof of Concept

5.1   Implementation

Overview. During the configuration process, the user specifies his choices step-by-step. As argued in the introduction, a configurator tool can support the user in many ways: displaying the cost of the current partial configuration, propagating the impact of the choices of the user, presenting remaining possible values

---

[2] We note that $\leq_p$ is a partial order and denote $min_{\leq_p}$ for all minimal elements of a set according to that order.

for variables, explaining why certain choices are impossible, checking validity of a finished configuration, completing the don't cares of a user (potentially optimizing a cost function), etc. This work started as a feasibility study about using a KB system for solving interactive configuration problems. In this section we will describe the developed application and implementation, based on the IDP system for the back-end, together with a GUI made in QML [16] as front-end.[3] This was done in cooperation with Adaptive Planet, a consulting company [1] which developed the user interface and an international banking company, who provided us with a substantial configuration problem to test our implementation. The goal was to develop a highly customizable application, for general configuration problems. The GUI is a blank canvas, which is unaware of the configuration problem at hand. The IDP KB system has a knowledge base (a theory), containing all domain knowledge, and a set with all parameters (uninterpreted terms) and IDP is used for all the inferences on that knowledge base, which provide the functionalities of the subtasks discussed in Sect. 4. The developed application had 300 parameters and 650 constraints. This domain knowledge was distilled from a spreadsheet that the banking company currently uses for their interactive configuration tasks. Two user interfaces are available for the user to choose from:

Wizard. In the wizard interface, the user is interrogated and he answers on subsequent questions selected by the system, using the *GetOpenTerms* inference. An important side note here is that the user can choose not to answer a specific question, for instance because he cannot decide as he is missing relevant information or because he is not interested in the actual value (at this point). These parameters can be filled in at a later timepoint by the user, or the system can fill in all parameters using autocompletion.

Drill-Down. In the drill-down interface, the user sees a list of the still open parameters, and can pick which one he wants to fill in next. This interface is useful if the user is a bit more knowledgeable about the specific configuration and wants to give the values in a specific order.

In both interfaces the user is assisted in the same way when he enters data. When he or the system selects a parameter, he is provided with a dropdown list of the possible values, using the *GetConsistentValues* inference. Before committing to a choice, he is presented with the consequences of his choice, using the calculate consequences inference. The nature of the system guarantees a correct configuration and will automatically give the user support using all information it has (from the knowledge base, or received from the user).

Evaluation. When evaluating the quality of software (especially when evaluating declarative methods), scalability (data complexity) is often seen as the most

---

[3] More info about this implementation, a downloadable demo and another example of a configuration system developed with IDP as an engine (a simpler course configuration demo) can be found at: http://www.configuration.tk.

important quality metric. Naturally when using an interactive configuration system, performance is important. However, in the configuration community it is known that reasoning about typical configuration problems is relatively easy and does not exhibit real exponential behavior [21]. In this experiment (a configuration task with 300 parameters and 650 constraints), our users reported a response time of a half second on average with outliers up to 2 seconds. Note that the provided implementation was a naive prototype and optimizing the efficiency of the implemented algorithms is still possible in a number of ways. Also, it is reasonable to expect the number of parameters to be limited, since humans need to fill in the configuration in the end. When developing a configuration system, challenges lie in the complexity of the knowledge, its high volatility and the complex functionalities to be built. In such cases, more relevant than scalability are the standard metrics of software engineering: providing good functionality, maintainability, reuse and extensibility.

Maintainability and Reuse. The information used in an IC system is volatile, it is for example depending on ever-changing company policies. As such, it is vital that when that information changes, the system can be easily adapted. When using custom software, all tasks using domain knowledge (like rules and policies) need their own program code. The domain knowledge is scattered all over the program. If this policy changes, a programmer has to find all snippets of program code that are relevant for guarding this policy and modify them. This results in a system that is hard to maintain, hard to adapt and error-prone. Every time the domain knowledge changes, a whole development cycle has to be run through again. The development of a KB system with a centrally maintained knowledge base makes the knowledge directly available, readable and adaptable.

Extensibility. Supporting all subtasks expressed above is important for a good configuration system, but it is also important to have the possibility to accommodate new subtasks. A good system should be easily extensible with new functionalities, preferably without duplicating domain knowledge. This is one of the key points of a KB system. New inferences can be developed and added, independent from the domain knowledge.

Functionality. For evaluating functionality, industrial partners involved in this project have tested the proof of concept and compared with their conventional software solutions. The most common approach to developing configuration tools is building custom software. Other frequently used technology to handle interactive configuration problems are spreadsheets and business rules systems. When starting this project, the users had the following major issues with these systems, for which conceptual, general solutions were given by our approach:

- **Unidirectional dataflow:** All these systems have an obligatory unidirectional dataflow. This fixes beforehand which parameters are input and which parameters are output. However, given a problem statement, it is not natural to make a distinction between input and output. Different users may have different information or different needs and regard different parameters as input. In our approach, this distinction is not made at all by our inferences.

- **Incomplete knowledge:** These systems have problems reasoning with incomplete knowledge, i.e., rules and functions can only compute their result when their input is complete and they also cannot use partial knowledge to deduce (partial) new knowledge, e.g., to eliminate configuration options. Our language does by nature accommodate for partial knowledge, and is able to represent every intermediate partial configuration. These partial configurations are used by the inferences to calculate possible total configurations, consequences, etc.

6   Related Work

In different branches of AI research, people have been focusing on configuration software in different settings. Axling et al. [3] represent domain knowledge in the SICStus Object Language and have a configuration system specific for configuring physical objects, e.g., computers. An ontology based method was also proposed in by Vanden Bossche et al. [22] using OWL. The first reason these approaches are less general is that it is precisely the goal of the KB paradigm to reuse the knowledge for different reasoning tasks. All these approaches are focused towards one specific inference: ontologies are focused on deduction, Prolog and rule systems are focused on backward/forward chaining, etc.

Tiihonen et al. developed a configuration system WeCoTin [21] WeCoTin uses Smodels, an ASP system, as inference engine, for propagating consequences of choices. In 2004, Hadzic et al. [9] started working on solving different aspects of interactive configuration. They described solutions for these problem using knowledge compilation techniques such as binary decision diagrams (BDD) and using Boolean satisfiability solving (SAT). Hadzic et al. [9] stressed the importance of a distinction between *configuration knowledge* and the *configuration task*. This is similar to our separation of concerns by separating knowledge from computation. The authors also implemented solvers and systems for solving interactive configuration and interactive reconfiguration in later work [10]. Overall, the goal of their work is to develop different algorithms to solve different aspects of configuration problems and not to study an abstract reasoning framework in which knowledge and computation are separated. The contributions of this paper are different: we analyzed IC problems from a Knowledge Representation point of view. It is a discussion of possible approaches and the importance of this point of view. We made a study of desired functionalities for an IC system and how we can define logical reasoning tasks to supply these functionalities. In this project a more expressive language was used than in other work that we are aware of. Subbarayan et al. [19] for example use propositional logic, that is extended to CP by Andersen et al. [2]. The expressivity of the language is crucial for the usability of the approach. It allows us to address a broader range of applications, moreover it is easier to formalize and maintain the domain knowledge. A first approach in using the KB paradigm for IC, was done by Vlaeminck et al. [23], also using the FO(·) IDP project. Our work extends this, by analyzing a real-life application and discussing new functionalities.

7   Challenges and Future Work

Interactive configuration problems are part of a broader kind of problems, namely service provisioning problems. Service provisioning is the problem domain of coupling service providers with end users, starting from the request until the delivery of the service. Traditionally, such problems start with designing a configuration system that allows users to communicate their wishes, for which we provided a knowledge-based solution. After all the information is gathered from a user, it is still necessary to make a plan for the production and delivery of the selected configuration. Hence the configuration problem is followed by a planning problem that shares domain knowledge with the configuration problem but that also has its own domain knowledge about providers of components, production processes, etc. This planning problem then leads to a monitoring problem. Authorisations could be required, payments need to be checked, or it could be that the configuration becomes invalid mid-process. In this case the configuration needs to be redone, but preferably without losing much of the work that is already done. Companies need software that can manage and monitor the whole chain, from initial configuration to final delivery and this without duplication of domain knowledge. This is a problem area where the KB approach holds great promise but where further research is needed to integrate the KB system with the environment that the company uses to follow up its processes.

Other future work may include language extensions to better support configuration-like tasks. A prime example of this are templates [5]. Oftentimes the theory of a configuration problem contains lots of constraints which are similar in structure. It seems natural to introduce a language construct to abstract away the common parts. Another useful language extension is reification, to talk about the symbols in a specification rather than about their interpretation. Reification allows the system to reason on a meta level about the symbol and for example assign symbols to a category like "Technical" or "Administrative".

8   Conclusion

The KB paradigm, in which a strict separation between knowledge and problem solving is proposed, was analyzed in a class of knowledge intensive problems: interactive configuration problems. As we discussed why solutions for this class are hard to develop, we proposed a novel approach to the configuration problem based on an existing KB system. We analyzed the functional requirements of an IC system and investigated how we can provide these, using logical inferences on a knowledge base. We identified interesting new inference methods and applied them to the interactive configuration domain. We studied this approach in context of a large application, for which we built a proof of concept, using the KB system as an engine, which we extended with the new inferences. As proof of concept, we solved a configuration problem for a large banking company. Results are convincing and open perspectives for further research in service provisioning.

References

1. Adaptive planet. http://www.adaptiveplanet.com/
2. Andersen, H.R., Hadzic, T., Pisinger, D.: Interactive cost configuration over decision diagrams. J. Artif. Intell. Res. (JAIR) **37**, 99–139 (2010)
3. Axling, T., Haridi, S.: A tool for developing interactive configuration. J. Logic Program. **19**, 658–679 (1994)
4. Bogaerts, B., Jansen, J., Bruynooghe, M., De Cat, B., Vennekens, J., Denecker, M.: Simulating dynamic systems using linear time calculus theories. TPLP **14**(4–5), 477–492 (2014)
5. Dasseville, I., van der Hallen, M., Janssens, G., Denecker, M.: Semantics of templates in a compositional framework for building logics (2015). abs/1507.06778
6. De Cat, B., Bogaerts, B., Bruynooghe, M., Denecker, M.: Predicate logic as a modelling language: The IDP system. In: CoRR (2014). abs/1401.6312
7. Denecker, M., Ternovska, E.: A logic of nonmonotone inductive definitions. ACM Trans. Comput. Log. **9**(2), 14:1–14:52 (2008)
8. Denecker, M., Vennekens, J.: Building a knowledge base system for an integration of logic programming and classical logic. In: Garcia de la Banda, M., Pontelli, E. (eds.) ICLP 2008. LNCS, vol. 5366, pp. 71–76. Springer, Heidelberg (2008)
9. Hadzic, T.: A BDD-based approach to interactive configuration. In: Wallace, M. (ed.) CP 2004. LNCS, vol. 3258, p. 797. Springer, Heidelberg (2004)
10. Hadzic, T., Andersen, H.R.: Interactive reconfiguration in power supply restoration. In: van Beek, P. (ed.) CP 2005. LNCS, vol. 3709, pp. 767–771. Springer, Heidelberg (2005)
11. Immerman, N., Vardi, M.Y.: Model checking and transitive-closure logic. In: Grumberg, O. (ed.) CAV 1997. LNCS, vol. 1254. Springer, Heidelberg (1997)
12. Kleene, S.C.: Introduction to Metamathematics. Van Nostrand, New York (1952)
13. Mitchell, D.G., Ternovska, E., Hach, F., Mohebali, R.: Model expansion as a framework for modelling and solving search problems. Technical report TR 2006–24, Simon Fraser University, Canada (2006)
14. Pelov, N., Denecker, M., Bruynooghe, M.: Well-founded and stable semantics of logic programs with aggregates. TPLP **7**(3), 301–353 (2007)
15. Pontelli, E., Son, T.C.: *Justifications* for logic programs under answer set semantics. In: Etalle, S., Truszczyński, M. (eds.) ICLP 2006. LNCS, vol. 4079, pp. 196–210. Springer, Heidelberg (2006)
16. Qml. http://qmlbook.org/
17. Schneeweiss, D., Hofstedt, P.: *FdConfig*: a constraint-based interactive product configurator. In: Tompits, H., Abreu, S., Oetsch, J., Pührer, J., Seipel, D., Umeda, M., Wolf, A. (eds.) INAP/WLP 2011. LNCS, vol. 7773, pp. 230–246. Springer, Heidelberg (2013)
18. Shlyakhter, I., Seater, R., Jackson, D., Sridharan, M., Taghdiri, M.: Debugging overconstrained declarative models using unsatisfiable cores. In: ASE, pp. 94–105. IEEE Computer Society (2003)

19. Subbarayan, S., Jensen, R.M., Hadzic, T., Andersen, H.R., Hulgaard, H., Møller, J.: Comparing two implementations of a complete and backtrack-free interactive configurator. In: Proceedings of Workshop on CSP Techniques with Immediate Application, CP 2004 (2004)

20. Syrjänen, T.: Debugging inconsistent answer set programs. In: Dix, J., Hunter, A. (eds.) NMR, pp. 77–84. Institut für Informatik, Technische Universität Clausthal, Clausthal-Zellerfeld (2006)

21. Tiihonen, J., Heiskala, M., Anderson, A., Soininen, T.: Wecotin - a practical logic-based sales configurator. AI Commun. **26**(1), 99–131 (2013)

22. Bossche, M.V., Ross, P., MacLarty, I., Van Nuffelen, B., Pelov, N.: Ontology driven software engineering for real life applications. In: 3rd International Workshop on Semantic Web Enabled Software Engineering (SWESE) (2007)

23. Vlaeminck, H., Vennekens, J., Denecker, M.: A logical framework for configuration software. In: Porto, A., López-Fraguas, F.J. (eds.) PPDP, pp. 141–148. ACM (2009)

24. Wittocx, J., Mariën, M., Denecker, M.: The idp system: a model expansion system for an extension of classical logic. In: Denecker, M. (ed.) LaSh, pp. 153–165. ACCO, Leuven (2008)

25. Wittocx, J., Vlaeminck, H., Denecker, M.: Debugging for model expansion. In: Hill, P.M., Warren, D.S. (eds.) ICLP 2009. LNCS, vol. 5649, pp. 296–311. Springer, Heidelberg (2009)

A GPU Implementation
of the ASP Computation

Agostino Dovier[1]([✉]), Andrea Formisano[2], Enrico Pontelli[3], and Flavio Vella[4]

[1] Dipartimento di Matematica e Informatica, Università di Udine, Udine, Italy
agostino.dovier@uniud.it
[2] Dipartimento di Matematica e Informatica, Università di Perugia, Perugia, Italy
formis@dmi.unipg.it
[3] Department of Computer Science, New Mexico State University, Las Cruces, USA
epontell@cs.nmsu.edu
[4] IAC-CNR and Dipartimento di Informatica,
Sapienza Università di Roma, Rome, Italy
vella@di.uniroma1.it

Abstract. *General Purpose Graphical Processing Units (GPUs)* are affordable multi-core platforms, providing access to large number of cores, but at the price of a complex architecture with non-trivial synchronization and communication costs. This paper presents the design and implementation of a conflict-driven ASP solver, that is capable of exploiting the parallelism offered by GPUs. The proposed system builds on the notion of *ASP computation*, that avoids the generation of unfounded sets, enhanced by conflict analysis and learning. The proposed system uses the CPU exclusively for input and output, in order to reduce the negative impact of the expensive data transfers between the CPU and the GPU. All the solving components, i.e., the management of nogoods, the search strategy, backjumping, the search heuristics, conflict analysis and learning, and unit propagation, are performed on the GPU, by exploiting *Single Instruction Multiple Threads (SIMT)* parallelism. The preliminary experimental results confirm the feasibility and scalability of the approach, and the potential to enhance performance of ASP solvers.

Keywords: ASP solvers · ASP computation · SIMT parallelism · GPUs

1 Introduction

Answer Set Programming (ASP) [24,26] has gained momentum in the logic programming and Artificial Intelligence communities as a paradigm of choice for a variety of applications. In comparison to other non-monotonic logics and knowledge representation frameworks, ASP is syntactically simple and, at the same

---

Research partially supported by INdAM GNCS-14, GNCS-15 projects and NSF grants DBI-1458595, HRD-1345232, and DGE-0947465. Hardware partially supported by NVIDIA under the *GPU Research Center Program*. A preliminary version of this work has been presented in [9].

M. Gavanelli and J. Reppy (Eds.): PADL 2016, LNCS 9585, pp. 30–47, 2016.
DOI: 10.1007/978-3-319-28228-2_3

time, very expressive. The mathematical foundations of ASP have been extensively studied. In addition, there exist a large number of building block results about specifying and programming using ASP (e.g., see [2,15] and the references therein). ASP has offered novel and highly declarative solutions in a wide variety of application areas, including planning, verification, systems diagnosis, web services composition, and phylogenetic inference.

An important push towards the success of ASP has come from the development of efficient ASP solvers, such as SMODELS [33] and CLASP [13]. In particular, systems like CLASP and its derivatives are competitive with the state-of-the-art in several domains, including competitive performance in SAT solving competitions. In spite of the efforts in developing fast ASP solvers, execution of large programs and programs requiring complex search patterns remains a challenging task, limiting the scope of applicability of ASP in several domains (e.g., planning).

In this work, we explore the use of parallelism as a viable approach to enhance performance of ASP inference engines. In particular, we are interested in devising techniques that can take advantage of recent architectural developments in the field of *General Purpose Graphical Processing Units (GPUs)*. Modern GPUs are multi-core platforms, offering massive levels of parallelism. Vendors like AMD and NVIDIA support the use of GPUs for general-purpose non-graphical applications, providing dedicated APIs and development environments. Languages and language extensions like *OpenCL* [19] and *CUDA* [27] support the development of general applications on GPUs. To the best of our knowledge, the use of GPUs for ASP computations has not been explored and, as demonstrated in this paper, it opens an interesting set of possibilities and issues to be resolved. It is a contribution of this paper to bring these opportunities and challenges to the attention of the logic programming community.

The work proposed in this paper builds on two existing lines of research. The exploitation of parallelism from ASP computations has been explored in several proposals, starting with the seminal work presented in [11,29], and later continued in several other projects (e.g., [1,14,28,30]). Most of the existing proposals have primarily focused on the parallelization of the search process used in the construction of answer sets, by distributing parts of the search tree among different processors/cores (i.e., *search parallelism*). Furthermore, the literature has focused on parallelization on traditional multi-core or Beowulf architectures. These approaches are not applicable in the context of GPUs, since the models of parallelization used on GPUs are profoundly different, as we discuss in this paper. GPUs are designed to operate with a very large number of lightweight threads, operating in a synchronous fashion; GPUs present a complex memory organization, that has great impact on parallel performance. These factors make existing parallel ASP models not directly scalable and/or applicable to GPUs.

The second line of research that supports our effort can be found in the recent developments in GPU-based computation for SAT solving and constraint programming. The work in [7] illustrates how to parallelize the search process employed by the DPLL SAT-solving procedure on GPUs; the results demonstrate the potential benefit of delegating to GPUs tails of the branches of the search tree. Several other proposals have appeared in the literature suggesting the use of GPUs to parallelize parts of the SAT solving process—e.g., the computation of variable heuristics [23]. In the context of constraint programming, [4] explores the parallelization on GPUs of constraint propagation, with emphasis on complex global constraints; [5] shows how to exploit GPUs to concurrently explore larger neighborhoods in the context of constraint-based local-search, improving the quality of the results. In [6], a GPU-based constraint solver is used for fast prediction of protein structures.

The main lesson learned from the above studies, and applied in this paper, is that, as long as (exact) search problems are concerned, the best use of GPUs is in the parallelization of the "easy" activities, such as constraint propagation. Therefore, the main focus of this work is to apply GPU parallelism to the various (polynomial time) operations associated to answer set computation, such as unit propagation, heuristic computation, conflict analysis, nogood management and learning. The control of the search is also handled by the GPU, but the exploration of the search tree itself is not parallelized. This approach is radically different from what presented in [7], which proposes the parallelization of the DPLL procedure through partitioning of the search space among different threads. The paper provides also an analysis of components of the typical ASP computation that are challenging to parallelize using the fine-grained SIMT-style parallelism. This is the case, for example, of the traditional algorithms for unfounded set check [13], whose parallelization on GPUs is complicated by the *reachability bottleneck* [20]. Approaches relying on coarse-grained parallelism, such as running several instances of the source pointers algorithm [32] to process each strongly connected component of the dependency graph, are orthogonal to our approach. We have circumvented this problem by implementing the search strategy described in [22], that was also successfully used for solving ASP programs with delayed grounding [8]. In spite of some of these limitations, the current results already show the scalability and feasibility of the overall approach, opening promising doors for the use of GPUs in ASP.

2   Background

2.1   Answer Set Programming

In this section, we will review the basic notions on ASP (e.g., [24,26]). Let us consider a logic language composed of a set of propositional atoms $\mathcal{P}$. An ASP rule has the form

$$p_0 \leftarrow p_1, \ldots, p_m, not\ p_{m+1}, \ldots, not\ p_n \tag{1}$$

where $n \geq 0$ and $p_i \in \mathcal{P}$. A rule that includes first-order atoms with variables is simply seen as a syntactic sugar for all its ground instances. Given a rule r, p_0 is referred to as the *head* of the rule ($head(r)$), while the set $\{p_1, \ldots, p_m, not\ p_{m+1}, \ldots, not\ p_n\}$ is referred to as the body of the rule $(body(r))$. In particular, $body^+(r) = \{p_1, \ldots, p_m\}$ and $body^-(r) = \{p_{m+1}, \ldots, p_n\}$. A *constraint* is a rule of the form:

$$\leftarrow p_1, \ldots, p_m, not\ p_{m+1}, \ldots, not\ p_n \qquad (2)$$

A *fact* is a rule of the form (1) with $n = 0$. A program Π is a collection of ASP rules. We will use the following notation: $atom(\Pi)$ denotes the set of all atoms in Π, while $rules(p) = \{r : head(r) = p\}$ denotes the set of all the rules that define the atom p.

Let Π be a program; its *positive dependence graph* $\mathcal{D}_\Pi^+ = (V, E)$ is a directed graph, where $V = atom(\Pi)$ and $E = \{(p, q) : r \in \Pi, head(r) = p, q \in body^+(r)\}$. In particular, we are interested in recognizing cycles in $\mathcal{D}_\Pi^+$: a program Π is *tight* (resp., *non-tight*) if there are no (resp., there are) cycles in $\mathcal{D}_\Pi^+$. A *strongly connected component* of $\mathcal{D}_\Pi^+$ is a maximal subgraph X of $\mathcal{D}_\Pi^+$ such that there exists a path between each pair of nodes in X.

The *semantics* of ASP programs is expressed in terms of *answer sets*. An *interpretation* is a set M of atoms; $p \in M$ (resp. $p \notin M$) denotes the fact that p is true (resp. false). An interpretation is a *model* of a rule r if either $head(r) \in M$, $body^+(r) \setminus M \neq \emptyset$, or $body^-(r) \cap M \neq \emptyset$. M is a model of a program Π if it is a model of each rule in Π. M is an *answer set* of a program Π if it is the subset-minimal model of the *reduct program* Π^M, where the reduct is obtained from Π and M by first removing from Π all rules r such that $M \cap body^-(r) \neq \emptyset$ and then removing all the negated atoms from the remaining rules. Π^M is a *definite program*, i.e., a set of rules that does not contain any occurrence of *not*. Definite programs are characterized by the fact that they admit a unique minimal model. Each answer set of a program Π is, in particular, a minimal model of Π (we refer the reader to [2] for a detailed treatment).

2.2   Answer Set Computation

Let us recall some of the techniques that we will exploit in our proposal, namely the notion of ASP computation [22] and some of the techniques used by CLASP [13].

The CLASP system explores a search space composed of all interpretations for the atoms in Π, organized as a binary tree. The successful construction of a branch in the tree corresponds to the identification of an answer set of the program. If a (possibly partial) assignment fails to be a model of the rules in the program, then backjumping procedures are used to backtrack to the node in the tree that caused the failure. The tree construction and the backjumping procedures in CLASP are implemented in such a way to guarantee that, if a branch is successfully constructed, then the outcome will be an answer set of the program. CLASP's search is also guided by special assignments of truth values to subsets of atoms that are known not to be extendable into an answer set—these are referred to as *nogoods* [31]. Assignments and nogoods are sets of assigned atoms—i.e., entities of the form Tp or Fp, denoting that p has been assigned **true** or **false**, respectively. Each assignment should also contain at most one element between Tp and Fp for each atom p. Given an assignment A, let $A^T = \{p : Tp \in A\}$ and $A^F = \{p : Fp \in A\}$. Note that A^T is an interpretation. A *total* assignment A is such that, for every atom p, $\{Tp, Fp\} \cap A \neq \emptyset$. Given a (possibly partial) assignment A and a nogood δ, we say that δ is *violated* if $\delta \subseteq A$. In turn, A is a *solution* for a set of nogoods Δ if no $\delta \in \Delta$ is violated by A. The concept of nogood can be used during deterministic propagation phases (*unit propagation*) to determine additional assignments. Given a nogood δ and a partial assignment A such that $\delta \setminus A = \{Fp\}$ (resp., $\delta \setminus A = \{Tp\}$), then we can infer the need to add Tp (resp., Fp) to A in order to avoid violation of δ.

We distinguish two types of nogoods. The *completion nogoods* [10] are derived from the Clark completion of a logic program; we will denote with $\Delta_{\Pi_{cc}}$ the set of completion nogoods for the program Π. The *loop nogoods* Λ_Π [21] are derived from the loop formulae of Π. Let Π be a program and A an assignment [13]:

- If Π is tight, then $atom(\Pi) \cap A^T$ is an answer set of Π if and only if A is a solution of $\Delta_{\Pi_{cc}}$.
- If Π is not tight, then $atom(\Pi) \cap A^T$ is an answer set of Π if and only if A is a solution of $\Delta_{\Pi_{cc}} \cup \Lambda_\Pi$.

In this paper, we focus on the completion nogoods (although the solver might deal with the others as well). Let us define the Clark completion Π_{cc} of a program Π. For each rule $r \in \Pi$: $head(r) \leftarrow body(r)$ we add to Π_{cc} the formulae

$$\beta_r \leftrightarrow \tau_r \wedge \eta_r \qquad \tau_r \leftrightarrow \bigwedge_{a \in body^+(r)} a \qquad \eta_r \leftrightarrow \bigwedge_{b \in body^-(r)} \neg b \qquad (3)$$

where β_r, τ_r, η_r are new atoms. For each $p \in atom(\Pi)$, the following formula is added to Π_{cc} (if $rules(p) = \emptyset$, then the formula reduces simply to $\neg p$):

$$p \leftrightarrow \bigvee_{r \in rules(p)} \beta_r \qquad (4)$$

The *completion nogoods* reflect the structure of the implications in the formulae in Π_{cc}:

- From the first formula above we have the nogoods: $\{F\beta_r, T\tau_r, T\eta_r\}, \{T\beta_r, F\tau_r\}$, and $\{T\beta_r, F\eta_r\}$.
- From the second and third formula above we have the nogoods: $\{T\tau_r, Fa\}$ for each $a \in body^+(r)$; $\{T\eta_r, Tb\}$ for each $b \in body^-(r)$; $\{F\tau_r\} \cup \{Ta : a \in body^+(r)\}$; and $\{F\eta_r\} \cup \{Fa : b \in body^+(r)\}$.
- From the last formula we have the nogoods: $\{Fp, T\beta_r\}$ for each $r \in rules(p)$ and $\{Tp\} \cup \{F\beta_r : r \in rules(p)\}$.

$\Delta_{\Pi_{cc}}$ is the set of all the nogoods defined as above plus the constraints (2) that introduce nogoods of the form $\{Tp_1, \ldots, Tp_m, Fp_{m+1}, \ldots, Fp_n\}$.

The work described in [22] provides a *computation-based* characterization of answer sets for programs with abstract constraints. One of the outcomes of that research is the development of a computation-based view of answer sets for logic programs; we will refer to this model as ASP COMPUTATIONS. The computation-based characterization is based on an incremental construction process, where the choices are performed at the level of what rules are actually applied to extend the partial answer set. Let T_Π be the immediate consequence operator of Π: if I is an interpretation, then

$$T_\Pi(I) = \left\{ \begin{array}{c} p_0 : p_0 \leftarrow p_1, \ldots, p_m, not\ p_{m+1}, \ldots, not\ p_n \in \Pi\ \wedge \\ \{p_1, \ldots, p_m\} \subseteq I \wedge \{p_{m+1}, \ldots, p_n\} \cap I = \emptyset \end{array} \right\} \quad (5)$$

An *ASP Computation* of a program Π is a sequence of interpretations $I_0 = \emptyset, I_1, I_2, \ldots$ satisfying the following conditions:

- $I_i \subseteq I_{i+1}$ for all $i \geq 0$ (*Persistence of Beliefs*)
- $I_\infty = \bigcup_{i=0}^\infty I_i$ is such that $T_\Pi(I_\infty) = I_\infty$ (*Convergence*)
- $I_{i+1} \subseteq T_\Pi(I_i)$ for all $i \geq 0$ (*Revision*)
- if $a \in I_{i+1} \setminus I_i$ then there is a rule $a \leftarrow body$ in Π such that I_j is a model of $body$ for each $j \geq i$ (*Persistence of Reason*).

I_0 can be the empty set or, more in general, a set of atoms that are logical consequences of Π. We say that a computation $I_0, I_1, \ldots$ converges to I if $I = \bigcup_{i=0}^\infty I_i$. The results in [22] prove that, given a ground program Π, an interpretation I is an answer set of Π if and only if there exists an ASP computation that converges to I. I determines the assignment A such that $A^T = I$ and $A^- = atom(\Pi) \setminus I$.

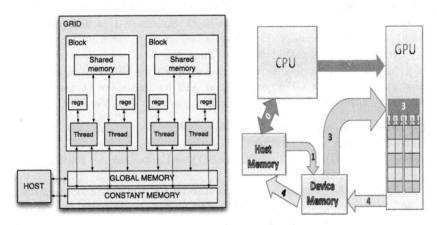

Fig. 1. CUDA Logical architecture   **Fig. 2.** Generic workflow in CUDA

2.3 CUDA

GPU computing is a general term indicating the use of the multi-cores available within modern GPUs for general purpose parallel computing. NVIDIA is one of the pioneering manufacturers in promoting GPU computing, especially thanks to its *Computing Unified Device Architecture (CUDA)* [27]. A GPU is composed of a collection of *Streaming Multi-processors (SMs)*; in turn, each SM contains a collection of computing cores (typically, 32 or 48). Each GPU provides access to both on-chip memory (used for thread registers and shared memory) and off-chip memory (used for L2 cache, global memory, and constant memory). The architecture of the GPU also determines the *GPU Clock* and the *Memory Clock* rates. The underlying conceptual model of parallelism supported by CUDA is *Single-Instruction Multiple-Thread (SIMT)*, where the same instruction is executed by different threads that run on identical cores, while data and operands may differ from thread to thread. CUDA's architectural model is represented in Fig. 1. A logical view of computations is introduced by CUDA, in order to define abstract parallel work and to schedule it among different hardware configurations. A typical CUDA program is a C/C++ program that includes parts meant for execution on the CPU (referred to as the *host*) and parts meant for parallel execution on the GPU (referred to as the *device*). The host program contains all the instructions necessary to initialize the data in the GPU, to define the number of threads and to manage the kernels. A kernel is a *device function*, namely, a set of instructions to be executed by many concurrent threads running on the GPU. The programmer organizes these threads in *thread blocks* and *grids* of blocks. Each thread in a block executes an instance of the kernel, and has a thread ID within its block. A grid is an array of blocks of threads that execute the same kernel, read data input from the global memory, and write results to the global memory. When a CUDA program on the host launches a grid of kernels, the blocks of the grid are distributed to the SMs with available execution capacity. The threads in the same block can share data, using shared high-throughput on-chip memory. The threads belonging to different blocks can only share data through the global memory. Thus, the block size allows the programmer to define the granularity of threads cooperation. Figure 1 shows the CUDA threads hierarchy. CUDA provides an API to interact with the GPU. A typical CUDA application can be summarized as follow (see Fig. 2):

Memory Allocation and Data Transfer. Before being processed by kernels, the data must be copied to GPU's global memory. The CUDA API supports memory allocation (`cudaMalloc()`) and data transfer to/from the host (`cudaMemcpy()`).

Kernel Definition. Kernels are defined as standard C functions; the annotation used to communicate to the CUDA compiler that a function should be treated as device function has the form:

$$\text{\_\_global\_\_ void kernelName(Formal Arguments).}$$

Kernel Execution. A grid of kernels can be launched from the host program by executing the call:

$$\text{kernelName} <<< \text{GridDim}, \text{TPB} >>> (\text{ActualArguments})$$

where `GridDim` is the number of blocks of the grid and `TPB` specifies the number of threads in each block.

Data Retrieval. After the execution of the device code, the host can retrieve the results through a transfer operation from global to host memory.

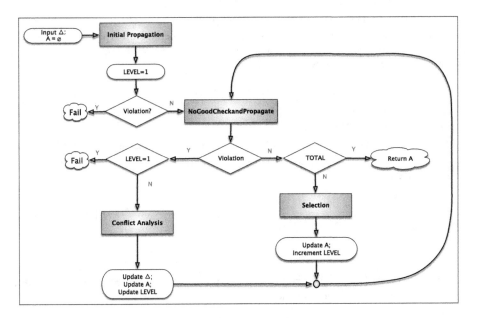

Fig. 3. CUD@ASP-computation: rectangle blocks exploit GPUs parallelism

3   Design of a Conflict-based CUDA ASP-Solver

In this section, we present the ASP solving procedure which exploits ASP computation, nogoods handling, and GPU parallelism. The ground program Π, as produced by the grounder GRINGO, is read by the CPU. The current implementation accepts as inputs programs possibly extended with choice rules and cardinality rules. Choice and cardinality rules are eliminated in advance by applying the technique described in [13]. In this prototype, we did not include weight rules and aggregates. The CPU computes the dependency graph of Π and its strongly connected components (using the classical Tarjan's algorithm) detecting, in particular, if the input program is tight. The CPU also computes the completion nogoods $\Delta_{\Pi_{cc}}$ and transfers them to the GPU. The CPU launches the various kernels summarized in Fig. 3. The rest of the computation is performed completely on the GPU. During this process, there are no memory transfers between the CPU and the GPU, with the exception of: **(1)** flow control flags, such as the "exit" flag, used to communicate whether the computation is terminated, and **(2)** the transfer of the computed answer set from the GPU to the CPU.

   The overall structure of the CUD@ASP-computation procedure (depicted in Fig. 3) is the conventional structure of an ASP solver. The differences lay in the selection heuristic (ASP computation) and in the parallelization of all the support functions involved. Each atom Π is uniquely identified by an *index* p. A vector A is used to represent the set of assigned atoms (with their truth values):

– $A[p] = 0$ if and only if the atom p is currently undefined;

Table 1. Main CUDA computations and the number of blocks/threads in each grid. TPB is the number of *threads-per-block* (in our experiments we empirically set it to 256). TPB* is the minimum between TPB and the number of nogoods related to recently assigned variables—See Sect. 3.2.

Main and auxiliary device computations	Blocks	Threads
InitialPropagation	⌈Num_Unit_Nogoods/TPB⌉	TPB
NoGoodCheckAndPropagate		
Binary/Ternary/General Completion Nogoods	Num_Rec_Assign_Vars	TPB*
Binary/Ternary/General Learned Nogoods	⌈Num_Nogoods/TPB⌉	TPB*
ConflictAnalysis		
MkNewNogood	1	1024
Backjump	⌈ Num_Tot_Atoms/TPB ⌉	TPB
Selection	1	TPB

- $A[p] = i$, $i > 0$ (resp., $A[p] = -i$) means that atom p has been assigned `true` (resp., `false`) at the decision level i.

The variable LEVEL represents the current *decision level*; this variable acts as a counter that keeps track of the number of *choices* that have been made in the computation of an answer set. These variables are stored and updated in the GPU. The vector A is transferred to the CPU as soon as an answer set is found.

In the rest of the section, we focus on the various kernels executed by the procedure CUD@ASP-computation. Concerning Fig. 3, rectangle blocks represent grids of kernels exploiting CUDA parallelism; each grid has its own number of blocks and of threads-per-block (TPB), as summarized in Table 1. We adopt the following notation: for each program atom p, $\overline{p}$ represents the atom with a truth value assigned; $\neg\overline{p}$ denotes instead the complement truth value with respect to $\overline{p}$. With Δ we refer to the variable storing the set of nogoods, initialized with those computed from the program Π and then monotonically increased during the computation.

3.1   The InitialPropagation Procedure

The set of nogoods Δ computed from the input program may include some unitary nogoods. A preliminary parallel computation partially initializes A by propagating them. Notice that the algorithm can be *restarted* several times— typically, this happens when more than one solution is requested. In such cases, the initial propagation also handles unit nogoods that have been learned in the previous executions. One grid of threads is launched with one thread for each unitary nogood (see Fig. 4). In particular, if k is the number of unitary nogoods, ⌈k/TPB⌉ blocks, with TPB threads each, are started. The sign of the literal p in each unitary nogood is analyzed and the entry $A[p]$ set accordingly. If one thread finds $A[p]$ already assigned in a inconsistent way, a Violation flag is set to true and the computation ends.

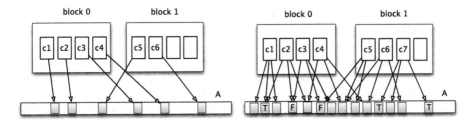

Fig. 4. Initial Propagation (left): a simple example of initial propagation, where $TPB = 4$ and 6 unitary nogoods have been identified. The propagation is executed in parallel running $2 = \lceil 6/4 \rceil$ thread blocks (cf. Sect. 3.1). **NoGoodCheckAndPropagate** (right): Assume $TPB = 4$ and that there are 7 nogoods with exactly 3 literals each. The truth values of such literals are checked in the current assignment A. Nogoods c2, and c3 are satisfied (at least one of their literals is false) while c7, having two satisfied literals, causes the propagation of its third literal (cf. Sect. 3.2).

The preliminary phase also includes a pre-processing step to enable special treatment of all other input nogoods, depending on their length, as described in the next section.

3.2 The NoGoodCheckAndPropagate Procedure

Given a partial assignment A, each nogood δ needs to be analyzed to detect whether: **(1)** δ is violated by A or **(2)** δ is not violated but there is exactly one literal in it that is unassigned in A (i.e., $\delta \setminus A = \{\overline{p}\}$, where $\overline{p} = Fp$ or $\overline{p} = Tp$)—in which case an inference step will add $\neg\overline{p}$ to A. The procedure is repeated until a fixpoint is reached.

To better exploit the SIMT parallelism and maximize the number of concurrently active threads, in each device computation the workload has to be divided among the threads of the grid as uniformly as possible. The set of nogoods is partitioned depending on their cardinality. Moreover, the **NoGoodCheckAndPropagate** is split in three steps, each one implemented by a different kernel grid. The first kernel grid deals with all the nogoods with exactly two literals; the second one processes the nogoods composed of three literals (cf. Fig. 4); the third grid processes all remaining nogoods.

All such kernels behave as follows. The execution of each iteration of **NoGoodCheckAndPropagate** is driven by the atoms that have already been assigned a truth value; in particular, in the first iteration, the procedure relies on the atoms that have been assigned by the **InitialPropagation**. The motivation is that only the atoms with an assigned truth value may trigger either a conflict or a propagation of a nogood. New assignments contribute to the following steps, either by enabling further propagations or by causing conflicts. Thus, each grid of kernels involves a number of blocks that is equal to the number of assigned atoms. The threads in each block process the nogoods that share the same assigned atom. The number of threads of each block is established by considering the number of occurrences of each assigned atom in the input nogoods. Observe that the dimension of the grid may change between two consecutive iterations of **NoGoodCheckAndPropagate**, and as such it is evaluated each time. Specific data structures (initialized once during the pre-processing phase) are used in order to determine, after each iteration of **NoGood-CheckAndPropagate** and for each assigned atom, which are the input nogoods to be considered in the next iteration. We observe that, despite the overhead of performing such a pre-processing, this selective treatment of nogoods proved to be very effective in practice, leading to several orders of magnitude of performance improvement with respect to a "blind" approach that treats all nogoods in the same manner. As mentioned, the third grid handles input nogood of cardinality greater than three. The processing of these nogoods is realized by implementing a standard technique based on *watched literals* [3]. In this case, each thread accesses the watched literals of a nogood and acts accordingly.

A similar approach is adopted to process those nogoods that are learned at run-time through the conflict analysis step (cf. Sect. 3.3). They are partitioned depending on their cardinality and processed by different grids, accordingly. In general, if n is the number of nogoods of one partition, the corresponding grid composes of $\lceil n/TPB \rceil$ blocks of TPB threads each. Each thread processes one learned nogood. *Watched literals* are exploited also for long learned nogoods.

During unit propagation, atoms may be assigned either `true` or `false` truth values. The assignment of `false` is not a critical component in ensuring stability, while assignment of `true` might lead to unfounded solutions. The **Selection** procedure, defined in Sect. 3.4, introduces only positively assigned atoms of the form β_r. Each β_r occurs in nogoods involving the "head" p and the auxiliary variables τ_r and η_r. In the subsequent call to **NoGoodCheckAndPropagate**, Tp and $T\eta_r$ are introduced in A. They are positive literals but asserting them does not invalidate stability of the final model, if any. This is because their truth values are strictly related to the supportedness of p, due to the choice of β_r by the **Selection** procedure. Moreover, the assignments Fb for $b \in body^-(r)$ are added, but being negative, they do not lead to unfounded solutions.

There are two cases when a positive, unsupported, literal may be assigned by unit propagation: **(1)** when the propagating nogood comes from a constraint of the initial program, and **(2)** when the nogood has been learned. In these cases, the literal is propagated anyway, but it is marked as "unsupported". The ASP computation described earlier would suggest not to propagate such positive assignment. However, performing such a propagation helps in the early detection of conflicts and significantly speeds up the search for a solution. Notice that these inferences have to be satisfied in the computed solution, because they are consequences of the conjunction of all selected literals. When a complete assignment is produced, for each marked atom an inspection is performed to check whether support for it has been generated after its assignment. Thanks to specific information gathered during the computation, this check is performed in constant time. If that is not the case, a restart is performed (for simplicity, this step is not depicted in Fig. 3).

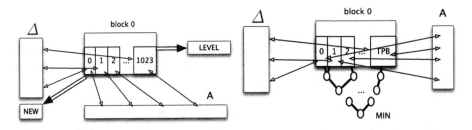

Fig. 5. ConflictAnalysis (left): one grid made of a single kernel block with 1024 threads analyzes the conflicts by performing backward resolution. For each learned nogood a new value for LEVEL is computed (Sect. 3.3). **Selection** (right): The Selection procedure assigns, in parallel, a heuristic score to each atom. Then, the best atom is determined by applying a parallel logarithmic reduction (cf. Sect. 3.4).

3.3   The ConflictAnalysis Procedure

The **ConflictAnalysis** procedure is used to resolve a conflict detected by the **NoGoodCheckAndPropagate**. The procedure identifies a LEVEL and an assignment $\bar{p}$ the computation should backjump to, in order to remove the nogood violation. This process allows classical backjumping in the search tree generated by the execution of CUD@ASP-computation [31]. This part of the solver is the one that is less suitable to SIMT parallelism, due to the fact that a (sequential) sequence of resolution steps must be encoded. This procedure ends with the identification of a unique implication point (UIP [25]) that determines the lower decision level/literal among those causing the detected conflicts. As default behavior, the solver selects one of the (possibly multiple) conflicts generated by **NoGoodCheckAndPropagate**. Heuristics can be applied to perform such a selection. In the current implementation priority is given to shorter nogoods. The kernels are run as a grid of a single block to facilitate synchronization— as we need to be sure that the first resolution step ends before the successive starts. The block contains a fixed number of threads (we use, by default, 1024 threads—see Fig. 5) and every thread takes care of one atom; if there are more atoms than threads involved in the learning, atoms are equally partitioned among threads. For each analyzed conflict, a new nogood is learned and added to Δ. This procedure takes also care of backtracking/backjumping, through the use of a specific grid of kernels (**Backjumping**). The target level for the backjump is computed and the data structures (e.g., the values of A and LEVEL) are updated accordingly. Notice that the prototype can learn from all the conflicts detected by the same run of **NoGoodCheckAndPropagate**. The number of conflicts to process can be specified through a command-line option. In case of multiple learned nogoods involving different "target" decision levels, the lowest level is selected.

3.4   The Selection Procedure

The purpose of this procedure is to determine an unassigned atom in the program. For each unassigned atom p occurring in the head of a clause in the original program, all nogoods reflecting the rule $\beta_r \leftarrow \tau_r, \eta_r$, such that $r \in rules(p)$ are analyzed to check whether $T\tau_r \in A$ and $F\eta_r \notin A$ (i.e., the rule is applicable). All p and all rules r that pass this test are evaluated according to a heuristic weight. Typical heuristics are used to rank the atoms. In particular, we consider the number of positive/negative occurrences of atoms in the program (by either simply counting the occurrences or by applying the *Jeroslow-Wang* heuristics) and the "activity" of atoms [16]. Using a logarithmic parallel reduction scheme, the rule r with highest ranking is selected (see Fig. 5). Then, $T\beta_r$ is added to A. In the subsequent execution of **NoGoodCheckAndPropagate**, Tp and $F\eta_r$ are also added to A. $F\eta_r$ imposes that all the atoms of $body^-(r)$ are set to false. This ensures the *persistence of beliefs* of the ASP computation.

4   Experimental Results

We have tested the software we have developed with six NVIDIA GPUs with different computing capabilities. The following table shows the micro-architecture codename, the number of cores, and the GPU clock of the GPUs. (Complete descriptions can be retrieved from NVIDIA website.)

GeForce cards	**Tesla** cards
GT520: Fermi, 48 cores, 1620 MHz	C2075: Tesla, 448 cores, 1147 MHz
GTX560: Fermi, 336 cores, 1800 MHz	K80: Kepler, 2496 cores, 562 MHz
GTX960: Maxwell, 1024 cores, 1278 MHz	K40: Kepler, 2880 cores, 745 MHz

Table 3 shows the results obtained for some of the benchmarks we used. Namely, those coming from the grounding of `stablemarriage`, `visitall`, `graph_colouring`, `labyrinth`, `ppm`, and `sokoban` programs and instances (material from ASP competitions—https://www.mat.unical.it/aspcomp2014/). As one might expect, running times depend on the card computing power. However, differences between the two macro families of cards (GeForce vs Tesla) emerge. In fact, GeForce cards are "real" GPUs, developed for graphical applications. Tesla cards are instead developed for computing purposes and are optimized for double precision floating point operations (including error correction checks). Figure 6 summarizes graphically the results, where instances are reordered according to running time, for a better rendering.

The best GTX card provides the best performance. The dominance of the GTX platform can be explained by the fact that the solver has been specifically developed for this type of architecture, while the Tesla machines have been used later only for testing. Some tuning of the code for the Tesla is expected to provide improved results and it is the focus of future work.

In Table 2 we compare the characteristics of the cards within the different two classes as well as the average speedups with respect to the less powerful card within each class. We assigned a POWER rating to each card, computed as the

Table 2. Brief summary of results. POWER is $\log_{10}(\text{noc} \cdot \text{gclo} \cdot \text{mclo})$.

	GT 520	GTX 560	GTX 960	C2075	K80	K40
AVERAGE SPEED-UP	1	1.81	2.72	1	1.2	1.3
noc: number of CORES	48	336	1024	448	2496	2880
gclo: GPU clock (MHz)	1620	1800	1278	1147	562	745
mclo: Memory Clock (MHz)	500	2004	3505	1566	2505	3004
POWER index	7.59	9.08	9.66	8.91	9.55	9.81

logarithm of the product of the number of GPU cores, the clock frequency of each core, and the clock of the memory. The measure is not a comprehensive measurement of all the architectural details of the cards we are using. However, the average speedup is well-approximated by the fraction of the ratio of the powers elevated to the cube. For instance, comparing the K40 and the C2057 one obtains $(\frac{9.81}{8.91})^3 \approx 1.3)$.

Table 3 summarizes the experimental results; the column *Answer* indicates whether the benchmark instances admits or not at least one answer set; the remaining columns provide the execution time in seconds for the different GPUs. The figures in boldface represent the best performance for each benchmark instance. The benchmarks marked *(*)* are among those that had been already used in our preliminary work [9]; note that the results presented in this paper show an improvement of 2 to 4 times with respect to the running times reported in [9].

The fact that the speedup is not the same in all experiments can be explained by how the propagation phase is performed by the kernels described in Sect. 3.2. Whenever a literal can be propagated in different ways, because it is the unique unassigned literal in several distinct nogoods, a race condition may occur involving the threads that process such nogoods. This may end up introducing a level of non-determinism in the computation. Furthermore, it is important to remember that different architectures may differ in the scheduling algorithms exploited to distribute tasks to the multi-processors. Since the specific sequence of inferences that produced a conflict is exploited by the conflict analysis step, the non-determinism of the generation of this sequence translates in the possibility of learning different nogoods. Since the learned nogoods drive the subsequent search, these differences may therefore affect the running time.

The system has been experimentally compared with CLASP; since our system does not implement any of the heuristics used by CLASP, we compared against CLASP with the heuristics disabled. For 8 of the 25 instances, CLASP fails to terminate within a 900-second time limit. Observe that, with the standard heuristics enabled, CLASP is still (much) faster than our system on all the benchmarks.

Several aspects of the current implementation deserve further investigation. As mentioned earlier, the unfounded set check, which is part of the CLASP implementation, represents a challenge to parallel implementation, especially due to the *reachability bottleneck* [18]. A fast implementation of this module would

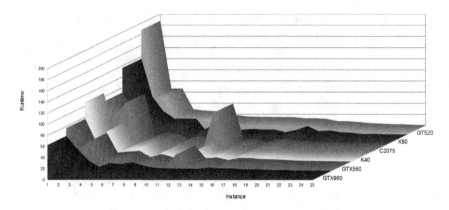

Fig. 6. A visualization of the experiments. The x axis reports the 25 studied instances (in decreasing order w.r.t. running time). The y axis shows running times in seconds. The GPU models are shown on the z axis.

allow us to use safely other search heuristics combined with the ASP computation. Conflict-driven learning suffers from the same problem (and currently takes roughly 50 % of the computation time). This is the real bottleneck, because of the intrinsic seriality of the algorithm used for conflict analysis.

The use of the ASP computation approach has the advantage of ensuring the stability of the determined models. As suggested in related literature (e.g., [17]), the restriction to branching heuristics may have an impact on the length of the search, compared to strategies that adopt unrestricted branching strategies (e.g., for model computation, coupled with explicit checks for stability). Analysis of these factors will be addressed as future work.

We are still working to speed-up this part as much as possible, but the current results already show the scalability and feasibility of the overall approach. Alternative approaches should be considered. A first attempt in developing alternative learning schemes, specifically designed to benefit from SIMT parallelism, can be found in [12]. Another possibility is to use a GPU thread as the "host" of the main loop (that is currently assigned to the CPU). This would reduce the running time for the transfer of flags at the end of any grid execution. On the other hand, *dynamic parallelism*—namely, the capability of launching a grid of kernels from a kernel—is supported only by the most recent devices. Finally, another interesting approach to consider is the execution of the final part of the search (i.e., subtrees of the search space located in the bottom-most part of the search tree) using an exhaustive search among all possible assignments for the remaining unassigned atoms (e.g., when 30-40 atoms are unassigned). This would exploit well the GPU parallelism. However, this would require the development of fast parallel algorithms for unfounded set extraction, in order to learn useful nogoods from non-stable total assignments.

Table 3. Performance of the GPU-based solver on instances from the 2014 ASP competition. In **boldface** the fastest execution of the benchmark, <u>underlined</u>, the fastest execution in the other class of GPUs. The rightmost column reports clasp timing where heuristics have been disabled. t.o. means more than 900 s (time out)

INSTANCE		Answer	GT 520	GTX 560	GTX 960	C2075	K80	K40	clasp*
0001-stablemarriage-0-0	*	Sat	11.73	6.84	**4.68**	9.41	15.52	<u>6.04</u>	t.o
0001-visitall-14-1	*	Sat	65.99	51.97	**18.56**	89.87	<u>42.08</u>	54.74	0.02
0002-stablemarriage-0-0	*	Sat	15.34	6.69	**4.97**	7.12	8.75	<u>6.15</u>	t.o
0003-stablemarriage-0-0		Sat	12.68	7.15	**4.66**	8.49	8.72	<u>7.62</u>	t.o
0003-visitall-14-1	*	Sat	66.07	<u>35.04</u>	39.61	65.97	67.83	**25.11**	0.01
0004-stablemarriage-0-0		Sat	14.87	8.02	**3.80**	9.76	9.28	<u>8.78</u>	t.o
0005-stablemarriage-0-0		Sat	15.19	29.55	**4.09**	72.01	<u>10.11</u>	19.70	t.o
0007-graph_colouring-125-0	*	Sat	29.00	16.51	**6.84**	<u>13.86</u>	28.90	16.00	44.71
0007-stablemarriage-0-0		Sat	12.79	<u>3.17</u>	6.27	**3.15**	4.23	3.40	t.o
0008-stablemarriage-0-0		Sat	7.64	4.53	**3.40**	5.18	7.58	<u>5.01</u>	t.o
0009-labyrinth-11-0	*	Sat	6.08	3.60	**2.26**	<u>3.39</u>	4.45	3.69	0.71
0009-stablemarriage-0-0		Sat	7.80	4.88	**3.16**	<u>4.90</u>	5.97	6.58	t.o
0010-graph_colouring-125-0	*	Sat	3.44	1.83	<u>1.52</u>	2.13	**1.24**	1.60	8.22
0039-labyrinth-11-0		Sat	24.39	<u>8.33</u>	15.45	9.38	4.03	**3.30**	0.02
0061-ppm-70-0	*	Unsat	2.19	1.08	**0.56**	0.90	0.94	<u>0.77</u>	0.05
0072-ppm-70-0	*	Unsat	2.25	1.57	**0.99**	<u>1.38</u>	1.76	1.63	0.03
0121-ppm-120-0	*	Unsat	15.79	8.16	**5.69**	<u>8.19</u>	10.86	8.94	0.31
0128-ppm-120-0	*	Sat	0.70	0.64	<u>0.25</u>	0.37	0.34	**0.24**	0.03
0129-ppm-120-0	*	Unsat	14.96	6.25	**4.19**	7.26	8.99	<u>7.18</u>	0.08
0130-ppm-90-0	*	Unsat	4.00	2.23	**1.63**	<u>2.32</u>	3.60	2.48	0.01
0153-ppm-90-0	*	Sat	1.18	0.89	**0.44**	0.66	0.71	<u>0.58</u>	0.02
0167-sokoban-15-1	*	Sat	25.43	19.48	**11.83**	<u>18.99</u>	28.24	23.59	0.01
0345-sokoban-17-1		Sat	187.87	76.86	**62.54**	<u>91.30</u>	135.95	106.73	0.93
0482-sokoban-15-1		Sat	26.67	18.20	**13.88**	<u>21.58</u>	29.09	23.60	0.24
0589-sokoban-15-1	*	Unsat	17.92	14.08	**9.65**	<u>15.18</u>	21.35	16.83	0.07
SUM			591.97	337.55	**230.92**	472.75	460.52	360.29	

5 Conclusions

We have presented the first ASP solver running on GPUs and experimentally proved that the approach scales well on the power of the devices. The solver is not yet ready to challenge the best ASP solvers, e.g., CLASP, with their default heuristics (although it proves to be faster as soon as the heuristics are removed). Those solvers include families of heuristics for driving the search that are not (yet) implemented in our solver. A sensible speedup will be obtained as soon as the conflict analysis will be implemented by exploiting a truly parallel schema. Another point to be addressed is the development of an ad-hoc parallel handling of the cardinality constraints/aggregates by suitable device functions instead of removing them in the pre-processing stage, thus removing relevant structural information.

References

1. Balduccini, M., Pontelli, E., El-Khatib, O., Le, H.: Issues in parallel execution of non-monotonic reasoning systems. Parallel Comput. **31**(6), 608–647 (2005)

2. Baral, C.: Knowledge Representation, Reasoning and Declarative Problem Solving. Cambridge University Press, Cambridge (2010)
3. Biere, A., Heule, M., van Maaren, H., Walsh, T. (eds.): Handbook of Satisfiability (Frontiers in Artificial Intelligence and Applications), vol. 185. IOS Press, Amsterdam (2009)
4. Campeotto, F., Dal Palù, A., Dovier, A., Fioretto, F., Pontelli, E.: Exploring the use of GPUs in constraint solving. In: Flatt, M., Guo, H.-F. (eds.) PADL 2014. LNCS, vol. 8324, pp. 152–167. Springer, Heidelberg (2014)
5. Campeotto, F., Dovier, A., Fioretto, F., Pontelli, E.: A GPU implementation of large neighborhood search for solving constraint optimization problems. In: Schaub, T., Friedrich, G., O'Sullivan, B. (eds.) ECAI 2014–21st European Conference on Artificial Intelligence - Including Prestigious Applications of Intelligent Systems (PAIS) 2014. Frontiers in Artificial Intelligence and Applications, vol. 263, pp. 189–194. IOS Press, Prague, Czech Republic (2014)
6. Campeotto, F., Dovier, A., Pontelli, E.: A declarative concurrent system for protein structure prediction on GPU. J. Exp. Theor. Artif. Intell. (JETAI) 27(5), 503–541 (2015)
7. Dal Palù, A., Dovier, A., Formisano, A., Pontelli, E.: CUD@SAT: SAT solving on GPUs. J. Exp. Theor. Artif. Intell. (JETAI) 27(3), 293–316 (2015)
8. Dal Palù, A., Dovier, A., Pontelli, E., Rossi, G.: GASP: answer set programming with lazy grounding. Fundamenta Informaticae 96(3), 297–322 (2009)
9. Dovier, A., Formisano, A., Pontelli, E., Vella, F.: Parallel execution of the ASP computation - an investigation on GPUs. In: De Vos, M., Eiter, T., Lierler, Y., Toni, F. (eds.) Technical Communications of the 31st International Conference on Logic Programming (ICLP 2015), Cork, Ireland, August 31 - September 4, 2015, vol. 1433, CEUR Workshop Proceedings (2015). CEUR-WS.org
10. Fages, F.: Consistency of Clark's completion and existence of stable models. Methods Logic Comput. Sci. 1(1), 51–60 (1994)
11. Finkel, R.A., Marek, V.W., Moore, N., Truszczynski, M.: Computing stable models in parallel. In: Answer Set Programming, Towards Efficient and Scalable Knowledge Representation and Reasoning, Proceedings of the 1st International ASP 2001 Workshop, Stanford (2001)
12. Formisano, A., Vella, F.: On multiple learning schemata in conflict driven solvers. In: Bistarelli, S., Formisano, A. (eds.) Proceedings of ICTCS 2014, vol. 1231, pp. 133–146. CEUR Workshop Proceedings, (2014). CEUR-WS.org
13. Gebser, M., Kaminski, R., Kaufmann, B., Schaub, T.: Answer set solving in practice. Morgan & Claypool Publishers, San Rafael (2012)
14. Gebser, M., Kaufmann, B., Schaub, T.: Multi-threaded ASP solving with clasp. TPLP 12(4–5), 525–545 (2012)
15. Gelfond, M.: Answer sets. In: van Harmelen, F., Lifschitz, V., Porter, B.W. (eds.) Handbook of Knowledge Representation. Foundations of Artificial Intelligence, vol. 3, pp. 285–316. Elsevier, Amsterdam (2008)
16. Goldberg, E., Novikov, Y.: BerkMin: a fast and robust SAT-solver. Discrete Appl. Math. 155(12), 1549–1561 (2007)
17. Järvisalo, M., Junttila, T.A., Niemelä, I.: Unrestricted vs restricted cut in a tableau method for boolean circuits. Ann. Math. Artif. Intell. 44(4), 373–399 (2005)
18. Kao, M., Klein, P.N.: Towards overcoming the transitive-closure bottleneck: efficient parallel algorithms for planar digraphs. J. Comput. Syst. Sci. 47(3), 459–500 (1993)
19. Khronos Group Inc., OpenCL: the open standard for parallel programming of heterogeneous systems (2015). http://www.khronos.org

20. Khuller, S., Vishkin, U.: On the parallel complexity of digraph reachability. Inf. Process. Lett. **52**(5), 239–241 (1994)
21. Lin, F., Zhao, Y.: ASSAT: computing answer sets of a logic program by SAT solvers. Artif. Intell. **157**(1), 115–137 (2004)
22. Liu, L., Pontelli, E., Son, T.C., Truszczynski, M.: Logic programs with abstract constraint atoms: the role of computations. Artif. Intell. **174**(3–4), 295–315 (2010)
23. Manolios, P., Zhang, Y.: Implementing survey propagation on graphics processing units. In: Biere, A., Gomes, C.P. (eds.) SAT 2006. LNCS, vol. 4121, pp. 311–324. Springer, Heidelberg (2006)
24. Marek, V.W., Truszczynski, M.: Stable models and an alternative logic programming paradigm (1998). CoRR, cs.LO/9809032
25. Marques-Silva, J.P., Sakallah, K.A.: GRASP: a search algorithm for propositional satisfiability. IEEE Trans. Comput. **48**(5), 506–521 (1999)
26. Niemelä, I.: Logic programs with stable model semantics as a constraint programming paradigm. Ann. Math. Artif. Intell. **25**(3–4), 241–273 (1999)
27. NVIDIA Corporation. NVIDIA CUDA Zone (2015). https://developer.nvidia.com/cuda-zone
28. Perri, S., Ricca, F., Sirianni, M.: Parallel instantiation of ASP programs: techniques and experiments. TPLP **13**(2), 253–278 (2013)
29. Cabalar, P.: Answer set; programming? In: Balduccini, M., Son, T.C. (eds.) Logic Programming, Knowledge Representation, and Nonmonotonic Reasoning. LNCS, vol. 6565, pp. 334–343. Springer, Heidelberg (2011)
30. Pontelli, E., Le, H.V., Son, T.C.: An investigation in parallel execution of answer set programs on distributed memory platforms: task sharing and dynamic scheduling. Comput. Lang. Syst. Struct. **36**(2), 158–202 (2010)
31. Rossi, F., van Beek, P., Walsh, T.: Handbook of Constraint Programming. Foundations of Artificial Intelligence. Elsevier Science Inc., New York (2006)
32. Simons, P., Niemelä, I., Soininen, T.: Extending and implementing the stable model semantics. Artif. Intell. **138**(1–2), 181–234 (2002)
33. Syrjänen, T., Niemelä, I.: The smodels system. In: Eiter, T., Faber, W., Truszczyński, M. (eds.) LPNMR 2001. LNCS (LNAI), vol. 2173, pp. 434–438. Springer, Heidelberg (2001)

The Picat-SAT Compiler

Neng-Fa Zhou[1][(✉)] and Håkan Kjellerstrand[2]

[1] CUNY Brooklyn College and Graduate Center, Brooklyn, USA
nzhou@acm.org
[2] Independent Researcher, Malmö, Sweden
http://www.hakank.org

Abstract. SAT has become the backbone of many software systems. In order to make full use of the power of SAT solvers, a SAT compiler must encode domain variables and constraints into an efficient SAT formula. Despite many proposals for SAT encodings, there are few working SAT compilers. This paper presents Picat-SAT, the SAT compiler in the Picat system. Picat-SAT employs the sign-and-magnitude log encoding for domain variables. Log-encoding for constraints resembles the binary representation of numbers used in computer hardware, and many algorithms and optimization opportunities have been exploited by hardware design systems. This paper gives the encoding algorithms for constraints, and attempts to experimentally justify the choices of the algorithms for the addition and multiplication constraints. This paper also presents preliminary, but quite encouraging, experimental results.

1 Introduction

SAT solvers' performance has drastically improved during the past 20 years, thanks to the inventions of techniques from conflict-driven clause learning, backjumping, variable and value selection heuristics, to random restarts [1,4,23]. SAT has become the backbone of many software systems, including specification languages for model generation and checking [9,17,18,22], planning [21,27], program analysis and test pattern generation [28], answer set programming [6,12], and solvers for general constraint satisfaction problems (CSPs) [15,19,29,31,33].

In order to fully exploit the power of SAT solvers, a compiler is needed to Booleanize constraints as formula in the conjunctive normal form (CNF) or some other acceptable form. The encodings of constraints have big impact on the runtime of SAT solvers [2]. Several encodings of domain variables have been proposed, including *sparse* encoding [13,33], *order* encoding [8,25,31], and *log* encoding [16]. Log-encoding has less propagation power than sparse encodings for certain constraints [11], but is much more compact than other encodings. The FznTini compiler [15] adopts two's complement representation for domain variables.

For each encoding, there are different ways to Booleanize constraints. The hardness of a CNF formula is normally determined by several parameters, such as the number of clauses and the number of variables. There is no commonly

© Springer International Publishing Switzerland 2016
M. Gavanelli and J. Reppy (Eds.): PADL 2016, LNCS 9585, pp. 48–62, 2016.
DOI: 10.1007/978-3-319-28228-2_4

accepted definition for the optimality of SAT formulas, and SAT compiler writers have to rely on intensive experimentation to find good formulas that are compact and enhance propagation opportunities for the used SAT solver.

We have developed a SAT compiler for Picat [35], called *Picat-SAT*, which adopts the *sign-and-magnitude* log-encoding for domain variables. Log-encoding for constraints resembles the binary representation of numbers used in computer hardware, and many algorithms and optimization opportunities have been exploited by hardware design systems. Despite many proposals for SAT encodings, there are few working SAT compilers, and there are basically no working SAT compilers that are based on log-encoding.[1]

In this paper, we describe the algorithms for Booleanizing constraints employed in Picat-SAT. All of the algorithms are either well known or can be easily derived from the well-known algorithms used in hardware designs. This paper attempts to experimentally justify the choices of the algorithms for the addition and multiplication constraints. This paper also compares Picat-SAT with the following solvers: Sugar and Azucar, two SAT compilers based on order-encoding, and the winning CP solvers of MiniZinc Challenge 2015. The experimental results show that Picat-SAT is competitive with Sugar and Azucar, and that Picat-SAT outperforms the MiniZinc Challenge winners on some of the benchmarks.

Section 2 gives the API of the constraint modules in Picat. Section 3 describes the sign-and-magnitude log encoding adopted in Picat-SAT for domain variables. Section 4 details the algorithms used in Picat-SAT for compiling constraints, including the *enumeration* algorithm for the addition constraint $X + Y = Z$, the *shift-and-add* algorithm for the multiplication constraint $X \times Y = Z$, the use of the Espresso logic optimizer for the table constraint, and the decomposition algorithms for global constraints. Section 5 presents and analyzes the experimental results. We also implemented a transformation algorithm for the addition constraint, and the Karatsuba algorithm for the multiplication constraint. These two algorithms are described in the appendices.

2 Picat's Constraint Modules

Picat is a simple, and yet powerful, logic-based multi-paradigm programming language aimed for general-purpose applications [34,35]. Picat provides solver modules, including the `sat`, `cp`, and `mip` modules. All these three modules implement the same set of basic linear constraints. The `cp` and `sat` modules also implement non-linear and global constraints, and the `mip` module also supports real-domain variables. The common interface that Picat provides for the solver modules allows seamless switching from one solver to another.

As a constraint programming language, Picat resembles CLP(FD): the operator `::` is used for domain constraints, the operators `#=`, `#!=`, `#>`, `#>=`, `#<`, and `#=<` are for arithmetic constraints, and the operators `#/\` (and), `#\/` (or), `#^` (xor), `#~` (not), `#=>` (if), and `#<=>` (iff) are for Boolean constraints. Picat supports many global constraints, such as `all_different/1`, `element/3`, and `cumulative/4`. In

---

[1] The FznTini compiler is not maintained.

addition to intensional constraints, Picat also supports extensional constraints, or *table constraints*.

For example, the following gives a program in Picat for solving the Sudoku problem:

```
import sat.

main =>
    Board = {{5,3,_,_,7,_,_,_,_},
             {6,_,_,1,9,5,_,_,_},
             {_,9,8,_,_,_,_,6,_},
             {8,_,_,_,6,_,_,_,3},
             {4,_,_,8,_,3,_,_,1},
             {7,_,_,_,2,_,_,_,6},
             {_,_,_,_,_,_,_,_,_},
             {_,_,_,_,_,_,_,_,_},
             {_,_,_,_,_,_,_,_,_}},
    sudoku(Board),
    foreach(Row in Board) writeln(Row) end.

sudoku(Board) =>
    N = Board.len,
    Vars = Board.vars(),
    Vars :: 1..N,
    foreach (Row in Board) all_different(Row) end,
    foreach (J in 1..N)
       all_different([Board[I,J] : I in 1..N])
    end,
    M = round(sqrt(N)),
    foreach (I in 1..M..N-M, J in 1..M..N-M)
       all_different([Board[I+K,J+L] : K in 0..M-1, L in 0..M-1])
    end,
    solve(Vars).
```

The first line imports the `sat` module, which defines the used built-ins by this program, including the operator `::`, the global constraint `all_different`, and the `solve` predicate for labeling variables. For a given board, the `sudoku` predicate retrieves the length of the board (`Board.len`), extracts the variables from the board (`Board.vars()`),[2] generates the constraints, and calls `solve(Vars)` to label the variables. The first `foreach` loop ensures that each row of `Board` has different values. The second `foreach` loop ensures that each column of `Board` has different values. The list comprehension `[Board[I,J] : I in 1..N]` returns the Jth column of `Board` as a list. Let M be the size of the sub-squares (M = `round(sqrt(N))`). The third `foreach` loop ensures that each of the N M×M squares has different values. As demonstrated by this example, Picat's language constructs such as functions, arrays, loops, and list comprehensions make Picat as powerful as other modeling languages, such as OPL [14] and MiniZinc [26], for CSPs.

3   The Sign-and-Magnitude Log Encoding

Picat-SAT employs the so called *log-encoding* for domain variables. For a domain variable, $\lceil log_2(n) \rceil$ Boolean variables are used, where n is the maximum absolute

---

[2] Picat supports the dot-notation for chaining function calls. The function call `Board.vars()` is the same as `vars(Board)`.

value in the domain. If the domain contains both negative and positive values, then another Boolean variable is used to represent the sign. In this paper, for a log-encoded domain variable X, $X.\mathtt{s}$ denotes the sign, $X.\mathtt{m}$ denotes the magnitude, which is a vector of Boolean variables $< X_{n-1} X_{n-2} \ldots X_1 X_0 >$.

This *sign-and-magnitude* encoding is simple, and is well suited to Booleanizing certain constraints, such as $\mathtt{abs}(X) = Y$ and $-X = Y$. However, this encoding requires a clause to disallow negative zero if the domain contains values of both signs. This extra clause is unnecessary if 2's complement encoding is used, as in [15]. Each combination of values of these Boolean variables represents a valuation for the domain variable. If there are holes in the domain, then disequality ($\neq$) constraints are generated to disallow assignments of those hole values to the variable. Also, inequality constraints ($\geq$ and $\leq$) are generated to prohibit assigning out-of-bounds values to the variable.

For small-domain variables that can be encoded with 14 bits, including the sign bit, Picat-SAT calls the logic optimizer, Espresso [5], to generate an optimal CNF formula. For example, for the domain constraint $X \; :: \; \mathtt{[-2,-1,2,1]}$, Espresso returns the following two CNF clauses:

$\mathtt{X_0} \lor \mathtt{X_1}$
$\neg\mathtt{X_0} \lor \neg\mathtt{X_1}$

which make it impossible to assign -3, 0, or 3 to $\mathtt{X}$.

4   Booleanization of Constraints

Picat-SAT flattens intensional constraints into *primitive, reified*, and *implicative* constraints. A primitive constraint is one of the following: $\Sigma_i^n B_i \; r \; c$ (r is $=$, $\geq$, or $\leq$, and c is 1 or 2) , $X \; r \; Y$ (r is $=$, $\neq$, $>$, $\geq$, $<$, or $\leq$), $\mathtt{abs}(X) = Y$, $-X = Y$, $X + Y = Z$, and $X \times Y = Z$, where B_i is a Boolean variable, and X, Y, and Z are integers or log-encoded integer domain variables.[3]

The sign-and-magnitude encoding facilitates Booleanization of some of the primitive constraints. For example, $\mathtt{abs}(X) = Y$ is translated to:

$X.\mathtt{m} = Y.\mathtt{m} \land Y.\mathtt{s} = 0$

and the constraint $-X = Y$ is translated to:

$(X.\mathtt{m} = Y.\mathtt{m}) \land (X.\mathtt{s} \neq Y.\mathtt{s} \lor X.\mathtt{m} = 0)$

The at-least-one constraint $\Sigma_i^n B_i \geq 1$ is encoded into one CNF clause:

$B_1 \lor B_2 \lor \ldots \lor B_n$

---

[3] The operators $\mathtt{div}$ and $\mathtt{mod}$ can be expressed by using the multiplication operator $\times$. In the implemented version of Picat-SAT, Pseudo-Boolean constraints are treated in the same way as other linear constraints, except for the special case $\Sigma_i^n B_i \; r \; c$ ($c = 1$ or 2).

The at-least-two constraint $\Sigma_i^n B_i \geq 2$ is converted into n at-least-one constraints: for each $n-1$ variables, the sum of the variables is at least one. The at-most-one constraint $\Sigma_i B_i \leq 1$ is encoded into CNF by using Jingchao Chen's algorithm [7], which splits the sequence of Boolean variables into two subsequences, and encodes the sum $\Sigma_i^n B_i$ as the Cartesian product of the two subsequences. The at-most-two constraint is converted into n at-most-one constraints. The exactly-one constraint $\Sigma_i^n B_i = 1$ is converted into a conjunction of an at-least-one constraint and an at-most-one constraint. The exactly-two constraint is compiled in the same way.

A recursive algorithm is utilized to encode each of the binary primitive constraints of the form $X \ r \ Y$, where r is $=, \neq, >, \geq, <,$ or $\leq$. For example, consider $X \geq Y$. This constraint is translated to the following:

$$X.s = 0 \wedge Y.s = 1 \ \vee$$
$$X.s = 1 \wedge Y.s = 1 \Rightarrow X.m \leq Y.m \ \vee$$
$$X.s = 0 \wedge Y.s = 0 \Rightarrow X.m \geq Y.m$$

Let $X.m = <X_{n-1}X_{n-2}\ldots X_1X_0>$ and $Y.m = <Y_{n-1}Y_{n-2}\ldots Y_1Y_0>$, where X_i and Y_i are Boolean variables, $i = 0,\ldots,n-1$. The following function returns the CNF formula for $X.m \geq Y.m$:

```
ge(<X_{n-1}X_{n-2}...X_1X_0>, <Y_{n-1}Y_{n-2}...Y_1Y_0>):
    if n = 1 then return the CNF formula for X_0 ≥ Y_0;
    return the CNF formula for X_{n-1} > Y_{n-1} ∨
        X_{n-1} = Y_{n-1} ∧ ge(<X_{n-2}...X_1X_0>, <Y_{n-2}...Y_1Y_0>);
```

A reified constraint has the form $B \Leftrightarrow C$, and an implicative constraint has the form $B \Rightarrow C$, where B is a Boolean variable and C is a primitive constraint. The reified constraint $B \Leftrightarrow C$ is equivalent to $B \Rightarrow C$ and $\neg B \Rightarrow \neg C$, where $\neg C$ is the negation of C. Let $C_1 \wedge \ldots \wedge C_n$ be the CNF formula of C after Booleanization. Then $B \Rightarrow C$ can be encoded into $C_1' \wedge \ldots \wedge C_n'$, where $C_i' = C_i \vee \neg B$ for $i = 1,\ldots,n$.

4.1 Booleanization of the Addition Constraint

This subsection considers the Booleanization of the constraint $X + Y = Z$, where the operands are log-encoded integers or integer-domain variables. If all of the operands are non-negative (i.e., $X.s = 0$ and $Y.s = 0$), then the constraint can be rewritten into the unsigned addition $X.m + Y.m = Z.m$. Let $X.m = X_{n-1}\ldots X_1X_0$, $Y.m = Y_{n-1}\ldots Y_1Y_0$, and $Z.m = Z_n\ldots Z_1Z_0$. The unsigned addition can be Booleanized by using logic adders as follows:

$$\begin{array}{r} X_{n-1} \ldots X_1 \ X_0 \\ + \ Y_{n-1} \ldots Y_1 \ Y_0 \\ \hline Z_n \ Z_{n-1} \ldots Z_1 \ Z_0 \end{array}$$

A half-adder is employed for $X_0 + Y_0 = C_1Z_0$, where C_1 the carry-out. For each other position i $(0 < i \leq n-1)$, a full adder is employed for $X_i + Y_i + C_i = C_{i+1}Z_i$. The top-most bit of Z, Z_n, is equal to C_n.

If any of the variables in the addition constraint has both negative and positive values in the domain, then the Booleanization of the constraint is not so straightforward. Although the compiler makes efforts not to create negative-domain variables when flattening constraints into primitive ones, some problem variables may be negative. Picat-SAT adopts the *enumeration* algorithm for the general addition constraint. We also implemented another algorithm, called *transformation*, which replaces negative domain values by non-negative domain values in the addition constraint. This algorithm is given in Appendix A, together with the experimental results that justify the choice of the enumeration algorithm.

The *enumeration* algorithm translates the addition constraint $X + Y = Z$ into the following conjunction of conditional constraints, each of which takes care of a combination of signs of the operands.

$$X.\mathtt{s} = 0 \wedge Y.\mathtt{s} = 0 \Rightarrow Z.\mathtt{s} = 0 \wedge X.\mathtt{m}+Y.\mathtt{m} = Z.\mathtt{m}$$
$$X.\mathtt{s} = 1 \wedge Y.\mathtt{s} = 1 \Rightarrow Z.\mathtt{s} = 1 \wedge X.\mathtt{m}+Y.\mathtt{m} = Z.\mathtt{m}$$
$$X.\mathtt{s} = 0 \wedge Y.\mathtt{s} = 1 \wedge Z.\mathtt{s} = 1 \Rightarrow X.\mathtt{m}+Z.\mathtt{m} = Y.\mathtt{m}$$
$$X.\mathtt{s} = 0 \wedge Y.\mathtt{s} = 1 \wedge Z.\mathtt{s} = 0 \Rightarrow Y.\mathtt{m}+Z.\mathtt{m} = X.\mathtt{m}$$
$$X.\mathtt{s} = 1 \wedge Y.\mathtt{s} = 0 \wedge Z.\mathtt{s} = 0 \Rightarrow X.\mathtt{m}+Z.\mathtt{m} = Y.\mathtt{m}$$
$$X.\mathtt{s} = 1 \wedge Y.\mathtt{s} = 0 \wedge Z.\mathtt{s} = 1 \Rightarrow Y.\mathtt{m}+Z.\mathtt{m} = X.\mathtt{m}$$

This encoding does not introduce extra new variables, except carry variables used in the Booleanization of the unsigned addition constraints. Since only one combination of signs is possible, one vector of carry variables can be used for the Booleanization of all of the unsigned addition constraints.

4.2   Booleanization of the Multiplication Constraint

This subsection considers the Booleanization of the constraint $X \times Y = Z$, where the operands are log-encoded integers or integer-domain variables. Since the sign of any operand is determined by the signs of the other two operands, this section only considers unsigned multiplication. Many algorithms have been used in the hardware-design community for fast multiplication. Picat-SAT adopts the *shift-and-add* algorithm for multiplication constraints. We also implemented Karatsuba's *divide-and-conquer* algorithm [20]. This algorithm is given in Appendix B, together with the experimental results that justify the choice of the shift-and-add algorithm.

Let $Y.\mathtt{m}$ be $Y_{n-1} \ldots Y_1 Y_0$. The *shift-and-add* algorithm generates the following conditional constraints for the multiplication constraint $X \times Y = Z$.

$$Y_0 = 0 \Rightarrow S_0 = 0$$
$$Y_0 = 1 \Rightarrow S_0 = X$$
$$Y_1 = 0 \Rightarrow S_1 = S_0$$
$$Y_1 = 1 \Rightarrow S_1 = (X << 1) + S_0$$
$$\vdots$$
$$Y_{n-1} = 0 \Rightarrow S_{n-1} = S_{n-2}$$

$$Y_{n-1} = 1 \Rightarrow S_{n-1} = (X << (n-1)) + S_{n-2}$$
$$Z = S_{n-1}$$

The operation $(X << i)$ shifts the binary string of X to left by i positions. Let the length of the binary string of X be m. The length of S_0 is m, that of S_1 is $m + 1$, and so on. So the total number of auxiliary Boolean variables that are used in S_i's is $\Sigma_{i=m}^{(n+m-2)} i$. In addition, auxiliary variables are used for carries in the additions. For example, in the addition $S_i = (X << i) + S_{i-1}$, $m + i$ auxiliary Boolean variables are needed.

This algorithm can be improved to reduce the number of new variables when Y is an integer. For the addition $S_i = (X << i) + S_{i-1}$, if S_{i-1} is a 0 vector, then the Boolean variables can be copied from X to S_i, and so no new variables are necessary. Booth's algorithm [3], which examines multiple digits of Y at once, can also be used to further reduce the number of variables if Y is a constant.[4]

4.3   Booleanization of the Table Constraint

In log-encoding, a table constraint can easily be converted into a truth table. Consider the constraint table_in({X,Y}, [{1,2},{1,3},{2,1},{2,2}, {3,1}]). Let X.m be $<X_1,X_0>$, and Y.m be $<Y_1,Y_0>$. Since the sign bits are known to be 0, they are ignored. The above table constraint can be represented as the truth table shown in Fig. 1. The task of compiling a table constraint amounts to finding a CNF formula to equivalently represent its truth table.

X_1	X_0	Y_1	Y_0
0	1	1	0
0	1	1	1
1	0	0	1
1	0	1	0
1	1	0	1

Fig. 1. The truth table of table_in({X,Y}, [{1,2},{1,3},{2,1},{2,2},{3,1}])

Just as for variables with small domains, Picat-SAT uses the logic optimizer, Espresso, to find compact SAT encodings for small truth tables. Espresso returns a *disjunctive-normal-form* (DNF) formula for a true table. In order to easily convert the DNF formula into CNF, Picat-SAT feeds Espresso with the complementary truth table, i.e., setting the output of *in* tuples to *0* and the output of *out* tuples to *1*. For example, Espresso returns the following DNF clauses for the complement of the truth table in Fig. 1.

$\neg X_0 \wedge Y_1 \wedge Y_0$
$X_1 \wedge X_0 \wedge Y_1$
$\neg X_1 \wedge \neg X_0$
$\neg X_1 \wedge \neg Y_1$
$\neg Y_1 \wedge \neg Y_0$

---

[4] Booth's algorithm has not yet been implemented in Picat-SAT.

The original truth table is represented as the negation of the DNF formula, which is a conjunction of the following CNF clauses:

$$X_0 \lor \neg Y_1 \lor \neg Y_0$$
$$\neg X_1 \lor \neg X_0 \lor \neg Y_1$$
$$X_1 \lor X_0$$
$$X_1 \lor Y_1$$
$$Y_1 \lor Y_0$$

Espresso is slow when the number of variables is large. For a truth table with more than 14 Boolean variables, Picat-SAT breaks the table down into smaller tables by enumerating part of the variables. For example, the Boolean table in Fig. 1 can be broken down into two tables, one assuming $X_1=1$ and the other assuming $X_1=0$.

4.4   Decomposition of Global Constraints

Picat-SAT decomposes global constraints into primitive ones in a straightforward manner. This subsection briefly overviews the algorithms adopted by Picat-SAT for decomposing several well-used global constraints.

all_different(L): Let L be $[E_1, E_2, \ldots, E_n]$. Picat-SAT decomposes this constraint into $E_i \neq E_j$ for $i, j = 1, \ldots, n, i < j$. For an *assignment-type* all-different constraint, in which the number of values in the domains is equal to the number of variables, Picat-SAT also generates the following redundant constraints: each value is assigned to exactly one variable.

circuit(L): Picat-SAT first generates all_different(L) for this constraint, which is guaranteed to be an assignment-type constraint. In order to prevent sub-cycles in the circuit, Picat-SAT uses a new variable, O_i, for each value i, which indicates the ordering number of i in the circuit, assuming the ordering number of value 1 being 1. Let L be $[E_1, E_2, \ldots, E_n]$. If $E_i = j$, then a constraint is generated to ensure that O_j is the successor of O_i, meaning that $O_j = O_i + 1$ if $O_i < n$, and $O_j = 1$ if $O_i = n$. This is a standard decomposition algorithm, which is used by other compilers, such as the mzn2fzn compiler [24].

cumulative(*Starts*, *Durations*, *Resources*, *Limit*): For the cumulative constraint, two basic decomposition algorithms exist, namely, *time decomposition* and *task decomposition* [10]. Let n be the number of tasks, S_i be the earliest start time, and E_i to the latest end time of task i, $i \in 1, \ldots, n$. The time-decomposition algorithm generates constraints to ensure the following: for each time point from $\min_{i=1}^{n}(S_i)$ to $\max_{i=1}^{n}(E_i)$-1, the total amount of resources consumed by the running tasks cannot exceed the resource limit. The task-decomposition algorithm only generates constraints to ensure that the resource limit is not exceeded at the start and end times of each of the tasks. Picat-SAT adopts the task decomposition algorithm. All of the resource constraints are pseudo-Boolean constraints. As mentioned above, Picat-SAT splits pseudo-Boolean constraints into adders and comparators, as it does for other arithmetic constraints.

element(I,L,V): Let L be $[E_1, E_2, \ldots, E_n]$. If L contains variables, Picat-SAT decomposes this constraint into the following : for each value i in 1..n, $I = i \Rightarrow V = E_i$; otherwise, if L is ground, Picat-SAT encodes the constraint as a table constraint.

5 Experimental Results

Picat-SAT, which is implemented in Picat, has about 5,000 lines of code, excluding comments. In addition to the encoding algorithms described in the paper, it also incorporates some specialization and optimization techniques. Picat-SAT eliminates common subexpressions in constraints. For example, when a reification constraint $B \Leftrightarrow C$ is generated, Picat-SAT tables it and reuses the variable B, rather than introducing a new variable for the primitive constraint C, when C is encountered again. Picat-SAT has been an entrant in the MiniZinc Challenge three times since 2013, and was the only purely SAT-based CSP solver in 2015. This section experimentally compares Picat-SAT, as implemented in Picat version 1.4, with two other SAT compilers, and reports on the Picat-SAT's performance in MiniZinc Challenge 2015.

Table 1 compares Picat-SAT with two other SAT compilers: Sugar and Azucar.[5] Sugar is a mature SAT compiler based on order encoding [30], and Azucar is a successor to Sugar based on compact order encoding [32]. The benchmarks are from Sugar's package. The all_different constraint is used in *golombRuler*, *knightTour*, and *nqueens*, and no other global constraints are used. The table

Table 1. A comparison of three SAT compilers

Benchmark	Picat			Sugar			Azucar		
	#vars	#cls	time	#vars	#cls	time	#vars	#cls	time
golombRuler-10–55	6438	27194	**36.50**	4584	190594	92.53	5635	44937	60.32
golombRuler-8	3024	12698	**0.22**	5111	422046	3.04	2988	35847	0.44
jss-ft10	13613	68880	5.90	76617	703313	6.24	8227	119126	**1.50**
knightTour-5	3051	21401	8.19	1296	20510	**0.83**	1667	9123	2.36
knightTour-7	11970	114818	374.36	4944	141818	99.68	5919	44059	**85.53**
magicSquare-5 × 5	2742	20302	1.68	3504	73717	0.72	2052	16239	**0.29**
magicSquare-9 × 9	33606	178328	**48.58**	60960	5463881	167.24	19405	317128	57.36
nqueens-200	1003112	3997099	1925.52	159196	18646098	**131.96**	284400	4004662	397.82
oss-gp03-01	785	3535	**0.19**	11126	46075	0.69	786	6231	2.13
oss-gp10-01	25540	139168	**2.90**	343189	6514888	40.40	17216	544880	5.79
socialGolfer-3-2-5	315	3360	0.12	810	2355	0.31	1680	5250	**0.10**
socialGolfer-6-3-7	9702	163863	**13.19**	22545	79236	13.78	46248	184980	14.04
tdsp-C1-1	6361	25187	0.67	1226	17631	**0.26**	4586	36997	0.64
tdsp-C2-1	16079	67032	5.09	2720	61572	**0.72**	11746	112436	7.12

---

[5] Efforts were also made to compare Picat-SAT with FznTini [15], a log-encoding based SAT compiler, and with meSAT [29], which supports the hybrid of order and sparse encodings. FznTini is for an old version of FlatZinc, and the default setting of meSAT did not perform better than Sugar on the benchmarks.

Table 2. MiniZinc Challenge scores on benchmarks that do not use global constraints

Benchmark	OR-Tools	Opturion CPX	iZplus	Picat-SAT
freepizza(MIN)	4.03	10.96	**12.00**	3.01
grid-colouring(MIN)	1.91	11.27	5.28	**11.54**
nmseq(SAT)	**13.46**	10.75	3.19	0.60
project-planning(MIN)	5.00	**14.67**	10.33	0.00
radiation(MIN)	0.00	**11.04**	8.56	10.40
triangular(MAX)	7.75	1.00	9.00	**12.25**
zephyrus(MIN)	**9.00**	7.50	7.50	6.00
(TOTAL)	41.16	67.19	55.86	43.79

shows the the size of the generated code (the number of variables, #vars, and the number of clauses, #cls) and the CPU time (in seconds) taken to run the generated code using Lingeling version 587f on a Cygwin notebook with 2.4 GHz Intel i5 and 4 GB RAM.[6]

It is not surprising that Picat-SAT generates more compact code than Sugar and Azucar for most of the benchmarks because log-encoding is known to be more compact than order-encoding. For the *knightTour* and *nqueens* benchmarks, both of which include the assignment-type `all_different` constraint, Picat-SAT uses more Boolean variables than Sugar and Azucar. This is because Picat-SAT generates redundant constraints to ensure that each value is assigned to exactly one variable.

Picat-SAT also compares favorably well with Sugar and Azucar in terms of CPU time on most of the benchmarks. Picat-SAT is significantly slower than Sugar and Azucar on *knightTour* and *nqueens*. These results reveal that Picat-SAT's choice algorithm for `all_different` is not the best.

Tables 2 and 3 show the points scored by Picat-SAT and the top three CP solvers in MiniZinc Challenge 2015. Table 2 shows the scores for the benchmarks that do not include global constraints,[7] and Table 3 shows the scores for the benchmarks that include global constraints. MiniZinc Challenge uses a scoring procedure based on the Borda count voting system; the higher a score is, the better. Despite the 0 score from the *project-planning* benchmark, Picat-SAT performed quite well on the benchmarks that do not include global constraints: it scored higher than OR-Tools, and could have performed better than iZplus had the points from *project-planning* been counted in. Picat-SAT is less competitive with the winners on the benchmarks that use global constraints. Picat-SAT scored 0 points on *is(Min)*, which uses `circuit` and `table`, on *largescheduling*,

---

[6] The CPU time does not include the compile time for any of the SAT compilers.

[7] Picat-SAT scored 0 on *project-planning* because `mzn2fzn` failed to specialize the `element` constraint, which prevented Picat's FlatZinc interpreter from functioning. It was understood that `mzn2fzn` would specialize generic global constraints into specific ones once the types of the arguments are known.

Table 3. MiniZinc Challenge scores on benchmarks that use global constraints

Benchmark	OR-Tools	Opturion CPX	iZplus	Picat-SAT
costas-array(SAT)	**7.35**	4.86	5.06	0.73
cvrp(MIN)	7.07	8.59	**12.30**	2.04
gfd-schedule(MIN)	2.48	10.53	**11.99**	5.00
is(MIN) TOTAL	7.56	7.88	**12.56**	0.00
largescheduling(MIN)	**13.00**	10.00	0.00	0.00
mapping(MIN)	2.00	**14.91**	7.00	5.09
multi-knapsack(MAX)	4.18	**10.75**	4.26	9.80
opd(MIN)	8.07	2.50	7.00	**12.43**
open_stacks(MIN)	10.10	5.19	2.00	**12.71**
p1f(MIN)	**14.53**	3.95	2.01	3.51
roster(MIN)	**11.72**	4.44	11.40	2.44
spot5(MAX)	8.00	6.68	2.34	**12.98**
tdtsp(MIN)	8.24	**11.26**	10.50	0.00
(TOTAL)	104.31	101.54	88.43	66.72

which uses `cumulative`, and on *tdsp(Min)*, which uses `inverse`. Overall, Picat-SAT had the highest scores on 5 of 20 benchmarks.

6   Concluding Remarks

This paper has described Picat-SAT, which employs the sign-and-magnitude log encoding for domain variabls. Log-encoding of domain variables resembles the binary representation of numbers used in computer hardware. It is a very compact encoding, and a large repository of algorithms has been developed by the hardware design community. Interestingly, few SAT compilers for general constraints have been developed that are based on this encoding. This is partly because of the negative research results reported on log-encoding's failure to maintain arc consistency, and partly because of the engineering effort required to implement the encoding. This paper has given the adapted algorithms employed by Picat-SAT, and has presented preliminary, but quite encouraging, experimental results.

One direction for future work is to examine more encoding algorithms and optimization techniques for Booleanizing constraints, especially global and pseudo-Boolean constraints. SMT solvers have been shown to be successful in handling various types of constraints, including arithmetic constraints. Another direction for future work is to compare Picat-SAT with SMT solvers on SMT-LIB benchmarks.

A   The Transformation Algorithm for $X + Y = Z$

The *transformation* algorithm replaces negative domain values by non-negative domain values in the addition constraint. For the constraint $X + Y = Z$, if any of the operands has a domain with negative values, this method finds the smallest integer k such that $\mathsf{abs}(X) < 2^{k-1}/$, $\mathsf{abs}(Y) < 2^{k-1}$, and $\mathsf{abs}(Z) < 2^k$, and transforms the original addition constraint to $Z' = X' + Y'$, where $X' = X + 2^{k-1}$, $Y' = Y + 2^{k-1}$, and $Z' = Z + 2^k$. The newly introduced variables X', Y', and Z' are guaranteed not to include negative values in their domains, and therefore the constraint $X' + Y' = Z'$ can be Booleanized as $X'.\mathsf{m} + Y'.\mathsf{m} = Z'.\mathsf{m}$.

The question is how to Booleanize the newly introduced constraints. Consider the constraint $X' = X + 2^{k-1}$. Let $X.\mathsf{m} = X_{k-1} \ldots X_n X_{n-1} \ldots X_1 X_0$, and $X'.\mathsf{m} = X'_{k-1} \ldots X'_1 X'_0$ ($k > n$, $X_i = 0$ for $i = k - 1, \ldots, n$). Note that 0s are added in the high end of $X.\mathsf{m}$ in order for it to have the same length as $X'.\mathsf{m}$. The constraint $X' = X + 2^{k-1}$ can be translated to a conjunction of the following two conditional constraints:

$$X.\mathsf{s} = 0 \Rightarrow X_0 = X'_0 \wedge \ldots \wedge X_{k-2} = X'_{k-2} \wedge X'_{k-1} = 1$$
$$X.\mathsf{s} = 1 \Rightarrow X.\mathsf{m} + X'.\mathsf{m} = 2^{k-1}$$

Note the unsigned addition $X.\mathsf{m} + X'.\mathsf{m} = 2^{k-1}$ can be Booleanized using a much simpler logic than for the general addition. In particular, no new variables are necessary for carries in the addition. In order for the constraint to hold, the following formula must hold:

$$X_0 = X'_0$$
$$\texttt{for } i = 1..k - 2$$
$$\quad X_{i-1} = 0 \wedge X'_{i-1} = 0 \Rightarrow X_i = X'_i$$
$$\quad X_{i-1} = 1 \wedge X'_{i-1} = 1 \Rightarrow X_i \neq X'_i$$
$$\quad X_{i-1} \neq X'_{i-1} \Rightarrow X_i \neq X'_i$$
$$X'_{k-1} = 0$$

The two Boolean variables at the lowest end, X_0 and X'_0, must be equal. Otherwise, the lowest bit of the sum cannot be 0. The intuition of the logic of the `for` loop is that if there is an 1 at some position, then there must be exactly one 1 at each of the higher positions in order for the sum to be equal to 2^{k-1}. Since no negative zero is allowed, at least one of X_is is 1. In order for the sum to be equal to 2^{k-1}, X'_{k-1} must be 0.

The idea of removing negative domain values through transformation is well known in linear programming. Unlike in linear programming, however, the transformation is only performed locally on negative-domain variables in addition constraints, and all other constraints, such as $\mathsf{abs}(X) = Y$, are not affected.

For a negative-domain variable X that occurs in multiple addition constraints, an optimization can be employed to avoid introducing new variables unnecessarily. The compiler memorizes the transformation $X' = X + 2^{k-1}$ in a table. In case the same transformation is required by another addition constraint, then the compiler fetches X' from the table, rather than introducing new variables.

Table 4 compares the enumeration (enum) and transformation (trans) algorithms, using the constraint $Z = X+Y$, where X and Y are in $-N..N$. The code size is not informative on which encoding is better: the enum encoding uses fewer variables but more clauses than the trans encoding.[8] The time shows that the enum encoding is favorable. This result led to the adoption the enum encoding by Picat-SAT for addition constraints.

Table 4. A comparison of two encodings for $Z = X + Y$

N	enum			trans		
	#vars	#cls	time(s)	#vars	#cls	time(s)
5000	56	1121	0.058	100	632	0.070
10000	60	1211	0.060	107	682	0.060
15000	60	1199	0.052	107	670	0.080
20000	64	1301	0.060	114	732	0.070
25000	64	1295	0.059	114	726	0.080

B Karatsuba's Divide and Conquer Algorithm for $X \times Y = Z$

Karatsuba's algorithm [20] is a well-known algorithm for multiplying big integers. It can be applied to numbers in any base. The basic idea of the algorithm is to divide and conquer, splitting large numbers into smaller numbers, until the numbers are small enough.

Let X and Y be two N-digit binary strings. If N is small enough, then the multiplication constraint is Booleanized using shift-and-add. If N is big, then this algorithm selects an integer M ($1 \leq M \leq N-1$) and splits both X and Y into two parts as follows:

$$X = X_h \times 2^M + X_l$$
$$Y = Y_h \times 2^M + Y_l$$

where X_l and Y_l are less than 2^M. The product $X \times Y$ is then

$$Z = X \times Y = Z_2 \times 2^{2M} + Z_1 \times 2^M + Z_0$$

where

$$Z_0 = X_l \times Y_l$$
$$Z_1 = (X_h + X_l)(Y_h + Y_l) - Z_2 - Z_0$$
$$Z_2 = X_h \times Y_h$$

---

[8] Note that the code size sometimes decreases with N because of the domain constraints.

The resulting formulas require three multiplications, plus some additions, subtractions, and shifts.

Table 5 compares the shift-and-add (saa) and Karatsuba (kara) algorithms, using the constraint $Z = X \times Y$, where X and Y are in $-N..N$. The base-case size for the Karatsuba algorithm is set to 3 (i.e., $X.\mathtt{m} \leq 7$ or $Y.\mathtt{m} \leq 7$).

Two observations can be made about the results: first, the code sizes only grow slightly with N no matter which algorithm is used; and second, kara uses more variables and generates more clauses than saa. The Karatsuba algorithm is well used for multiplying big integers and its advantage cannot be witnessed unless the operands are really big. Nevertheless, big domains rarely occur in CSPs. This experimental comparison naturally resulted in the adoption of the shift-and-add algorithm by Picat-SAT for multiplication constraints.

Table 5. A comparison of two encodings for $Z = X \times Y$

N	saa			kara		
	#vars	#cls	time(s)	#vars	#cls	time(s)
5000	443	2880	0.236	1380	6872	0.382
10000	512	3357	0.270	1594	7931	0.425
15000	513	3353	0.271	1595	7927	0.442
20000	585	3831	0.226	1845	9175	0.481
25000	585	3827	0.223	1845	9171	0.491

References

1. Biere, A., Heule, M., van Maaren, H., Walsh, T. (eds.): Handbook of Satisfiability. IOS Press, Amsterdam (2009)
2. Bjork, M.: Successful SAT encoding techniques. JSAT Addendum (2009)
3. Booth, A.D.: A signed binary multiplication technique. Q. J. Mech. Appl. Math. **IV**, 236–240 (1951)
4. Bordeaux, L., Hamadi, Y., Zhang, L.: Propositional satisfiability and constraint programming: a comparative survey. ACM Comput. Surv. **38**(4), 1–54 (2006)
5. Brayton, R.K., Hachtel, G.D., McMullen, C.T., Sangiovanni-Vincentelli, A.L.: Logic Minimization Algorithms for VLSI Synthesis. Kluwer Academic Publishers, Boston (1984)
6. Brewka, G., Eiter, T., Truszczyński, M.: Answer set programming at a glance. Commun. ACM **54**(12), 92–103 (2011)
7. Chen, J.: A new SAT encoding of the at-most-one constraint. In: Proceeding of the 9th International Workshop of Constraint Modeling and Reformulation (2010)
8. Crawford, J.M., Baker, A.B.: Experimental results on the application of satisfiability algorithms to scheduling problems. In: AAAI, pp. 1092–1097 (1994)
9. Boulanger, J.L. (ed.): Formal Methods Applied to Industrial Complex Systems: Implementation of the B Method. Wiley, New York (2014)
10. Francis, K.G., Stuckey, P.J.: Explaining circuit propagation. Constraints **19**(1), 1–29 (2014)

11. Gavanelli, M.: The log-support encoding of CSP into SAT. In: CP, pp. 815–822 (2007)
12. Gebser, M., Kaufmann, B., Neumann, A., Schaub, T.: Conflict-driven answer set solving. In: IJCAI, pp. 386–392 (2007)
13. Ian Gent, P.: Arc consistency in SAT. In: ECAI, pp. 121–125 (2002)
14. Van Hentenryck, P.: Constraint and integer programming in OPL. INFORMS J. Comput. **14**, 345–372 (2002)
15. Huang, J.: Universal Booleanization of constraint models. In: CP, pp. 144–158 (2008)
16. Iwama, K., Miyazaki, S.: SAT-varible complexity of hard combinatorial problems. IFIP Congress **1**, 253–258 (1994)
17. Jackson, D.: Software Abstractions: Logic, Language, and Analysis. MIT Press, Cambridge (2012)
18. Jackson, E.K.: A module system for domain-specific languages. Theory Pract. Logic Program. **14**(4–5), 771–785 (2014)
19. Jeavons, P., Petke, J.: Local consistency and SAT-solvers. JAIR **43**, 329–351 (2012)
20. Karatsuba, A., Ofman, Y.: Multiplication of many-digital numbers by automatic computers. In: Proceeding the USSR Academy of Sciences, vol. 145 pp. 293–294 (1962)
21. Kautz, H.A., Selman, B.: Planning as satisfiability. In: ECAI, pp. 359–363 (1992)
22. Lamport, L.: Specifying Systems: The TLA+ Language and Tools for Hardware and Software Engineers. Addison-Wesley (2004)
23. Malik, S., Zhang, L.: Boolean satisfiability: from theoretical hardness to practical success. Commun. ACM **52**(8), 76–82 (2009)
24. Marriott, K., Stuckey, P.J., De Koninck, L., Samulowitz, H.: A MiniZinc tutorial. http://www.minizinc.org/downloads/doc-latest/minizinc-tute.pdf
25. Metodi, A., Codish, M.: Compiling finite domain constraints to SAT with BEE. Theory Pract. Logic Program. **12**(4–5), 465–483 (2012)
26. Nethercote, N., Stuckey, P.J., Becket, R., Brand, S., Duck, G.J., Tack, G.R.: MiniZinc: towards a standard CP modelling language. In: Bessière, C. (ed.) CP 2007. LNCS, vol. 4741, pp. 529–543. Springer, Heidelberg (2007)
27. Rintanen, J.: Planning as satisfiability: heuristics. Artif. Intell. **193**, 45–86 (2012)
28. Drechsler, R., Eggersglüß, S.: High Quality Test Pattern Generation and Boolean Satisfiability. Springer, New York (2012)
29. Stojadinovic, M., Maric, F.: meSAT: multiple encodings of CSP to SAT. Constraints **19**(4), 380–403 (2014)
30. Sugar. bach.istc.kobe-u.ac.jp/sugar/
31. Tamura, N., Taga, A., Kitagawa, S., Banbara, M.: Compiling finite linear CSP into SAT. Constraints **14**(2), 254–272 (2009)
32. Tanjo, T., Tamura, N., Banbara, M.: Azucar: a SAT-based CSP solver using compact order encoding. In: Cimatti, A., Sebastiani, R. (eds.) SAT 2012. LNCS, vol. 7317, pp. 456–462. Springer, Heidelberg (2012)
33. Walsh, T.: SAT v CSP. In: Dechter, R. (ed.) CP 2000. LNCS, vol. 1894, p. 441. Springer, Heidelberg (2000)
34. Zhou, N.-F., Fruhman, J.: A User's Guide to Picat. http://picat-lang.org
35. Zhou, N.-F., Kjellerstrand, H., Fruhman, J.: Constraint Solving and Planning with Picat. Springer, Heidelberg (2015)

Functional Programming

Default Rules for Curry

Sergio Antoy[1] and Michael Hanus[2]([⊠])

[1] Computer Science Department, Portland State University, Portland, OR, USA
antoy@cs.pdx.edu
[2] Institut für Informatik, CAU Kiel, 24098 Kiel, Germany
mh@informatik.uni-kiel.de

Abstract. In functional logic programs, rules are applicable independently of textual order, i.e., any rule can potentially be used to evaluate an expression. This is similar to logic languages and contrary to functional languages, e.g., Haskell enforces a strict sequential interpretation of rules. However, in some situations it is convenient to express alternatives by means of compact default rules. Although default rules are often used in functional programs, the non-deterministic nature of functional logic programs does not allow to directly transfer this concept from functional to functional logic languages in a meaningful way. In this paper we propose a new concept of default rules for Curry that supports a programming style similar to functional programming while preserving the core properties of functional logic programming, i.e., completeness, non-determinism, and logic-oriented uses of functions. We discuss the basic concept and sketch an initial implementation of it which exploits advanced features of functional logic languages.

1   Motivation

Functional logic languages combine the most important features of functional and logic programming in a single language (see [7,15] for recent surveys). In particular, the functional logic language Curry [17] conceptually extends Haskell with common features of logic programming, i.e., non-determinism, free variables, and constraint solving. Moreover, the amalgamated features of Curry support new programming techniques, like *deep* pattern matching through the use of *functional patterns*, i.e., evaluable functions at pattern positions [4].

For example, suppose that we want to compute two elements x and y in a list l with the property that the distance between the two elements is n, i.e., in l there are $n - 1$ elements between x and y. We will use this condition in the n-queens program discussed later. Of course, there may be many pairs of elements in a list satisfying the given condition ("++" denotes the concatenation of lists):

```
dist n (_++[x]++zs++[y]++_) | n == length zs + 1 = (x,y)
```

Defining functions by case distinction through pattern matching is a very useful feature. Functional patterns make this feature even more convenient. However, in functional logic languages, this feature is slightly more delicate because of the

M. Gavanelli and J. Reppy (Eds.): PADL 2016, LNCS 9585, pp. 65–82, 2016.
DOI: 10.1007/978-3-319-28228-2_5

possibility of functional patterns, which typically stand for an infinite number of standard patterns, and because there is no textual order among the rules defining a function. The variables in a functional pattern are bound like the variables in ordinary patterns.

As a simple example, consider an operation `isSet` intended to check whether a given list represents a set, i.e., does not contain duplicates. In Curry, we might implement it as follows:

```
isSet (_++[x]++_++[x]++_) = False
isSet _                   = True
```

The first rule uses a functional pattern: it returns `False` if the argument matches a list where two identical elements occur. The intent of the second rule is to return `True` if no identical elements occur in the argument. However, according to the semantics of Curry, which ensures completeness w.r.t. finding solutions or values, *all* rules are tried to evaluate an expression. Therefore, the second rule is always applicable to calls of `isSet` so that the expression `isSet [1,1]` will be evaluated to `False` *and* `True`.

The unintended application of the second rule can be avoided by the additional requirement that this rule should be applied only if no other rule is applicable. We call such a rule a *default rule* and mark it by adding the suffix `'default` to the function's name (in order to avoid a syntactic extension of the base language). Thus, if we define `isSet` with the rules

```
isSet (_++[x]++_++[x]++_) = False
isSet'default _           = True
```

then `isSet [1,1]` evaluates only to `False` and `isSet [0,1]` only to `True`.

In this paper we propose a concept for default rules for Curry, define its precise semantics, and discuss implementation options. In the next section, we review the main concepts of functional logic programming and Curry. Our intended concept of default rules is informally introduced in Sect. 3. Some examples showing the convenience of default rules for programming are presented in Sect. 4. In order to avoid the introduction of a new semantics specific to default rules, we define the precise meaning of default rules by transforming them into already known concepts in Sect. 5. Options to implement default rules efficiently are sketched and evaluated in Sect. 6 before we relate our proposal to other work and conclude.

2   Functional Logic Programming and Curry

Before presenting the concept and implementation of default rules in more detail, we briefly review those elements of functional logic languages and Curry that are necessary to understand the contents of this paper. More details can be found in recent surveys on functional logic programming [7,15] and in the language report [17].

Curry is a declarative multi-paradigm language combining in a seamless way features from functional, logic, and concurrent programming (concurrency is irrelevant as our work goes, hence it is ignored in this paper). The syntax of Curry is close to Haskell [21], i.e., type variables and names of defined operations usually start with lowercase letters and the names of type and data constructors start with an uppercase letter. $\alpha \rightarrow \beta$ denotes the type of all functions mapping elements of type α into elements of type β (where β can also be a functional type, i.e., functional types are "curried"), and the application of an operation f to an argument e is denoted by juxtaposition ("$f\ e$"). In addition to Haskell, Curry allows *free (logic) variables* in conditions and right-hand sides of rules and expressions evaluated by an interpreter. Moreover, the patterns of a defining rule can be non-linear, i.e., they might contain multiple occurrences of some variable, which is an abbreviation for equalities between these occurrences.

Example 1. The following simple program shows the functional and logic features of Curry. It defines an operation "++" to concatenate two lists, which is identical to the Haskell encoding. The second operation, dup, returns some list element having at least two occurrences:[1]

```
(++) :: [a]  →  [a]  →  [a]
[]       ++ ys = ys
(x:xs) ++ ys = x : (xs ++ ys)

dup :: [a]  →  a
dup xs | xs == _ ++ [x] ++ _ ++ [x] ++ _
           = x      where x free
```

Function calls can contain free variables. They are evaluated lazily where free variables as demanded arguments are non-deterministically instantiated. Hence, the condition of the rule defining dup is solved by instantiating x and the anonymous free variables "_". This evaluation method corresponds to narrowing [22,24], but Curry narrows with possibly non-most-general unifiers to ensure the optimality of computations [3].

Note that dup is a *non-deterministic operation* since it might deliver more than one result for a given argument, e.g., the evaluation of dup [1,2,2,1] yields the values 1 and 2. Non-deterministic operations, which are interpreted as mappings from values into sets of values [13], are an important feature of contemporary functional logic languages. Hence, there is also a predefined *choice* operation:

```
x ? _  =  x
_ ? y  =  y
```

Thus, the expression "0 ? 1" evaluates to 0 and 1 with the value non-deterministically chosen.

Some operations can be defined more easily and directly using *functional patterns* [4]. A functional pattern is a pattern occurring in an argument of the left-hand side of a rule containing defined operations (and not only data constructors and variables). Such a pattern abbreviates the set of all standard patterns

---

[1] Note that Curry requires the explicit declaration of free variables, as x in the rule of dup, to ensure checkable redundancy.

to which the functional pattern can be evaluated (by narrowing). For instance, we can rewrite the definition of dup as

```
dup (_++[x]++_++[x]++_) = x
```

Functional patterns are a powerful feature to express arbitrary selections in tree structures, e.g., in XML documents [14]. Details about their semantics and a constructive implementation of functional patterns by a demand-driven unification procedure can be found in [4].

Set functions [6] allow the encapsulation of non-deterministic computations in a strategy-independent manner. For each defined function f, f_S denotes the corresponding set function. f_S encapsulates the non-determinism caused by evaluating f except for the non-determinism caused by evaluating the arguments to which f is applied. For instance, consider the operation decOrInc defined by

```
decOrInc x = (x-1) ? (x+1)
```

Then "decOrInc$_S$ 3" evaluates to (an abstract representation of) the set $\{2,4\}$, i.e., the non-determinism caused by decOrInc is encapsulated into a set. However, "decOrInc$_S$ (2?5)" evaluates to two different sets $\{1,3\}$ and $\{4,6\}$ due to its non-deterministic argument, i.e., the non-determinism caused by the argument is not encapsulated. This property is desirable and essential to define and implement default rules by a transformational approach, as shown in Sect. 5. In the following section, we discuss default rules and their intended semantics.

3   Default Rules: Concept and Informal Semantics

Default rules are often used in both functional and logic programming. In languages in which rules are applied in textual order, such as Haskell and Prolog, losely speaking every rule is a default rule of all the preceding rules. For instance, the following standard Haskell function takes two lists and return the list of corresponding pairs, where excess elements of a longer list are discarded:

```
zip (x:xs) (y:ys) = (x,y) : zip xs ys
zip _       _      = []
```

The second rule is applied only if the first rule is not applicable, i.e., if one of the argument lists is empty. We can avoid the consideration of rule orderings by replacing the second rule with rules for the patterns not matching the first rule:

```
zip (x:xs) (y:ys) = (x,y) : zip xs ys
zip (_:_)  []     = []
zip []     _      = []
```

In general, this coding is cumbersome since the number of additional rules increases if the patterns of the first rule are more complex (e.g., we need three additional rules for the function zip3 combining three lists). Moreover, this coding might be impossible in conjunction with some functional patterns, as in the first rule of isSet above. Some functional patterns conceptually denote an infinite set of standard patterns (e.g., [x,x], [x,_,x], [_,x,_,x],...) and the complement of this set is infinite too.

In Prolog, one often uses the "cut" operator to implement the behavior of default rules. For instance, zip can be defined as a Prolog predicate as follows:

```
zip([X|Xs],[Y|Ys],[(X,Y)|Zs]) :- !, zip(Xs,Ys,Zs).
zip(_,_,[]).
```

Although this definition behaves as intended for instantiated lists, the completeness of logic programming is destroyed by the cut operator. For instance, the goal zip([],[],[]) is provable, but Prolog does not compute the answer {Xs=[],Ys=[],Zs=[]} for the goal zip(Xs,Ys,Zs).

These examples show that neither the functional style nor the logic style of default rules is suitable for functional logic programming. The functional style, based on textual order, curtails non-determinism. The logic style, based on the *cut* operator, destroys the completeness of some computations. Thus, a new concept of default rules is required for functional logic programming if we want to keep the strong properties of the base language, in particular, a simple to use non-determinism and the completeness of logic-oriented evaluations. Before presenting the exact definition of default rules, we introduce them informally and discuss their intended semantics.

We intend to extend a "standard" function definition by one default rule. Hence, a function definition with a default rule has the following form ($\overline{o_k}$ denotes a sequence of objects $o_1 \ldots o_k$):[2]

$$f \ \overline{t_k^1} \ | \ c_1 \ = \ e_1$$

$$\vdots$$

$$f \ \overline{t_k^n} \ | \ c_n \ = \ e_n$$

$$f\text{'default } \overline{t_k^{n+1}} \ | \ c_{n+1} \ = \ e_{n+1}$$

We call the first n rules *standard rules* and the final rule the *default rule* of f. Informally, the default rule is applied only if no standard rule is applicable, where a rule is applicable if the pattern matches and the condition is satisfied. Hence, an expression $e = f \ \overline{s_k}$, where $\overline{s_k}$ are expressions, is evaluated as follows:

1. If there is a standard rule whose left-hand side matches e and the condition is satisfied (i.e., evaluable to True), the default rule is ignored to evaluate e.
2. If no standard rule can be applied, the default rule is used to evaluate e.
3. If some argument is non-deterministic, the previous points apply independently for each non-deterministic choice of the combination of arguments. In particular, if an argument is a free variable, it is non-deterministically instantiated to all its possible values before deciding whether the default rule is chosen.

As usual in a non-strict language like Curry, arguments of an operation application are evaluated as they are demanded by the operation's pattern

---

[2] We consider only conditional rules since an unconditional rule can be regarded as a conditional rule with condition True.

matching and condition. However, any non-determinism or failure during argument evaluation is not passed inside the condition evaluation. A precise definition of "inside" is in [6, Definition 3]. This behavior is quite similar to set functions to encapsulate internal non-determinism. Therefore, we will exploit set functions to implement default rules.

Before discussing the advantages and implementation of default rules, we explain and motivate the intended semantics of our proposal. First, it should be noted that this concept distinguishes non-determinism outside and inside a rule application. This difference is irrelevant in purely functional programming but essential in functional logic programming.

Example 2. Consider the operation `zip` defined with a default rule:

```
zip (x:xs) (y:ys) = (x,y) : zip xs ys
zip'default _ _   = []
```

Since the standard rule is applicable to `zip [1] [2]`, the default rule is ignored so that this expression is solely reduced to `(1,2):zip [] []`. Since the standard rule is not applicable to `zip [] []`, the default rule is applied and yields the value `[]`. Altogether, the only value of `zip [1] [2]` is `[(1,2)]`. However, if some argument has more than one value, we use the evaluation principle above for each combination. Thus, the call `zip ([1] ? []) [2]` yields the two values `[(1,2)]` and `[]`.

These considerations are even more relevant if the evaluation of the condition might be non-deterministic, as the following example shows.

Example 3. Consider an operation to look up values for keys in an association list:

```
lookup key assoc   | assoc == (_ ++ [(key,val)] ++ _)
                   = Just val              where val free
lookup'default _ _ = Nothing
```

Note that the condition of the standard rule can be evaluated in various ways. In particular, it can be evaluated (non-deterministically) to `True` and `False` for a fixed association list and key. Therefore, using if-then-else (or an `otherwise` branch as in Haskell) instead of the default rule might lead to unintended results.

If we evaluate `lookup 2 [(2,14),(3,17),(2,18)]`, the condition of the standard rule is satisfiable so that the default rule is ignored. Since the condition has the two solutions $\{val \mapsto 14\}$ and $\{val \mapsto 18\}$, we yield the values `Just 14` and `Just 18`. If we evaluate `lookup 2 [(3,17)]`, the condition of the standard rule is not satisfiable but the default rule is applicable so that we obtain the result `Nothing`.

On the other hand, non-deterministic arguments might trigger different rules to be applied. Consider the expression `lookup (2 ? 3) [(3,17)]`. Since the non-determinism in the arguments leads to independent evaluations of the expressions `lookup 2 [(3,17)]` and `lookup 3 [(3,17)]`, we obtain the results `Nothing` and `Just 17`.

Similarly, free variables as arguments might lead to independent results since free variables are equivalent to non-deterministic values [5]. For instance, the expression `lookup 2 xs` yields the value `Just v` with the binding $\{xs \mapsto (2,v):\_\}$, but also the value `Nothing` with the binding $\{xs \mapsto []\}$ (as well as many other solutions).

The latter desirable property has also implications for the handling of failures occurring when arguments are evaluated. For instance, consider the expression `lookup 2 failed` (where `failed` is a predefined operation which always fails whenever it is evaluated). Because the evaluation of the condition of the standard rule demands the evaluation of `failed` and the subsequent failure comes from "outside" the condition, the entire expression evaluation fails instead of returning the value `Nothing`. This is motivated by the fact that we need the value of the association list in order to check the satisfiability of the condition and, thus, to decide the applicability of the standard rule, but this value is not available.

Example 4. To see the consequences of an alternative design decision, consider the following contrived definition of an operation that checks whether its argument is the unit value () (which is the only value of the unit type):

```
isUnit x | x == () = True
isUnit'default _    = False
```

In our proposal, the evaluation of "`isUnit failed`" fails. In an alternative design (like Prolog's if-then-else construct), one might skip any failure during condition checking and proceed with the next rule. In this case, we would return the value `False` for the expression `isUnit failed`. This is quite disturbing since the (deterministic!) operation `isUnit`, which has only one possible input value, could return two values: `True` for the call `isUnit ()` and `False` for the call `isUnit failed`. Moreover, if we call this operation with a free variable, like `isUnit x`, we obtain the single binding $\{x \mapsto ()\}$ and value `True` (since free variables are never bound to failures). Thus, either our semantics would be incomplete for logic computations or we compute too many values. In order to get a consistent behavior, we require that failures of arguments demanded for condition checking lead to failures of evaluations.

4 Examples

To show the applicability and convenience of default rules for functional logic programming, we sketch a few more examples in this section.

Example 5. Default rules are important in combination with functional patterns, since functional patterns denote an infinite set of standard patterns which often has no finite complement. Consider again the operation `lookup` as introduced in Example 3. With functional patterns and default rules, this operation can be conveniently defined:

```
lookup key (_ ++ [(key,val)] ++ _) = Just val
lookup'default _  _                 = Nothing
```

Example 6. Functional patterns are also useful to check the deep structure of arguments. In this case, default rules are useful to express in an easy manner that the check is not successful. For instance, consider an operation that checks whether a string contains a float number (without an exponent but with an optional minus sign). With functional patterns and default rules, the definition of this predicate is easy:

```
isFloat (("-" ? "") ++ n1 ++ "." ++ n2)
        | (all isDigit n1 && all isDigit n2) = True
isFloat'default _ = False
```

Example 7. In the classical *n*-queens puzzle, one must place *n* queens on a chess board so that no queen can attack another queen. This can be solved by computing some permutation of the list [1..*n*], where the *i*-th element denotes the row of the queen placed in column *i*, and check whether this permutation is a safe placement. The latter property can easily be expressed with functional patterns and default rules where the non-default rule fails on a non-safe placement:

```
safe (_++[x]++zs++[y]++_) | abs (x-y) == length zs + 1 = failed
safe'default xs = xs
```

Hence, a solution can be obtained by computing a safe permutation:

```
queens n = safe (permute [1..n])
```

This example shows that default rules are a convenient way to express negation-as-failure from logic programming.

Example 8. This programming pattern can also be applied to solve the map coloring problem. Our map consists of the states of the Pacific Northwest and a list of adjacent states:

```
data State = WA | OR | ID | BC
adjacent = [(WA,OR),(WA,ID),(WA,BC),(OR,ID),(ID,BC)]
```

Furthermore, we define the available colors and an operation that associates (non-deterministically) some color to a state:

```
data Color = Red | Green | Blue
color x = (x, Red ? Green ? Blue)
```

A map coloring can be computed by an operation `solve` that takes the information about potential colorings and adjacent states as arguments, i.e., we compute correct colorings by evaluating the initial expression

```
solve (map color [WA,OR,ID,BC]) adjacent
```

The operation `solve` fails on a coloring where two states have an identical color and are adjacent, otherwise it returns the coloring:

```
solve (_++[(s1,c)]++_++[(s2,c)]++_) (_++[(s1,s2)]++_) = failed
solve'default cs _ = cs
```

5   Transformational Semantics

In order to define a precise semantics of default rules, one could extend an existing logic foundation of functional logic programming (e.g., [13]) to include a meaning of default rules. This approach has been partially done in [19] but without considering the different sources of non-determinism (inside, outside) which is important for our intended semantics, as discussed in Sect. 3. Fortunately, the semantic aspects of these issues have already been discussed in the context of encapsulated search [6,11] so that we can put our proposal on these foundations. Hence, we do not develop a new logic foundation of functional logic programming with default rules, but we provide a transformational semantics, i.e., we specify the meaning of default rules by a transformation into existing constructs of functional logic programming.

We start the description of our transformational approach by explaining the translation of the default rule for `zip`. A default rule is applied only if no standard rule is applicable (because the rule's pattern does not match the argument or the rule's condition is not satisfiable). Hence, we translate a default rule into a regular rule by adding the condition that no other rule is applicable. For this purpose, we generate from the original standard rules a set of "test applicability only" rules where the right-hand side is replaced by a constant (here: the unit value "()"). Thus, the single standard rule of `zip` produces the following new rule:

```
zip'TEST (x:xs) (y:ys) = ()
```

Now we have to add to the default rule the condition that `zip'TEST` is not applicable. Since we are interested in the failure of attempts to apply `zip'TEST` to the actual argument, we have to check that this application has no value. Furthermore, non-determinism and failures in the evaluation of actual arguments must be distinguished from similar outcomes caused by the evaluation of the condition.

All these requirements call for the encapsulation of a search for values of `zip'TEST` where "inside" and "outside" non-determinism are distinguished and handled differently. Fortunately, set functions [6] (as sketched in Sect. 2) provide an appropriate solution to this problem. Since set functions have a strategy-independent denotational semantics [11], we will use them to specify and implement default rules. Using set functions, one could translate the default rule into

```
zip xs ys | isEmpty (zip'TEST_S xs ys) = []
```

Hence, this rule can be applied only if all attempts to apply the standard rule fail. To complete our example, we add this translated default rule as a further alternative to the standard rule so that we obtain the transformed program

```
zip'TEST (x:xs) (y:ys) = ()
zip (x:xs) (y:ys) = (x,y) : zip xs ys
zip xs ys | isEmpty (zip'TEST_S xs ys) = []
```

Thanks to the logic features of Curry, one can use this definition also to generate appropriate argument values for `zip`. For instance, if we evaluate the equation `zip xs ys == []` with the Curry implementation KiCS2 [10], the search space is finite and computes, among others, the solution {`xs=[]`}.

Unfortunately, this scheme does not yield the best code to ensure optimal computations. To understand the potential problem, consider the following function:

```
f 0 1 = 1
f _ 2 = 2
```

Intuitively, the best strategy to evaluate a call to `f` is a case distinction on the second argument, since its value is demanded by both rules. Formally, `f` is an *inductively sequential* function [1] since the rules can be organized in a structure called "definitional tree" [1] that expresses the following pattern matching strategy:

1. Evaluate the second argument (to head normal form).
2. If its value is 2, apply the second rule.
3. If its value is 1, evaluate the first argument and try to apply the first rule.
4. Otherwise, no rule is applicable.

In particular, if `loop` denotes a non-terminating operation, the call `f loop 2` evaluates to 2. This is in contrast to Haskell [21] which performs pattern matching from left to right so that Haskell loops on this call. This strategy has been extended to functional logic programming (*needed narrowing* [3]) and is known to be optimal for inductively sequential programs. It is also used in Curry but extended to overlapping rules in order to cover general functional logic programs.

Now consider the following default rule for `f`:

```
f'default _ x = x
```

If we apply our transformation scheme sketched above, we obtain the following Curry program:

```
f'TEST 0 1 = ()
f'TEST _ 2 = ()

f 0 1 = 1
f _ 2 = 2
f x y | isEmpty (f'TESTₛ x y) = y
```

As a result, the definition of `f` is no longer inductively sequential since the left-hand sides of the first and third rule overlap. Since there is no argument demanded by all rules of `f`, the rules could be applied independently. In fact, the Curry implementation KiCS2 [10] loops on the call `f loop 2` (since it tries to evaluate the first argument in order to apply the first rule), whereas it yields the result 2 without the default rule.

To avoid this undesirable behavior when adding default rules, we could try to use the same strategy for the standard rules and the test in the default rule. This can be done by translating the original standard rules into an auxiliary operation and redefining the original operation into one that either applies the standard rules or the default rules. For our example, we transform the definition of f (with the default rule) into the following functions:

```
f'TEST 0 1 = ()              f'INIT 0 1 = 1
f'TEST _ 2 = ()              f'INIT _ 2 = 2

f'DFLT x y | isEmpty (f'TESTS x y) = y

f x y = f'INIT x y ? f'DFLT x y
```

Now, both f'TEST and f'INIT are inductively sequential so that the optimal needed narrowing strategy can be applied, and f simply denotes a choice (without an argument evaluation) between two expressions that are evaluated optimally. Observe that at most one of these expressions is reducible. As a result, the Curry implementation KiCS2 evaluates f loop 2 to 2 and does not run into a loop.

The overall transformation of default rules can be described by the following scheme (its simplicity is advantageous to obtain a comprehensible definition of the semantics of default rules). The function definition

$$f \ \overline{t_k^1} \ | \ c_1 = e_1$$

$$\vdots$$

$$f \ \overline{t_k^n} \ | \ c_n = e_n$$
$$f\text{'default} \ \overline{t_k^{n+1}} \ | \ c_{n+1} = e_{n+1}$$

is transformed into (where $f\text{'TEST}$, $f\text{'INIT}$, $f\text{'DFLT}$ are new function names):

$$f\text{'TEST} \ \overline{t_k^1} \ | \ c_1 = () \qquad f\text{'INIT} \ \overline{t_k^1} \ | \ c_1 = e_1$$

$$\vdots \qquad\qquad\qquad\qquad \vdots$$

$$f\text{'TEST} \ \overline{t_k^n} \ | \ c_n = () \qquad f\text{'INIT} \ \overline{t_k^n} \ | \ c_n = e_n$$

$$f\text{'DFLT} \ \overline{t_k^{n+1}} \ | \ \text{isEmpty} \ (f\text{'TEST}_S \ \overline{t_k^{n+1}}) \ \&\& \ c_{n+1} = e_{n+1}$$
$$f \ \overline{x_k} = f\text{'INIT} \ \overline{x_k} \ ? \ f\text{'DFLT} \ \overline{x_k}$$

Note that the patterns and conditions of the original rules are not changed. Hence, this transformation is also compatible with other advanced features of Curry, like functional patterns, "as" patterns, non-linear patterns, local declarations, etc. Furthermore, if an efficient strategy exists for the original standard rules, the same strategy can be applied in the presence of default rules. This property can be formally stated as follows:

Proposition 1. *Let $\mathcal{R}$ be a program without default rules, and $\mathcal{R}'$ be the same program except that default rules are added to some operations of $\mathcal{R}$. If $\mathcal{R}$ is overlapping inductively sequential, so is $\mathcal{R}'$.*

Proof. Let f be an operation of $\mathcal{R}$. The only interesting case is when a default rule of f is in $\mathcal{R}'$. Operation f of $\mathcal{R}$ produces four different operations of $\mathcal{R}'$: f, $f\text{'DFLT}$, $f\text{'INIT}$, and $f\text{'TEST}$. The first two are overlapping inductively sequential since they are defined by a single rule. The last two are overlapping inductively sequential when f of $\mathcal{R}$ is overlapping inductively sequential since they have the same definitional tree as f modulo a renaming of symbols. $\square$

The above proposition could be tightened a little when operation f is non-overlapping. In this case three of the four operations produced by the transformation are non-overlapping as well. Proposition 1 is important for the efficiency of computations. In overlapping inductively sequential systems, needed redexes exist and can be easily and efficiently computed [2]. If the original system has a strategy that reduces only needed redexes, the transformed system has a strategy that reduces only needed redexes. This ensures that optimal computations are preserved by the transformation regardless of non-determinism.

This result is in contrast to Haskell (or Prolog), where the concept of default rules is based on a sequential testing of rules, which might inhibit optimal evaluation and prevent or limit non-determinism. Hence, our concept of default rules is more powerful than existing concepts in functional or logic programming (see also Sect. 7).

We now relate values computed in the original system to those computed in the transformed system and vice versa. As expected, extending an operation with a default rule preserves the values computed without the default rule.

Proposition 2. *Let $\mathcal{R}$ be a program without default rules, and $\mathcal{R}'$ be the same program except that default rules are added to some operations of $\mathcal{R}$. If e is an expression of $\mathcal{R}$ that evaluates to the value t w.r.t. $\mathcal{R}$, then e evaluates to t w.r.t. $\mathcal{R}'$.*

Proof. Let $f\ \overline{t_k} \to u$ w.r.t. $\mathcal{R}$, for some expression u, a step of the evaluation of e. The only interesting case is when a default rule of f is in $\mathcal{R}'$. By the definitions of f and f'INIT in $\mathcal{R}'$, $f\ \overline{t_k} \to f$'INIT $\overline{t_k} \to u$ w.r.t. $\mathcal{R}'$. A trivial induction on the length of the evaluation of e completes the proof. $\square$

The converse of Proposition 2 does not hold because $\mathcal{R}'$ typically computes more values than $\mathcal{R}$—that is the reason why there are default rules. The following statement relates values computed in $\mathcal{R}'$ to values computed in $\mathcal{R}$.

Proposition 3. *Let $\mathcal{R}$ be a program without default rules, and $\mathcal{R}'$ be the same program except that default rules are added to some operations of $\mathcal{R}$. If e is an expression of $\mathcal{R}$ that evaluates to the value t w.r.t. $\mathcal{R}'$, then either e evaluates to t w.r.t. $\mathcal{R}$ or some default rule of $\mathcal{R}'$ is applied in $e \xrightarrow{*} t$ in $\mathcal{R}'$.*

Proof. Let A denote an evaluation $e \xrightarrow{*} t$ in $\mathcal{R}'$ that never applies default rules. For any operation f of $\mathcal{R}$, the steps of A are of two kinds: (1) $f\ \overline{t_k} \to f$'INIT $\overline{t_k}$ (2) f'INIT $\overline{t_k} \to t'$, for some expressions $\overline{t_k}$ and t'. If we remove from A the steps of kind (1) and replace f'INIT with f, we obtain an evaluation of e to t in $\mathcal{R}$. $\square$

In Curry, by design, the textual order of the rules is irrelevant. A default rule is a constructive alternative to a certain kind of failure. For these reasons, a single default rule, as opposed to multiple default rules without any order, is conceptually simpler and adequate in practical situations. Nevertheless, a default rule of a function f may invoke an auxiliary function with multiple ordinary rules thus producing the same behavior of multiple default rules of f.

6   Implementation

The implementation of default rules for Curry based on the transformational approach is available as a preprocessor. The preprocessor is integrated into the compilation chain of the Curry systems PAKCS [16] and KiCS2 [10]. In some future version of Curry, one could also add a specific syntax for default rules and transform them in the front end of the Curry system.

The transformation scheme shown in the previous section is mainly intended to specify the precise meaning of default rules (similarly to the specification of the meaning of guards in Haskell [21]). Although this transformation scheme leads to a reasonably efficient implementation, the actual implementation can be improved in various ways. For instance, the generated functions f'TEST and f'INIT might duplicate some work to check the patterns and the conditions of the standard rules. This can be avoided by a more sophisticated (but less comprehensible) transformation scheme where the common parts of the definitions of f'TEST and f'INIT are somehow joined into a single function definition.

Further improvements are possible for specific classes of programs. For instance, consider a function where functional patterns are not used and all standard rules are unconditional. If the left-hand side of the default rule overlaps with the left-hand side of some standard rule, one can compute the complement of the patterns of the standard rules and replace the default rule with patterns from this complement that are compatible with the default pattern. Since the complement might be infinite, one has to find a finite representation of it by considering the size of the standard patterns. For instance, the complement of the pattern ((x:xs),(y:ys)) can be represented by the set {((x:xs),[]), ([],_)} (there are also other possible representations). Hence, we can replace the default rule of zip (Example 2) by two rules and obtain the definition shown at the beginning of Sect. 3 and avoid the use of any encapsulated search operation (which is usually less efficient than a case distinction).

As a further example, consider the following definition of the Boolean conjunction:

```
and True   True  = True
and'default _ _ = False
```

By computing the complement pattern of the first rule, we obtain the following transformed definition:

```
and True   True  = True
and True   False = False
and False _       = False
```

Note that this definition is inductively sequential so that it can be evaluated with the optimal needed narrowing strategy [3].

Although the computation of pattern complements is expensive in general [18], it can be done with limited efforts in most practical cases, as shown above. For instance, pattern complements can be computed in a constructive manner with definitional trees. One has to construct a definitional tree for the pattern of the default rule, extend it up to the size of all patterns of standard rules, and remove the overlaps with patterns of standard rules in order to obtain the remaining patterns for the default rule. The precise description of this method requires a number of technical definitions which are omitted from this paper due to space restrictions.

To show the practical advantage of the transformation with pattern complements, we evaluated a few simple operations defined in a typical functional programming style with default rules. For instance, the computation of the last element of a list can be defined with a default rule as follows:

```
last [x] = x
last'default (_:xs) = last xs
```

Our final example extracts all values in a list of optional ("Maybe") values:

```
catMaybes []            = []
catMaybes (Just x : xs) = x : catMaybes xs
catMaybes'default (_:xs) = catMaybes xs
```

Figure 1 shows the run times (in seconds) to evaluate the operations discussed in this section with the different transformation schemes (i.e., the scheme of Sect. 5 and the improvements with pattern complements presented in this section) and different Curry implementations (where "call size" denotes the number of calls to and and the lengths of the input lists for the other examples). All benchmarks were executed on a Linux machine (Debian Jessie) with an Intel Core i7-4790 (3.60 Ghz) processor and 8GB of memory. The results clearly indicate the advantage of computing pattern complements, in particular for PAKCS, which has a less sophisticated implementation of set functions than KiCS2.

System:	PAKCS [16]				KiCS2 [10]			
Operation:	zip	and	last	catMaybes	zip	and	last	catMaybes
Call size:	1000	100000	2000	2000	1000000	1000000	100000	1000000
Sect. 5:	3.66	8.46	2.53	2.45	2.72	1.35	0.38	0.40
Sect. 6:	0.01	0.25	0.01	0.01	0.04	0.08	0.01	0.01

Fig. 1. Performance comparison of different schemes for different compilers for some operations discussed in this section.

7   Related Work

In this section, we compare our proposal of default rules for Curry with existing proposals for other rule-based languages.

The functional programming language Haskell [21] has no explicit concept of default rules. Since Haskell applies the rules defining a function sequentially from top to bottom, it is a common practice in Haskell to write a "catch all" rule as a final rule to avoid writing several nearly identical rules (see example `zip` at the beginning of Sect. 3). Thus, our proposal for default rules increases the similarities between Curry and Haskell. However, our approach is more general, since it also supports logic-oriented computations, and it is more powerful, since it ensures optimal evaluation for inductively sequential standard rules, in contrast to Haskell (as shown in Sect. 5).

Since Haskell applies rules in a sequential manner, it is also possible to define more than one default rule for a function, e.g., where each rule has a different specificity. This cannot be directly expressed with our default rules where at most one default rule is allowed. However, one can obtain the same behavior by introducing a sequence of auxiliary functions where each function has one default rule.

The logic programming language Prolog [12] is based on backtracking where the rules defining a predicate are sequentially applied. Similarly to Haskell, one can also define "catch all" rules as the final rules of predicate definitions. In order to avoid the unintended application of these rules, one has to put "cut" operators in the preceding standard rules. As already discussed in Sect. 3, these cuts are only meaningful for instantiated arguments so that the completeness of logic programming is destroyed. Hence, this kind of default rules can be used only if the predicate is called in a particular mode, in contrast to our approach.

Various encapsulation operators have been proposed for functional logic programs [9] to encapsulate non-deterministic computations in some data structure. Set functions [6] have been proposed as a strategy-independent notion of encapsulating non-determinism to deal with the interactions of laziness and encapsulation (see [9] for details). One can also use set functions to distinguish successful and non-successful computations, similarly to negation-as-failure in logic programming, exploiting the possibility to check result sets for emptiness. When encapsulated computations are nested and performed lazily, it turns out that one has to track the encapsulation level in order to obtain intended results, as discussed in [11]. Thus, it is not surprising that set functions and related operators fit quite well to our proposal. Actually, many explicit uses of set functions in functional logic programming to implement negation-as-failure can be implicitly and more tersely encoded with our concept of default rules, as shown in Examples 7 and 8.

Default rules and negation-as-failure have been also explored in [19,23] for functional logic programs. In these works, an operator, `fails`, is introduced to check whether every reduction of an expression to a head-normal form is not successful. [19] proposes the use of this operator to define default rules for functional logic programming. However, the authors propose a scheme where the default rule is applied if no standard rule was able to compute a head normal form. This is quite unusual and in contrast to functional programming (and our proposal) where default rules are applied if pattern matches or conditions of standard rules fail, but the computations of the rules' right-hand sides are not taken into account to decide whether a default rule should be applied. The same applies to an early proposal for default rules in an eager functional logic language [20].

Since the treatment of different sources of non-determinism and their interaction were not explored at that time, nested computations with failures are not considered by these works. As a consequence, the operator `fails` might yield unintended results if it is used in nested expressions. For instance, if we use `fails` instead of set functions to implement the operation `isUnit` defined in Example 4, the evaluation of `isUnit failed` yields the value `False` in contrast to our intended semantics.

Finally, we proposed in [8] to change Curry's rule selection strategy to a sequential one. However, it turned out that this change has drawbacks w.r.t. the evaluation strategy, since formerly optimal reductions are no longer possible in particular cases. For instance, consider the function `f` defined in Sect. 5 and the call `f loop 2`. In a sequential rule selection strategy, one starts by testing whether the first rule is applicable. Since both arguments are demanded by this rule, one might evaluate them from left to right (as done in the implementation [8]) so that one does not terminate. This problem is avoided with our proposal which returns `2` even in the presence of a default rule for `f`. Moreover, the examples presented in [8] can be expressed with default rules in a similar way.

8   Conclusions

We proposed a new concept of default rules for Curry. Default rules are available in many rule-based languages, but a sensible inclusion into a functional logic language is demanding. Therefore, we used advanced features for encapsulating search to define and implement default rules. Thanks to this approach, typical logic programming features, like non-determinism and evaluating functions with unknown arguments, are still applicable with our new semantics. This distinguishes our approach from similar concepts in logic programming which simply cut alternatives.

Our approach can lead to more elegant and comprehensible declarative programs, as shown by several examples in this paper. Moreover, many uses of negation-as-failure, which are often implemented in functional logic programs by complex applications of encapsulation operators, can easily be expressed with default rules.

Since encapsulated search is more costly than simple pattern matching, we have also shown some opportunities to implement default rules by computing pattern complements. For future work it might be interesting to find more general techniques to transform default rules into case distinctions and tests.

Acknowledgements. The authors are grateful to Sandra Dylus for her suggestions to improve this paper. This material is based in part upon work supported by the National Science Foundation under Grant No. 1317249.

References

1. Antoy, S.: Definitional trees. In: Kirchner, H., Levi, G. (eds.) ALP 1992. LNCS, vol. 632, pp. 143–157. Springer, Heidelberg (1992)

2. Antoy, S.: Optimal non-deterministic functional logic computations. In: Hanus, M., Heering, J., Meinke, K. (eds.) ALP/HOA 1997. LNCS, vol. 1298, pp. 16–30. Springer, Heidelberg (1997)

3. Antoy, S., Echahed, R., Hanus, M.: A needed narrowing strategy. J. ACM **47**(4), 776–822 (2000)

4. Antoy, S., Hanus, M.: Declarative programming with function patterns. In: Hill, P.M. (ed.) LOPSTR 2005. LNCS, vol. 3901, pp. 6–22. Springer, Heidelberg (2006)

5. Antoy, S., Hanus, M.: Overlapping rules and logic variables in functional logic programs. In: Etalle, S., Truszczyński, M. (eds.) ICLP 2006. LNCS, vol. 4079, pp. 87–101. Springer, Heidelberg (2006)

6. Antoy, S., Hanus, M.: Set functions for functional logic programming. In: Proceedings of the 11th ACM SIGPLAN International Conference on Principles and Practice of Declarative Programming (PPDP 2009), pp. 73–82. ACM Press (2009)

7. Antoy, S., Hanus, M.: Functional logic programming. Commun. ACM **53**(4), 74–85 (2010)

8. Antoy, S., Hanus, M.: Curry without success. In: Proceedings of the 23rd International Workshop on Functional and (Constraint) Logic Programming (WFLP 2014). CEUR Workshop Proceedings, vol. 1335, pp. 140–154. CEUR-WS.org (2014)

9. Braßel, B., Hanus, M., Huch, F.: Encapsulating non-determinism in functional logic computations. J. Funct. Logic Program. **2004**(6) (2004)

10. Braßel, B., Hanus, M., Peemöller, B., Reck, F.: KiCS2: a new compiler from Curry to Haskell. In: Kuchen, H. (ed.) WFLP 2011. LNCS, vol. 6816, pp. 1–18. Springer, Heidelberg (2011)

11. Christiansen, J., Hanus, M., Reck, F., Seidel, D.: A semantics for weakly encapsulated search in functional logic programs. In: Proceedings of the 15th International Symposium on Principle and Practice of Declarative Programming (PPDP 2013), pp. 49–60. ACM Press (2013)

12. Deransart, P., Ed-Dbali, A., Cervoni, L.: Prolog - The Standard: Reference Manual. Springer, Heidelberg (1996)

13. González-Moreno, J.C., Hortalá-González, M.T., López-Fraguas, F.J., Rodríguez-Artalejo, M.: An approach to declarative programming based on a rewriting logic. J. Logic Program. **40**, 47–87 (1999)

14. Hanus, M.: Declarative processing of semistructured web data. In: Technical Communications of the 27th International Conference on Logic Programming. Leibniz International Proceedings in Informatics (LIPIcs), vol. 11, pp. 198–208 (2011)

15. Hanus, M.: Functional logic programming: from theory to Curry. In: Voronkov, A., Weidenbach, C. (eds.) Programming Logics. LNCS, vol. 7797, pp. 123–168. Springer, Heidelberg (2013)

16. Hanus, M., Antoy, S., Braßel, B., Engelke, M., Höppner, K., Koj, J., Niederau, P., Sadre, R., Steiner, F.: PAKCS: The Portland Aachen Kiel Curry System (2015). http://www.informatik.uni-kiel.de/~pakcs/

17. Hanus, M. (ed.): Curry: An integrated functional logic language (vers. 0.8.3) (2012). http://www.curry-language.org

18. Krauss, A.: Pattern minimization problems over recursive data types. In: Proceedings of the 13th ACM SIGPLAN International Conference on Functional Programming (ICFP 2008), pp. 267–274. ACM Press (2008)

19. López-Fraguas, F.J., Sánchez-Hernández, J.: A proof theoretic approach to failure in functional logic programming. Theory Pract. Logic Program. **4**(1), 41–74 (2004)

20. Moreno-Navarro, J.J.: Default rules: an extension of constructive negation for narrowing-based languages. In: Proceedings of Eleventh International Conference on Logic Programming, pp. 535–549. MIT Press (1994)

21. Peyton Jones, S. (ed.): Haskell 98 Language and Libraries—The Revised Report. Cambridge University Press, Cambridge (2003)
22. Reddy, U.S.: Narrowing as the operational semantics of functional languages. In: Proceedings of IEEE International Symposium on Logic Programming, Boston, pp. 138–151 (1985)
23. Sánchez-Hernández, J.: Constructive failure in functional-logic programming: from theory to implementation. J. Univ. Comput. Sci. **12**(11), 1574–1593 (2006)
24. Slagle, J.R.: Automated theorem-proving for theories with simplifiers, commutativity, and associativity. J. ACM **21**(4), 622–642 (1974)

Generic Matching of Tree Regular Expressions over Haskell Data Types

Alejandro Serrano$^{(\boxtimes)}$ and Jurriaan Hage

Department of Information and Computing Sciences,
Utrecht University, Utrecht, The Netherlands
{A.SerranoMena, J.Hage}@uu.nl

Abstract. *Tree regular expressions* are a generalization of string regular expressions to tree-shaped data. In this paper we apply the theory of tree regular expressions to extend pattern matching on Haskell data types. We define the operations in a *data type-generic way*, looking at data types as fixed-points of pattern functors and using the Generic implementation available in the GHC Haskell compiler.

Keywords: Tree regular expressions · Generic programming · Haskell

1 Introduction

Pattern matching is one of the key ingredients of functional programming. It allows defining functions by cases, looking at the structure of the value under consideration. It is indeed the core of value inspection in Haskell, ML and its many derivatives, and available in Common Lisp (as the **destructuring-bind** macro), Clojure (packaged in **core.match**) and many others. It seems reasonable to ask ourselves how to enhance the expressivity of this fundamental construct.

In this paper, we focus on pattern matching in a particular language, namely Haskell [8]. In Haskell, a data type is defined via a series of constructors, like in the following example which represents the structure of arithmetic expressions with literals, addition and product:

> **data** *ArithExpr = Literal Integer*
> | *Plus   ArithExpr ArithExpr*
> | *Times ArithExpr ArithExpr*

Values in a data type are formed by applying these constructors to arguments of the types specified by their constructors. For example, the *ArithExpr* representation of $3 + (2 * 4)$ is:

> *Plus (Literal 3) (Times (Literal 2) (Literal 4))*

A. Serrano and J. Hage—This work was supported by the Netherlands Organisation for Scientific Research (NWO) project on "DOMain Specific Type Error Diagnosis (DOMSTED)" (612.001.213).

M. Gavanelli and J. Reppy (Eds.): PADL 2016, LNCS 9585, pp. 83–98, 2016.
DOI: 10.1007/978-3-319-28228-2_6

It is important to notice that values in Haskell can be seen in general as trees.[1] Each node in the tree corresponds to a constructor application, and their children correspond to the arguments. Our example can be depicted as follows:

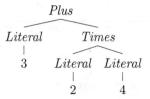

Functions are defined by cases, each targeting values with a specific structure, that is, a specific tree shape. Furthermore, parts of the tree can be captured and made available under a name throughout the execution. As an example, the following piece of code traverses an arithmetic expression and simplifies all appearances of expressions of the form $a + 0$, $0 + a$, $a * 1$ and $1 * a$ to a:

```
simpl :: ArithExpr → ArithExpr
simpl (Plus   x (Literal 0)) = simpl x
simpl (Plus   (Literal 0) x) = simpl x
simpl (Plus   x y)           = Plus  (simpl x) (simpl y)
simpl (Times x (Literal 1)) = simpl x
simpl (Times (Literal 1) x) = simpl x
simpl (Times x y)            = Times (simpl x) (simpl y)
simpl (Literal n)            = Literal n
```

This definition is very clear, but it has also a lot of repetition in the cases we want to simplify. OCaml includes disjunctive patterns [5], allowing us to express this algorithm in a much more compact form:

```
fun simpl x = match x with
  | Plus   y (Literal 0) | Plus   (Literal 0) y
  | Times y (Literal 1) | Times (Literal 1) y → simpl y
  | Plus   x y                                → Plus  (simpl x) (simpl y)
  | Times x y                                → Times (simpl x) (simpl y)
  | Literal n                                → Literal n
```

Being able to express this kind of patterns directly inside Haskell is one of the goals of this paper.

There are situations where we want to check the shape of a value up to an unbounded depth. One example is re-associating expressions, such as ensuring that when using our *ArithExpr* data types, a sum of the form:

$$(a + b) + ((c + d) + e)$$

is converted into a right-associated form:

$$(((a + b) + c) + d) + e$$

---

[1] Haskell allows the definition of cyclic structures, such as *ones* = $1 : ones$. Those values are not simple trees, but rather rational trees.

We can definitely write a function which performs this duty, but using our tree regular expressions, it becomes a one-liner:

$assocSum :: ArithExpr \rightarrow ArithExpr$
$assocSum\ (Plus\ \square\ \square\ |\ leaves)\ ^{*,\square} = foldl1\ Plus\ leaves$

The key ingredient in this case is the iteration expressed via the $*$ operation, which happens in the positions marked by holes $\square$. If the match is successful, the leaves of the tree can be accessed throught the *leaves* binding in the body of the function. Having that information in place, we can just fold using the *Plus* constructor to get the desired shape.

This ability to iterate the matching an unbounded number of times is useful in other scenarios, which usually require recursion or folding over the value:

- Inside a compiler, sometimes we need to match an n-ary function application represented by nested binary application constructs. This was indeed our primary motivation to develop the library presented in this paper.
- In some cases, validation of terms in a data structure needs a complicated traversal. As an example, think of checking that every *Literal* in an *ArithExpr* is a positive number. Using iteration in patterns, accessing those values becomes trivial.

This paper presents a Haskell library, namely `t-regex`[2], in which all the previous extensions to pattern matching are available. It does so by leveraging the power of *tree regular expressions*, which are described in Sect. 2. The implementation is based on the fixed-point view on data (Sect. 3) with support from GHC Generics, and it is described in Sect. 4. Tree regular expressions have a larger range of application than merely pattern matching: they can also be used to generate arbitrary values and to implement attribute grammars with regular look-ahead, but we do not describe those due to lack of space.

2   Tree Regular Expressions

In the world of *strings* we find the well-known concepts of automaton, regular grammar and regular expression. Those three mechanisms provide different views on the problem of describing a set of strings, but at the very end we know that all three have the same expressive power. If we move from strings to the context of *trees*, the similar concepts of tree automaton, tree regular grammar and tree regular expression emerge. The encyclopaedic reference for tree automata is Comon et al. [3].

In order to be precise, let us introduce some definitions. A *ranked alphabet* is a pair $\mathcal{F} = \langle \hat{\mathcal{F}}, arity \rangle$, where $\hat{\mathcal{F}}$ is a finite set and $arity$ is a function $\hat{\mathcal{F}} \rightarrow \mathbb{N}$. The set $\hat{\mathcal{F}}$ represents the constructors used to build values of a data type. We

---

[2] Available at http://hackage.haskell.org/package/t-regex.

denote $\mathcal{F}_p$ the set of elements in $\hat{\mathcal{F}}$ whose arity is exactly p. The set of *ground trees* over $\mathcal{F}$, $T(\mathcal{F})$, is defined as the smallest set such that:[3]

- $\mathcal{F}_0 \subseteq T(\mathcal{F})$,
- if $f \in \mathcal{F}_p$ and $t_1, \ldots, t_p \in T(\mathcal{F})$, then $f(t_1, \ldots, t_p) \in T(\mathcal{F})$.

We shall depict ground trees as in the previous section, using internal nodes for elements in $\mathcal{F}_p$ with $p \geqslant 1$, and leaves corresponding to elements in $\mathcal{F}_0$.

In order to define *tree regular expressions*[4] over a ranked alphabet $\mathcal{F}$, we first need to enlarge the alphabet with an infinite set of *holes* $\mathcal{H} = \{\Box_1, \Box_2, \ldots\}$, whose purpose shall become clear in a moment. The set of regular expressions over $\mathcal{F}$ with holes $\mathcal{H}$, $R(\mathcal{F}, \mathcal{H})$, is inductively defined as:

- $\emptyset \in R(\mathcal{F}, \mathcal{H})$,
- $\top \in R(\mathcal{F}, \mathcal{H})$,
- if $x \in \mathcal{F}_0$ or $x \in \mathcal{H}$, then $x \in R(\mathcal{F}, \mathcal{H})$,
- if $f \in \mathcal{F}_p$ and $t_1, \ldots, t_p \in R(\mathcal{F}, \mathcal{H})$, then $f(t_1, \ldots, t_p) \in R(\mathcal{F}, \mathcal{H})$,
- if $r_1, r_2 \in R(\mathcal{F}, \mathcal{H})$, then $r_1 \,|\, r_2 \in R(\mathcal{F}, \mathcal{H})$,
- if $r_1, r_2 \in R(\mathcal{F}, \mathcal{H})$ and $\Box \in \mathcal{H}$, then $r_1 \cdot_\Box r_2 \in R(\mathcal{F}, \mathcal{H})$,
- if $r \in R(\mathcal{F}, \mathcal{H})$ and $\Box \in \mathcal{H}$, then $r^{*,\Box} \in R(\mathcal{F}, \mathcal{H})$.

Intuitively, the $|$, $\cdot_\Box$ and $^{*,\Box}$ operators correspond to choice, concatenation and iteration, respectively. The constants $\emptyset$ and $\top$ are used to represent an impossible match and a pattern which matches any term, respectively.

Let us fix for the following examples a ranked alphabet corresponding to arithmetic expressions, $\mathcal{F}_0 = \mathbb{N}$, $\mathcal{F}_1 = \{Literal\}$ and $\mathcal{F}_2 = \{Plus, Times\}$. The regular expression that matches both $0 + x$ and $x + 0$ is simply:

$$Plus(Literal(0), \top) \,|\, Plus(\top, Literal(0))$$

The reader might be wondering why the concatenation and iteration operations need to be annotated with a hole, whereas no annotation is used in string regular expressions. The reason is that, in contrast to strings, trees might grow in more than one place, and one needs to be explicit about which is chosen when putting together two regular expressions. *Holes* are the mechanism used for *describing positions* in a tree.

For example, the regular expression $Times(\Box_1, \Box_2)$ leaves the two argument positions open, which can be later replaced by different regular expressions:

$$Times(\Box_1, \Box_2) \cdot_{\Box_1} Literal(0) = Times(Literal(0), \Box_2)$$
$$Times(\Box_1, \Box_2) \cdot_{\Box_2} Literal(0) = Times(\Box_1, Literal(0))$$

On the other hand, the expression $Times(\Box, \Box)$ forces both positions to be filled with the same element:

$$Times(\Box, \Box) \cdot_\Box Literal(0) = Times(Literal(0), Literal(0))$$

---

[3] Note that, in order to keep the exposition simple, our definition does not involve typing information. However, our implementation enforces that only well-typed tree shapes are described.

[4] We shall drop the word *tree* from now on.

Holes are also used in the iteration combinator to describe the position where iteration should take place. As a very simple example, we can describe arithmetic expressions whose literals always are the number 2.

$$(Plus(\square, \square) \mid Times(\square, \square) \mid Literal(2))^{*,\square}$$

We can represent this regular expression graphically. In the following picture, dashed arrows represent references from a hole to the corresponding regular expression filling it.

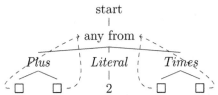

Each regular expression defines a *language*, that is, a set of trees which are matched by it. First of all, we need an auxiliary operation of *substitution* of mutually distinct holes by trees, $t\{\square_1 \mapsto t_1, \ldots, \square_n \mapsto t_n\}$, which we refrain from defining here (see Comon et al. [3] for the complete description of this operation). This operation is then lifted from trees to languages

$$L\{\square_1 \mapsto L_1, \ldots, \square_n \mapsto L_n\} = \{t\{\square_1 \mapsto t_1, \ldots, \square_n \mapsto t_n\} \mid t \in L, t_i \in L_i\}$$

Armed with substitutions, we can define the notions of n-th *iteration* and *closure* of a language as follows:

$$\begin{aligned} L^{0,\square} &= \{\square\} \\ L^{n+1,\square} &= L^{n,\square} \cup L\{\square \mapsto L^{n,\square}\} \end{aligned} \qquad L^{*,\square} = \bigcup_{n \geqslant 0} L^{n,\square}$$

Finally, we can describe the *language defined by a regular expression* r, $[\![r]\!]$:

$$\begin{aligned} [\![\emptyset]\!] &= \emptyset \\ [\![\top]\!] &= T(\mathcal{F}) \\ [\![x]\!] &= \{x\}, \text{if} x \in \mathcal{F}_0 \text{or} x \in \mathcal{H} \\ [\![f(r_1, \ldots, r_n)]\!] &= \{f(t_1, \ldots, t_n) \mid t_1 \in [\![r_1]\!], \ldots, t_n \in [\![r_n]\!]\} \\ [\![r_1 \mid r_2]\!] &= [\![r_1]\!] \cup [\![r_2]\!] \\ [\![r_1 \cdot_\square r_2]\!] &= [\![r_1]\!]\{\square \mapsto [\![r_2]\!]\} \\ [\![r^{*,\square}]\!] &= [\![r]\!]^{*,\square} \end{aligned}$$

Our task is now to find a way to describe regular expressions over an arbitrary Haskell data type, along with a *match r t* function which returns *True* if and only if $t \in [\![r]\!]$.

3   Fixed-Point View and Generics

In order to work generically over Haskell data types, we adopt a *fixed-point view* on data similar to the **regular** library [9]. This means that we assume that each data type is defined as *Fix f* for some pattern functor *f*, where *Fix* defines the least fixed-point of a functor:

newtype *Fix f = Fix { unFix :: f (Fix f) }*

For a simple data type, its pattern functor has almost the same shape as its definition. However, a new type argument is added to the data type, which accounts for recursion. Instead of directly including recursive occurrencess in the data type, we use that new type argument. For example, our *ArithExpr* turns into:[5]

data *ArithExprP r = LiteralP Integer*
          | PlusP   r r
          | TimesP   r r

We can almost get back our original *ArithExpr* by taking:

type *ArithExpr = Fix ArithExprP*

The "almost" in the previous sentence comes from the fact that we now need to wrap constructors from the pattern functor inside an extra *Fix*. Our running example $2 + (3 * 4)$ now reads:

Fix (PlusP (Fix (LiteralP 2))
          (Fix (TimesP (Fix (LiteralP 3)) (Fix (LiteralP 4)))))

The GHC compiler ships since version 7.8 with an extension called *pattern synonyms* which helps us reducing much of the syntactic overhead of explicit *Fix* constructors. If we define the following synonyms:

pattern *Literal n = Fix (LiteralP n)*
pattern *Plus   a b = Fix (PlusP   a b)*
pattern *Times a b = Fix (TimesP a b)*

we can get back the same syntax for our running example $2 + (3 * 4)$:

Plus (Literal 2) (Times (Literal 3) (Literal 4))

A pattern functor allows us to separate the constructors, corresponding to a ranked alphabet, from the construction of values by recursion, which is captured by *Fix*. The next step is to treat any set of constructors in a generic way, so we can implement matching once and for all data types. For that we employ *data type-generic* programming: our implementation accomodates itself to the shape of the data being matched.

There are a handful of libraries bringing data type-generic programming to Haskell. In this work, we use the integrated support for Generics in GHC [6].

---

[5] Throughout this paper, we suffix constructors in pattern functors with the letter *P*.

The *generic universe* used to describe data types with one argument, similar to those taken as argument by *Fix*, is made of the following basic blocks:

data *V1*   *p*
data *U1*   *p* = *U1*
data (*f* ⊕ *g*)   *p* = *L1* (*f p*) | *R1* (*g p*)
data (*f* ⊗ *g*)   *p* = *f p* ⊗ *g p*
newtype *K1 c p* = *K1*   *c*
newtype *Par1 p* = *Par1 p*

- *V1* represents data types without any constructor.
- In the case of a constructor without arguments (like [] in the case of lists), the constructor is represented using *U1*.
- When a data type has more than one constructor, the choice combinator ⊕ is used to combine the representations of each of the constructors.
- When more than one argument is needed, these are combined with ⊗. The list of values is then represented as a nested tuple.
- Arguments to a constructor can be of two types. First, we might refer to the last type argument (the one we use to represent recursion). In that case, we use *Par1*. The other possibility is to refer to any other type τ; we need to use a constant *K1* τ to describe this situation.[6]

For each data type for which data type-generic support is desired, an instance of *Generic1* needs to exist. Such an instance packs together the representation of the data type along with conversion functions between actual data type values and its generic view.

class *Generic1 f* **where**
  type *Rep1 f* :: * → *
  from1 :: *f a* → *Rep1 f a*
  to1 :: *Rep1 f a* → *f a*

The attractiveness of using the integrated GHC Generics support is that the compiler is able to derive *Generic1* automatically for a pattern functor, by adding a **deriving** *Generic1* to the data type definition. If we do so for our *ArithExprP* data type, we get back the following definition of *Rep1*:[7]

K1 Integer ⊕ (*Par1* ⊗ *Par1*) ⊕ (*Par1* ⊗ *Par1*)

When implementing a generic function, the code for each of the basic blocks which make up the representation of a data type needs to be given. We do so by

---

[6] To be completely accurate, there is a third combinator *Rec1* which is used to describe recursion in which the type argument appears wrapped in another functor, like the second argument to (:) in the definition of lists.

[7] The actual implementation also includes *metadata* about the types and constructors, which we omit here.

defining a type class for which an instance is written for each of the blocks, and a wrapper function which performs the neccessary conversions back and forth between generic views and calls the functions in the type class.

As an example of the definition of a function in a data type-generic way, let us write a generic equality function *geq*. We start writing an initial wrapper and a corresponding *GEq* type class:

$geq :: (Generic1\ f, GEq\ (Rep1\ f)) \Rightarrow Fix\ f \rightarrow Fix\ f \rightarrow Bool$
$geq\ (Fix\ x)\ (Fix\ y) = geq_-\ (from1\ x)\ (from1\ y)$

class *GEq f* **where**
    $geq_- :: f\ a \rightarrow f\ a \rightarrow Bool$

The instances for the simpler cases of *GEq* are as follows:

instance *GEq V1* **where**
    $geq_-\ \_\ \_ = \bot$
instance *GEq U1* **where**
    $geq_-\ U1\ U1 = True$
instance *Eq c* $\Rightarrow$ *GEq (K1 c)* **where**
    $geq_-\ (K1\ x)\ (K1\ y) = x \equiv y$
instance *(GEq f, GEq g)* $\Rightarrow$ *GEq (f $\oplus$ g)* **where**
    $geq_-\ (L1\ x)\ (L1\ y) = geq_-\ x\ y$
    $geq_-\ (R1\ x)\ (R1\ y) = geq_-\ x\ y$
    $geq_-\ \_\ \qquad \_ \qquad = False$
instance *(GEq f, GEq g)* $\Rightarrow$ *GEq (f $\otimes$ g)* **where**
    $geq_-\ (x1 \otimes x2)\ (y1 \otimes y2) = geq_-\ x1\ y1 \wedge geq_-\ x2\ y2$

The next instance to write is that of the type parameters. Since we are going to use the data type with *Fix*, everytime we use *Par1* we know we are referring to the same data type. But the compiler does not know this fact, so the definition referring to the initial function is rejected:

instance *GEq Par1* **where**
    $geq_-\ (Par1\ x)\ (Par1\ y) = geq\ x\ y$

The solution is not to change the function definition, but to refine the type signature in *GEq* to work only on fixed-points of representable pattern functors:

class *GEq f* **where**
    $geq_- :: (Generic1\ g, GEq\ (Rep1\ g)) \Rightarrow f\ (Fix\ g) \rightarrow f\ (Fix\ g) \rightarrow Bool$

The same style of generic function definition is used several times throughout this paper. The key remark is the special care we need to take for the *Par1* case, by adding extra constraints to the type signature in the type class.

4   Haskell Implementation

The definition of *Fix* for a pattern functor corresponds closely to the definition of $T(\mathcal{F})$ for a ranked alphabet. In order to implement matching of tree regular expressions we shall start by providing a similar definition, but for $R(\mathcal{F}, \mathcal{H})$. The corresponding Haskell type, *Regex f*, is given below.

data *Regex* $(f :: * \rightarrow *)$
    $= Empty$
    | *Any*
    | *In* $(f \ (Regex \ f))$
    | *Regex f* ||| *Regex f*

Note that we do not include a specific constructor for concatenation, iteration or holes; instead, we shall define them by using higher-order abstract syntax. The data-free cases *Empty* and *Any* correspond to $\emptyset$ and $\top$ regular expressions, respectively. The ||| combinator also follows closely the definition of |. When a constructor for the underlying pattern functor f is to be used, the *In* case must be used. It is similar to the *Fix* constructor, but the recursive positions are not filled by trees, but with other regular expressions.

The definition of concatenation and iteration for regular expressions is tied to the notion of a hole. In this work, we are going to represent holes by variable binders in the Haskell term language: this technique is known as *higher-order abstract syntax* [10]. Thus, the tree regular expression with a hole:

$$Plus \ (Literal \ 0 \ \Box)$$

is represented as the following λ-abstraction with one binder:

$\lambda k \rightarrow In \ (PlusP \ (In \ (LiteralP \ 0)) \ k)$

Concatenation becomes simply function application (\$). Furthermore, we can ensure statically that when peforming substitution in a hole, the required amount of holes exist in the regular expression. Continuing with the previous example, the regular expression

$$Plus(Literal \ 0, \Box) \cdot_\Box Times(\top, \top)$$

is represented by the following Haskell term:

$(\lambda k \rightarrow In \ (PlusP \ (In \ (LiteralP \ 0)) \ k)) \ \$ \ (In \ (TimesP \ Any \ Any))$

The only construct left to define is iteration. In order to do so, we invoke the following property of tree regular expressions:

$$r^{*,\Box} = r \cdot_\Box r^{*,\Box}$$

In Haskell terms, the rule reads as a definition for iteration:

$$iter :: (Regex\ f \to Regex\ f) \to Regex\ f$$
$$iter\ r = r\ \$\ iter\ r$$

The lazy behavior of Haskell is key to make this definition work.

Now that we have all basic operations, we can express the shape whose aim is to match arithmetic expressions which only use the number 2:

$$iter\ (\lambda k \to In\ (PlusP\ k\ k)\ |||\ In\ (TimesP\ k\ k)\ |||\ In\ (LiteralP\ 2))$$

Notice that, by the way we have encoded holes in our Haskell representation, we ensure that a value of type $Regex\ f$ does not have any unbound holes in it.

4.1   Matching

Once we have all the pieces in place, writing a function which checks whether a value matches a regular expression is not a complicated task. The function *matches* that we are looking for has the type

$$matches :: (Generic1\ f, GMatches\ (Rep1\ f))$$
$$\Rightarrow Regex\ f \to Fix\ f \to Bool$$

where *GMatches* is the type class used to implement the data type-generic part. This function takes care of the data-type-independent parts of regular expressions, such as choice:

```
matches Empty    _      = False
matches Any      _      = True
matches (In r) (Fix t) = matches_ (from1 r) (from1 t)
matches (r1 ||| r2) t   = matches r1 t ∨ matches r2 t
```

The entrance to the data type-generic part is in the *In* case. Indeed, we can see that in the corresponding equations we find calls to *from1* to move to the generic view of data types. The great thing is that, given that both the regular expression and the value are built from the same functor, we just need to compare the generic structure of both. This is the task of *matches_*, defined in the *GMatches* type class. Taking into account the considerations about the structure of the generic function from the previous section, this type class and its instances are defined as follows:

```
class GMatches f where
    matches_ :: (Generic1 g, GMatches (Rep1 g))
              ⇒ f (Regex g) → f (Fix g) → Bool
instance GMatches U1 where
    matches_ _ _ = True
instance Eq c ⇒ GMatches (K1 c) where
    matches_ (K1 r) (K1 t) = x ≡ y
```

instance *GMatches Par1* **where**
  matches_ (Par1 r) (Par1 t) = matches' r t

instance *(GMatches f, GMatches g) ⇒ GMatches (f ⊕ g)* **where**
  matches_ (L1 r) (L1 t) = matches_ r t
  matches_ (R1 r) (R1 t) = matches_ r t
  matches_ _   _   = False

instance *(GMatches f, GMatches g) ⇒ GMatches (f ⊗ g)* **where**
  matches_ (r1 ⊗ r2) (t1 ⊗ t2) i s = matches_ r1 t1 ∧ matches_ r2 t2

One problem with this definition is that any type apart from the pattern functor is compared by equality (notice the *Eq c* constraint in the *GMatches (K1 i c)* case). This might not be the desired behavior every time. For example, if we use *ArithExprP*, we can write regular expressions which match instances of *LiteralP n* for each number *n* (that is, *LiteralP 0*, *LiteralP 1* and so on), but not a regular expression which matches *LiteralP n regardless* of *n*.

In order to support a version of *Any* but for any data type, we introduce a small hack.[8] The main idea is to throw an exception for this case, which should be later captured. Defining a new exception type and throwing one of them is done using the interface given by GHC [7].

data *DoNotCheckThis = DoNotCheckThis* **deriving** *(Show, Typeable)*

instance *Exception DoNotCheckThis*

† :: *a*
† *= throw DoNotCheckThis*

Then, the code for *K1* is refined to cope with this exception:

instance *Eq c ⇒ GMatches (K1 c)* **where**
  matches_ (K1 r) (K1 t) = unsafePerformIO $
    (evaluate $ *r ≡ t)* ‘*catch*‘ *(λ(_ :: DoNotCheckThis) → return True)*

Since we need to catch exceptions, we are bound to use the *IO* monad. However, in this case it is safe to use the *unsafePerformIO* escape hatch, since we know that the comparison between *r* and *t* either returns a Boolean or throws a *DoNotCheckThisException* from a use of †.

The only glitch left is to ensure that the exception, when thrown, is thrown in the correct context: laziness might defer evaluation until some other point in time. Luckily, the GHC exceptions module provides us with a *evaluate::a → IO a* function which forces evaluation to WHNF, which is enough for our purposes.

4.2   Capturing

Up to now, we have support for checking that a term complies with the specification given by a regular expression. However, full pattern matching is more

---

[8] The hack involves *unsafePerformIO*, so some people might not catalog this as such.

powerful: in addition to checks we might also obtain parts of the tree under a specific binding. For example, if you are working with *ArithExpr* values, you can write a pattern *Plus x y* and then use *x* and *y* in the body of the function. When this branch is executed, *x* and *y* take the value of the arguments to *Plus*: we say that those values are *captured* by the pattern under the bindings *x* and *y*.

The first thing that we need to notice is that, whereas usual pattern matching might only capture one value per binding, the structure of regular expressions involving iteration creates bindings with possibly more than one value. For example, if we capture all the literals when matching a tree of two's under the same binding, this binding might end up with a lot of *Literal* 2 trees.

There are several choices when facing this problem. One solution is to save all the captures in the order they were found. Another one is to keep just the first, or the last, capture. If the type has some notion of ordering, keeping them well-ordered is another possibility. In any case, it seems that the correct abstraction is the *Alternative* type class, which supports creating empty containers and joining two of them:

class *Applicative m* ⇒ *Alternative m* **where**
    empty :: *m a*
    (⟨|⟩) :: *m a* → *m a* → *m a*

Thus, if we want to obtain all captures, we just instantiate the match using the list type. If instead only the first one is wanted, we just need to choose *Maybe* as the container.

The second point to consider is how to name each of the captures that might be obtained. Our approach is to allow the user of the library to choose whatever type they like as names, given that they can be compared, so that captures for the same name can be collected. Only *Regex f* gets an extra parameter for the type of captures, and reads:

data *Regex c f* = ...   -- previous constructors
       | *c* ⇐ *Regex c f*

The more general operation of matching a term against a regular expression and capturing some subtrees is now called *match*. Instead of a simple Boolean, it returns a *Maybe* which signals whether the matching succeded or not, wrapping a map from *c* to the captures. The signature is now:

match :: (*Generic1 f*, *GMatch* (*Rep1 f*), *Ord c*, *Alternative m*)
    ⇒ *Regex c f* → *Fix f* → *Maybe* (*Map c* (*m* (*Fix f*)))

In the new version of the algorithm, a successful match is represented by returning an empty map wrapped in a *Just*. When a capture is requested, the current tree *t* is inserted into the map of captures, combining it via (⟨|⟩) with other captures already present.

```
import Data.Map as M   -- operations over key-value maps
match Empty     _    = Nothing
match Any       _    = Just M.empty
match (In r) (Fix t) = match_ (from1 r) (from1 t)
match (r1 ||| r2) t  = match r1 t ⟨|⟩ match r2 t
match (c ⇐ r)   t    = M.insertWith (⟨|⟩) c (pure t) ⟨$⟩ match r t
```

Most of the instances of *GMatch* can be used without changes in the new capture scenario. We need to upgrade *U1* and *K1* to return an empty map instead of plainly *True*. When two arguments of a constructor are matched with ⊗, each of them will return information about their captures, which we need to put together.

instance *GMatch U1* **where**
   $match_{-} \_ \_ \_ = Just\ M.empty$
instance *Eq c* ⇒ *GMatch* (*K1 c*) **where**
   $match_{-}$ (*K1 r*) (*K1 t*) = *guard* (*r* ≡ *t*) ≫ *return M.empty*
instance (*GMatch f*, *GMatch g*) ⇒ *GMatch* (*f* ⊗ *g*) **where**
   $match_{-}$ (*r1* ⊗ *r2*) (*t1* ⊗ *t2*) =
      M.unionWith (⟨|⟩) ⟨$⟩ $match_{-}$ *r1 t1* ⟨*⟩ $match_{-}$ *r2 t2*

4.3   Examples

Let us return to the examples from the introduction, and see how they are expressed using our library for tree regular expressions. The first function to be defined is *simpl*: we mentioned that it can be expressed in a nice way by using disjunction. In particular, the tree regular expression corresponding to the first equation reads:

```
matchSimple :: Regex String ArithExprP
matchSimple = In (PlusP  (In (LiteralP 0)) ("y" ⇐ Any))
          ||| In (PlusP  ("y" ⇐ Any)      (In (LiteralP 0)))
          ||| In (TimesP (In (LiteralP 1)) ("y" ⇐ Any))
          ||| In (TimesP ("y" ⇐ Any)      (In (LiteralP 1)))
```

Note that for simplicity we have decided to use strings as capture identifiers. In practice, one might want to use a type-safer alternative.

In order to check whether a value corresponds to that expression, we use the *match* function. If the call returns a *Just* value, we know that the match was successful and that we may obtain the value from the substitution. Note that in the call to *match* we implicitly need to choose the *Alternative* instance about how several values are combined: in this case we opt for [ ]:

```
simpl x | Just s ← matches matchSimple x = simpl (head (s M. !! "y"))
```

The information about captured variables is available as the variable *s*. Given that it is of *Map* type, we use the corresponding operator !! to look for the value in the "y" identifier. We have discussed that this value is a list, and thus we need to call *head* to obtain its only value. The rest of the equations for *simpl* stay the same as in the original definition.

The second example is even easier to translate, since we already found the tree regular expression which checks the shape and captures the values we are interested in. The bulk of the work is representing it via a Haskell term:

$$pluses :: Regex\ String\ ArithExprP$$
$$pluses = iter\ (\lambda k \rightarrow In\ (PlusP\ k\ k)\ |||\ "\texttt{leaves}" \Lleftarrow Any)$$
$$assocSum :: ArithExpr \rightarrow ArithExpr$$
$$assocSum\ e\ |\ Just\ s \Lleftarrow match\ pluses\ e = foldr1\ Sum\ (s\ M.!!\ "\texttt{leaves}")$$

4.4 Integration with Pattern Matching Syntax

We are now close to being able to use regular expressions as enhanced pattern match constructs. However, the way in which we obtain the results by *match* is not appealing: it forces us to choose a type to name captures, and then to perform lookups over the obtained map. Instead, we aim to reuse Haskell binding forms as names, which are directly bound to the corresponding captures whenever the match is successful.

Unfortunately, we cannot do this using bare Haskell. However, Template Haskell [12] enables us to use meta-programming facilities, and to create a syntactic form which fulfills these requirements. We refrain from explaining it thoroughly due to lack of space, but the actual implementation of our `t-regex` library includes support for using tree regular expressions in the place where a pattern match is expected.

As an example, here is a function which can be written with our library, which obtains all literal leaves from an *ArithExpr*. The *ns* binding in the regular expression is shown in the body of the function as a list of matches; for that reason we can use *map* over it.

$$numbers\ [\,rx\ |\ iter\ (\lambda k \rightarrow In\ (PlusP\ k\ k)\ |||\ In\ (TimesP\ k\ k)$$
$$|||\ ns \Lleftarrow In\ (LiteralP\ \dagger))\,|]$$
$$= map\ (\lambda(LiteralP\ n) \rightarrow n)\ ns$$

5 Related Work

Tree Automata [4]. It is well-known that tree regular expressions correspond to languages matchable by tree automata [3]. This relation can be used to build a tree automata for patterns we want to check, which are later applied to the terms to match. This technique is used by Fähndrich et al. [4], although using regular term equations instead of regular expressions. Tree automata are also used by Bagrak and Shivers [1] to implement tree regular expressions for Scheme.

We have not made any empirical comparison, but it should be expected for a minimized tree automaton to perform better than our generic matching. Integrating their work on already-existing compiler requires modification, though, whereas our library uses data type-generic operations already available in GHC.

Regular Expression Patterns for Lists [2]. The main difference is that their work focuses on patterns for lists, whereas ours extends to any Haskell data type which can be represented in the Generic framework. On the other hand, patterns in Broberg et al. [2] can depend on both the structure of the list and the data contained on it. Our approach does not directly allow this two-level matching: we need to combine both data types in a single one.

Type-Safe Pattern Combinators [11]. The main difference here is that we reuse the constructors that define the original data type, keeping the syntax closer to usual pattern matching. On the other hand, new pattern combinators need to be provided for each new data type that we want to match upon. The main advantage of pattern combinators is that they are not limited to traversing the structure of the tree, they can perform other kinds of checks on the values. For example, tree regular expression cannot express an invariant such as "the value in this position must be greater than the one in this other place". In that respect, pattern combinators are more powerful; tree regular expressions only allow matching on a regular structure.

References

1. Bagrak, I., Shivers, O.: trx: regular-tree expressions, now in scheme. In: Fifth Workshop on Scheme and Functional Programming (2004)
2. Broberg, N., Farre, A., Svenningsson, J.: Regular expression patterns. In: Proceedings of the Ninth ACM SIGPLAN International Conference on Functional Programming. ICFP 2004, pp. 67–78. ACM, New York (2004)
3. Comon, H., Dauchet, M., Gilleron, R., Löding, C., Jacquemard, F., Lugiez, D., Tison, S., Tommasi, M.: Tree automata techniques and applications, release October, 12th 2007 (2007). http://www.grappa.univ-lille3.fr/tata
4. Fähndrich, M., Boyland, J.: Statically checkable pattern abstractions. In: Jones, S.L.P., Tofte, M., Berman, A.M. (eds.) Proceedings of the 1997 ACM SIGPLAN International Conference on Functional Programming (ICFP 1997), Amsterdam, The Netherlands, 9–11 June 1997, pp. 75–84. ACM (1997)
5. Leroy, X., Doligez, D., Frisch, A., Garrigue, J., Rémy, D., Vouillon, J.: The OCaml system release 4.02. http://caml.inria.fr/pub/docs/manual-ocaml/
6. Magalhães, J.P., Dijkstra, A., Jeuring, J., Löh, A.: A generic deriving mechanism for Haskell. In: Proceedings of the Third ACM Haskell Symposium on Haskell, Haskell 2010, pp. 37–48. ACM, New York (2010)
7. Marlow, S.: An extensible dynamically-typed hierarchy of exceptions. In: Haskell 2006: Proceedings of the 2006 ACM SIGPLAN workshop on Haskell
8. Marlow, S., et al.: Haskell 2010 language report. https://www.haskell.org/onlinereport/haskell2010/
9. Van Noort, T., Rodriguez, A., Holdermans, S., Jeuring, J., Heeren, B.: A lightweight approach to datatype-generic rewriting. In: Proceedings of the ACM SIGPLAN Workshop on Generic Programming, WGP 2008, pp. 13–24. ACM, New York (2008)
10. Pfenning, F., Elliott, C.: Higher-order abstract syntax. SIGPLAN Not. **23**(7), 199–208 (1988)

11. Rhiger, M.: Type-safe pattern combinators. J. Funct. Programm. **19**(2), 145–156 (2009)
12. Sheard, T., Peyton Jones, S.: Template meta-programming for Haskell. SIGPLAN Not. **37**(12), 60–75 (2002)

A Size-Proportionate Bijective Encoding of Lambda Terms as Catalan Objects Endowed with Arithmetic Operations

Paul Tarau[(⊠)]

Department of Computer Science and Engineering,
University of North Texas, Denton, USA
paul.tarau@unt.edu

Abstract. We describe a size-proportionate bijection between lambda terms in a compressed de Bruijn notation and the Catalan family of combinatorial objects implemented as a Haskell type class, that has as instances binary trees and multiway-trees with empty leaves, as well as standard bitstring-represented natural numbers.

By building on previous work that defines arithmetic operations on instances of this family, we extend lambda calculus with efficient arithmetic operations.

At the same time, operations like normalization of lambda terms are made available to members of the Catalan family of combinatorial objects.

As a practical application to software testing we derive a mechanism for generating large random lambda terms from Rémy's algorithm for efficient generation of random binary trees.

Keywords: Lambda calculus · compressed de Bruijn terms · Tree-based numbering systems · Ranking and unranking of lambda terms · Normalization with higher order abstract syntax · Random generation of large lambda terms

1 Introduction

Bijective encodings of tree-like structures go back to Ackermann's bijection between natural numbers and hereditarily finite sets [1]. They are relatively easy to design if one does not care about one side of the bijection exponentially exploding in size, as it is the case, for instance, with Ackermann's bijection.

With significant effort, such size-proportionate bijections between term algebras and the set of natural numbers represented with the usual binary notation are defined in [21], using ranking of balanced parentheses languages and a generalization of Cantor's pairing function [5,16] to tuples. However, the binary search and complex computations involved in the ranking algorithms limit the encoding described in [21] to relatively small terms and numbers not larger than about 2000 bits.

© Springer International Publishing Switzerland 2016
M. Gavanelli and J. Reppy (Eds.): PADL 2016, LNCS 9585, pp. 99–116, 2016.
DOI: 10.1007/978-3-319-28228-2_7

A more revolutionary approach has been sketched out in [23]. Instead of trying to adjust the bijective Gödel numbering scheme to be size-proportionate as a bijection to bitstring-represented numbers, [23] replaces its target: natural numbers are represented as binary trees. This paper generalizes that approach to an arbitrary member of the Catalan family of combinatorial objects [20], on which the usual arithmetic operations are defined. At the same time, it lifts a limitation on the size-proportionate encoding of [23] where that property is lost unless de Bruijn indices fit in a fixed size word. The generalization of binary-tree arithmetic to Catalan objects, on which we rely in this paper, is described extensively in the unpublished arxiv draft [22], a subset of which is covered in [25].

Following [22], a Haskell type class will be used to abstract away the number representation. This has the benefit of having arithmetic operations implemented by any instance of the Catalan family of combinatorial objects. It will also enable trying out our algorithms on the usual "human friendly" natural numbers, which can be seen, via a bijective transformation, as such an instance.

The arithmetic operations performed with the Catalan family based numbering system can work with numbers comparable in size with Knuth's "arrow-up" notation. These computations have a worst case and average case complexity that is comparable with the traditional binary numbers, while their best case complexity outperforms binary numbers by an arbitrary tower of exponents factor.

More importantly, encodings of lambda terms, that can be seen as a tree-to-tree transformation, are naturally size-proportionate.

Our bijective encoding to tree-based number systems will provide the means to derive an algorithm for the generation of random lambda terms from well-known random generation algorithms for binary trees (Rémy's algorithm). Random lambda terms (and in particular, the very large ones our encoding enables) can be useful for testing tools where they play the role of an intermediate language, like compilers for functional languages and proof assistants.

By adding a normal order reducer of our lambda terms we provide a uniform representation for computations with lambda terms, and efficient arithmetic operations - two essential building blocks of modern functional languages.

Together, these have applications to implementation of domain specific languages, compiler stages and proof assistants relying on lambda terms as their intermediate language.

The paper is organized as follows. Section 2 introduces the compressed de Bruijn terms and bijective transformations from them to standard lambda terms. Section 3 describes mappings from lambda terms to Catalan families of combinatorial objects. These mappings lead to size-proportionate ranking and unranking algorithms for lambda terms. Section 4 gives an algorithm for normal order reduction of lambda terms that also extends to their Catalan encodings. Section 5 relates combinatorial generation of Catalan objects and that of lambda terms. Section 6 introduces algorithms for generation of random lambda terms. Section 7 discusses related work. Section 8 concludes the paper.

The paper is organized as literate Haskell program. The code in the paper is available at http://www.cse.unt.edu/~tarau/research/2015/XDB.hs, tested with GHC 7.10.2. It defines a module that includes code from [25] (file GCcat.hs, a superset of which is available from the arXiv draft [22]), which defines a type class for arithmetic operations with Catalan objects, generically. It also includes Haskell library packages needed for the generation of random binary trees.

```
module XDB where
import GCat
import System.Random
import Math.Combinat.Trees
```

To achieve a size-proportionate bijective Gödel numbering scheme, all our arithmetic computations will be performed with members of the type class `Cat` which provides a generic implementation in terms of members of the Catalan family of combinatorial objects [22], in particular binary or multiway trees with empty leaves.

2 A Compressed Representation of de Bruijn Terms

We will summarize here a compressed representation for lambda terms in de Bruijn notation introduced as Prolog program in [24], that will facilitate defining a bijection to tree-represented natural numbers.

2.1 De Bruijn Indices

De Bruijn indices [4,13] provide a *name-free* representation of lambda terms. All terms that can be transformed by a renaming of variables (α-conversion) will share a unique representation. Variables following lambda abstractions are omitted and their occurrences are marked with positive integers *counting the number of lambdas until the one binding them* is found on the way up to the root of the term.

We represent them using the constructor `Ab` for application, `Lb` for lambda abstractions (that we will call shortly *binders*) and `Vb` for marking the integers corresponding to the de Bruijn indices. This gives the Haskell data type `B a` as the definition of the de Bruijn terms *parameterized by the type* `a` *of the indices used by* `Vb`.

```
data B a = Vb a | Lb (B a) | Ab (B a) (B a) deriving (Eq,Show,Read)
```

For instance, when the parameter `a` is specialized to ordinary integers, the S combinator $\lambda x.\lambda y.\lambda z.(x\ z)\ (y\ z)$ is represented as `Lb (Lb (Lb (Ab (Ab (Vb 2) (Vb 0)) (Ab (Vb 1) (Vb 0)))))`, corresponding to the fact that `Vb 2` is bound by the outermost lambda (three steps away, counting from 0) and the occurrences of `Vb 0` are bound each by the closest lambda on the way to the root, represented by the third constructor `Lb`.

2.2   Compressed de Bruijn Terms

Iterated lambdas (represented as a block of constructors `Lb` in the de Bruijn notation) can be seen as a successor arithmetic representation of a number that counts them. So it makes sense to represent that number in a more efficient numbering system. Note that in de Bruijn notation blocks of lambdas can wrap either applications or variable occurrences represented as indices. This suggests using just two constructors: `Vx` indicating in a term `Vx k n` that we have `k` lambdas wrapped around the de Bruijn index `Vb n` and `Ax`, indicating in a term `Ax k x y` that `k` lambdas are wrapped around the application `Ab x y`.

We call the terms built this way with the constructors `Vx` and `Ax` *compressed de Bruijn terms*. They are specified by The Haskell data type `X`.

```
data X a = Vx a a | Ax a (X a) (X a) deriving (Eq,Show,Read)
```

For instance, the S combinator `Lb (Lb (Lb (Ab (Ab (Vb 2) (Vb 0)) (Ab (Vb 1) (Vb 0)))))` in de Bruijn notation, will be represented as `Ax 3 (Ax 0 (Vx 0 2) (Vx 0 0)) (Ax 0 (Vx 0 1) (Vx 0 0))`, with the outermost constructor `Ax` encoding the three `Lb` binders and k=0 elsewhere indicating the presence of no lambda binder in (front of) applications `Ax k` or indices `Vx k`. Note also that lambda binders counted by `k` in a leaf term `Vx k n` can bind at most one variable as no application splits the tree below them.

Open and Closed Terms. Lambda terms might contain *free variables* not associated to any binders. Such terms a called *open*. Any syntactically well formed term of types `B` and `X` is an open term. A *closed* term is such that each variable occurrence is associated to a binder. Closed terms can be easily identified by ensuring that the lambda binders on a given path from root outnumber the de Bruijn index of a variable occurrence ending the path.

To facilitate size-proportionate encodings of lambda terms, arithmetic operations in this paper will be performed in terms of tree instances of the type class `Cat`, *described in the companion paper* [25], *a superset of which is available as* [22]. The function `isClosedX` checks that a compressed de Bruijn term is closed by trying to find a lambda binding every index on the way up to the root of the lambda tree. The addition operation `add` and successor function `s`, defined for instances of the type class `Cat` (see [22,25]), will be used to count binders and the comparison operation `cmp` (see [22]) will ensure that binders on the way down from the root outnumber index values at the leaves of the lambda tree.

```
isClosedX :: Cat a ⇒ X a → Bool
isClosedX t = f t e where
  f (Vx k n) d = LT==cmp n (add d k)
  f (Ax k x y) d = f x d' && f y d' where d' = add d k
```

Example 1. `isClosedX` *on the K combinator* $\lambda x_0.(\lambda x_1. \ x_0)$, *written* `(Vx 2 1)` *as a compressed de Bruijn term, and a similar small open term. Note the use of both* `Cat` *instances* `N` *and* `T` *parameterizing our (compressed) de Bruijn terms.*

```
*XDB> isClosedX (Vx 2 1)
True
*XDB> isClosedX (Vx 2 2)
False
*XDB> isClosedX (Vx (C E (C E E)) (C E E))
True
*XDB> isClosedX (Vx (C E (C E E)) (C E (C E E)))
False
```

2.3   Converting from de Bruijn to Compressed de Bruijn Terms

The function b2x converts from the usual de Bruijn representation to the compressed one. It proceeds by case analysis on Vb, Ab, Lb and counts the binders Lb as it descends toward the leaves of the tree. Its steps are controlled by the successor function s that increments the counts when crossing a binder.

```
b2x :: (Cat a) ⇒ B a → X a
b2x (Vb x) = Vx e x
b2x (Ab x y) = Ax e (b2x x) (b2x y)
b2x (Lb x) = f e x where
  f k (Ab x y) = Ax (s k) (b2x x) (b2x y)
  f k (Vb x) = Vx (s k) x
  f k (Lb x) = f (s k) x
```

2.4   Converting from Compressed de Bruijn to de Bruijn Terms

The function x2b converts from the compressed to the usual de Bruijn representation. It reverses the effect of b2x by expanding the k in V k n and A k x y into k Lb binders (no binders when k=0). The function iterLam performs this operation in both cases, and the predecessor function s' computes the decrements at each step.

```
x2b :: (Cat a) ⇒ X a → B a
x2b (Vx k x)  = iterLam k (Vb x)
x2b (Ax k x y) = iterLam k (Ab (x2b x) (x2b y))

iterLam :: Cat a ⇒ a → B a → B a
iterLam k x | e_ k = x
iterLam k x = iterLam (s' k) (Lb x)
```

Proposition 1. *The functions* b2x *and* x2b, *having as domains and range open terms, are inverses.*

Example 2. *The conversion between types* B *and* X *of the combinator* $Y = \lambda x_0.$ $(\lambda x_1.(x_0 \ (x_1 \ x_1)) \ \lambda x_2.(x_0 \ (x_2 \ x_2)))$.

```
*XDB> b2x (Lb (Ab (Lb (Ab (Vb 1) (Ab (Vb 0) (Vb 0))))
          (Lb (Ab (Vb 1) (Ab (Vb 0) (Vb 0))))))
Ax 1 (Ax 1 (Vx 0 1) (Ax 0 (Vx 0 0) (Vx 0 0)))
```

```
          (Ax 1 (Vx 0 1) (Ax 0 (Vx 0 0) (Vx 0 0)))
*XDB> x2b it
Lb (Ab (Lb (Ab (Vb 1) (Ab (Vb 0) (Vb 0))))
          (Lb (Ab (Vb 1) (Ab (Vb 0) (Vb 0))))))
```

This bijection allows borrowing algorithms between the two representations. The function isClosedB tests if a term in de Bruijn notation is closed.

```
isClosedB :: Cat a ⇒ B a → Bool
isClosedB = isClosedX . b2x
```

3   Ranking and Unranking as a Catalan Embedding of Compressed de Bruijn Terms

We will derive an encoding of the compressed de Bruijn terms into objects of type Cat, such that the binary tree instance of type Cat is size-proportionate with the encoded term.

The intuition behind the algorithm is that we want leaf nodes of the lambda term to encode into leaves or small trees close to the leaves and application nodes to encode into internal nodes of the binary tree, as much as possible.

3.1   Ranking Compressed de Bruijn Terms

The function x2t implements such an encoding.

```
x2t :: Cat a ⇒ X a → a
x2t (Vx k n) | e_ k && e_ n = n
x2t (Vx k n) = c (s' (s' (c (n,k))),e)
x2t (Ax k a b) = c (k,q) where q = c (x2t a,x2t b)
```

Note that leaves Vx k x are encoded either as empty leaves of the binary tree or as subtrees with the right branch an empty leaf. To ensure the encoding is bijective, we will need to decrement the result of the constructor c twice in the second rule, with the predecessor function s' to ensure that this case leaves no gaps in the range of the function x2t. For application nodes Ax k a b we recurse on nodes a and b and then we put the branches together with the constructor c. When c=C or c=M, this results in a tree of a size proportionate to the compressed de Bruijn term.

3.2   Unranking Compressed de Bruijn Terms

The decoding function t2x reverses the steps of the encoder x2t.

Case analysis on the right branch of the binary tree will tell if it is a leaf node or an internal node of the lambda tree, in which case the increment in x2t, needed for bijectivity, is reversed by applying the successor function s twice before applying the deconstructor c'.

```
t2x :: Cat a ⇒ a → X a
t2x x | e_ x = Vx x x
t2x z = f y where
  (x,y) = c' z
  f y | e_ y = Vx k n where (n,k) = c' (s (s x))
  f y | c_ y = Ax x (t2x a) (t2x b) where (a,b) = c' y
```

Proposition 2. *The functions* t2x *and* x2t, *converting between open compressed de Bruijn terms and corresponding instances of* Cat, *are inverses.*

Example 3. *The work of* t2x *and* x2t *on* Cat *instance* N.

```
*XDB> t2x 1234
Ax 0 (Vx 0 0) (Ax 1 (Vx 0 0) (Ax 0 (Vx 1 0) (Ax 1 (Vx 0 0) (Vx 0 0))))
*XDB> x2t it
1234
*XDB> t it
C E (C E (C (C E E) (C E (C E (C (C E E) (C (C E E) (C E E))))))
*XDB> map (x2t.t2x) [0..15]
[0,1,2,3,4,5,6,7,8,9,10,11,12,13,14,15]
```

Note however that when using the instance N of Cat which implies the usual binary number representation, the encoding is, as expected, not size proportionate.

This precludes the use of the usual random number generators returning integers in binary notation to generate very large random lambda terms. We will circumvent this problem by using instead an algorithm that (uniformly) generates random binary trees (see Sect. 6).

We define the unranking function t2b and the ranking function b2t for de Bruijn terms, as follows.

```
t2b :: Cat a ⇒ a → B a
t2b = x2b . t2x

b2t :: Cat a ⇒ B a → a
b2t = x2t . b2x
```

Proposition 3. *The functions* t2b *and* b2t *converting between open de Bruijn terms and corresponding instances of* Cat, *are inverses.*

Example 4. *The encoding and decoding of the de Bruijn form of the pairing combinator* $\lambda x_0. \lambda x_1. \lambda x_2.((x_2\ x_0)\ x_1)$ *to ordinary binary numbers and binary trees.*

```
*XDB> b2t (Lb (Lb (Lb (Ab (Ab (Vb 0) (Vb 2)) (Vb 1)))))
1389505070847794345082851820104254894239239815
        98768676847349100809495755679247
*XDB> t it
C (C (C E E) E) (C (C E (C E (C (C E (C E (C E E))) E))) (C (C E E) E))
*XDB> t2b it
```

```
Lb (Lb (Lb (Ab (Ab (Vb E) (Vb (C E (C E E)))) (Vb (C E E)))))
*XDB> b2t it
C (C (C E E) E) (C (C E (C E (C (C E (C E (C E E))) E))) (C (C E E) E))
*XDB> n it
13895050708477943450828518201042548942392398159876867684734910080949575556792247
*XDB> t2b it
Lb (Lb (Lb (Ab (Ab (Vb 0) (Vb 2)) (Vb 1))))
```

To facilitate comparison, it is useful to define the functions `sizeT` that returns the number of internal nodes of the binary tree view of a Catalan object and `sizeX` returning the size of a lambda term in compressed de Bruijn form, in which numeric components `k` and `n` are also measured with `sizeT`.

```
sizeT :: Cat t ⇒ t → t
sizeT x | e_ x = x
sizeT x = s (add (sizeT a) (sizeT b)) where (a,b) = c' x

sizeX :: Cat a ⇒ X a → a
sizeX (Vx k n) = add (sizeT k) (sizeT n)
sizeX (Ax k a b) = s (add (sizeT k) (add (sizeX a) (sizeX b)))
```

Example 5. *The sum of the two sizes on an initial segment of* $\mathbb{N}$ *illustrates the fact that the bijection* `t2x` *is indeed size-proportionate.*

```
*Main> sum (map (sizeT) [0..10000])
114973
*Main> sum (map (sizeX.t2x) [0..10000])
75288
```

Proposition 4. *The average time complexity of* `t2x` *and* `x2t` *is* $O(n)$ *for input size* n *and their worst case time complexity is* $O(n \, log^*(n))$ *when working on instance* T *(binary trees).*

Proof. It follows from the fact that the average complexity of `c`, `c'` `s` and `s'` is constant time, the worst case complexity of `s` and `s'` is $O(log^*(n))$ and that $O(n)$ of these are performed by `t2x` and `x2t`.

3.3   Conversion to/from a Canonical Representation of Lambda Terms with Integer Variable Names

We represent standard lambda terms [2] by using the constructors `Ls` for lambda abstractions, `As` for applications and `Vs` for variable occurrences.

```
data S a = Vs a | Ls a (S a) | As (S a) (S a) deriving (Eq,Show,Read)
```

The function `b2s` converts from the de Bruijn representation to lambda terms whose canonical names are provided by natural numbers. We will call them terms in *standard notation*.

```
b2s :: Cat a ⇒ B a → S a
b2s a = f a e [] where
  f :: (Cat a) ⇒ B a → a → [a] → S a
  f (Vb i) _ vs =  Vs (at i vs)
  f (Lb a) v vs = Ls v (f a (s v) (v:vs))
  f (Ab a b) v vs = As (f a v vs) (f b v vs)

at i (x:_) | e_ i = x
at i (_:xs) = at (s' i) xs
```

Note the use of the helper function at that associates to an index i a variable in position i on the list vs. As we initialize in b2s when calling helper function f the list of index variables to [], we enforce that only closed terms (having no free variables) are accepted.

The inverse transformation is defined by the function s2b.

```
s2b  :: Cat a ⇒ S a → B a
s2b x = f x [] where
  f :: Cat a ⇒ S a → [a] → B a
  f (Vs x) vs = Vb  (at x vs)
  f (As x y) vs = Ab (f x vs) (f y vs)
  f (Ls v y) vs = Lb a where a = f y (v:vs)
```

Note again the use of at, this time to locate the index i on the list of variables vs. By initializing vs with [] in the call to helper function f, we enforce that only closed terms are accepted.

Proposition 5. *The functions s2b and b2s, converting between closed de Bruijn terms and closed standard terms, are inverses.*

Example 6. *The bijection defined by the functions s2b and b2s on the term* $\lambda x_0.(\lambda x_1.(x_0\ (x_1\ x_1))\ \lambda x_2.(x_0\ (x_2\ x_2)))$.

```
*XDB> b2s (Lb (Ab (Lb (Ab (Vb 1) (Ab (Vb 0) (Vb 0))))
          (Lb (Ab (Vb 1) (Ab (Vb 0) (Vb 0))))))
Ls 0 (As (Ls 1 (As (Vs 0) (As (Vs 1) (Vs 1))))
          (Ls 1 (As (Vs 0) (As (Vs 1) (Vs 1)))))
*XDB> s2b it
Lb (Ab (Lb (Ab (Vb 1) (Ab (Vb 0) (Vb 0))))
          (Lb (Ab (Vb 1) (Ab (Vb 0) (Vb 0)))))
```

4   Normalization with Tree-Based Arithmetic Operations

We will now describe an evaluation mechanism for the (Turing-complete) language of closed lambda terms, called *normal order reduction* [19]. A mapping between de Bruijn terms and *a new data type that mimics standard lambda terms, except for representing binders as functions in the underlying implementation language*, will be used both ways to evaluate and then return the result as a de Bruijn term.

4.1   Representing Lambdas as Functions in the Implementation Language

The data type H represents leaves Vh of the lambda tree and applications Ah the same way as the standard lambda terms of type S. However, Lambda binders, meant to be substituted with terms during β-reduction steps are represented as functions from the domain H to itself.

```
data H a = Vh a | Lh (H a → H a) | Ah (H a) (H a)
```

4.2   A HOAS-style Normal Order Reducer

Normal order evaluation [19] ensures that if a normal form exists, it is found after a finite number of steps. In lambda-calculus based functional languages computing a normal form, normalization can be achieved through a HOAS (Higher-Order Abstract Syntax) mechanism, that borrows the substitution operation from the underlying "meta-language". To this end, lambdas are implemented as functions which get executed (usually lazily) when substitutions occur. We refer to [18] for the original description of this mechanism, widely used these days for implementing embedded domain specific languages and proof assistants in languages like Haskell or ML.

The function nf implements normalization of a term of type H, derived from a closed de Bruijn term. At each normalization step, when encountering a binder of the form Lh f, the normalizer nf traverses it and it is composed with f. At each application step Ah f a, if the left branch is a lambda, it is applied to the reduced form of the right branch, as implemented by the helper function h. Otherwise, the application node is left unchanged.

```
nf :: H a → H a
nf (Vh a) = Vh a
nf (Lh f)   = Lh (nf . f)
nf (Ah f a) = h (nf f) (nf a) where
  h :: H a → H a → H a
  h (Lh g) x = g x
  h g x = Ah g x
```

The result of implementing lambdas as functions is that we not only borrow substitutions from the underlying Haskell system but also the underlying (normal) order of evaluation.

4.3   Closed Terms to/from HOAS

To implement conversion from the type H to the type B the function h2b traverses the application nodes. As in the case of our other transformers, the (simple) numerical computations involved in the transformations will be performed using the arithmetic on Catalan objects of type Cat.

```
h2b :: Cat a ⇒ H a → B a
h2b t = h e t where
  h d  (Lh f)  = Lb  (h d'  (f (Vh d'))) where d' = s d
  h d  (Ah a b) = Ab (h d a) (h d b)
  h d  (Vh d')  = Vb (sub d d')

b2h :: Cat a ⇒ B a → H a
b2h t = h t [] where
  h :: Cat a ⇒  B a  → [H a] → H a
  h (Lb a) xs  = Lh (λx → h a (x:xs))
  h (Ab a b) xs = Ah (h a xs) (h b xs)
  h (Vb i) xs  = at i xs
```

Example 7. *Testing that* h2b *is a left inverse of* h2b.

```
*XDB> (h2b . b2h) (Lb (Lb (Lb (Ab (Ab (Vb 0)
                              (Vb 2)) (Vb 1)))))
Lb (Lb (Lb (Ab (Ab (Vb 0) (Vb 2)) (Vb 1))))
```

While so called "exotic terms" are possible in the data type H to which no terms of type B correspond, the terms brought to the H side by b2h and back by h2b are identical.

4.4 Evaluating Closed Lambda Terms

As our normal order reduction is borrowed via a HOAS mechanism from the underlying Haskell system, evaluation is restricted to closed terms. Instead of getting help form a Maybe type, it is simpler to define its result as the trivial open term Vb e for all open terms.

We obtain a normal order reducer for de Bruijn terms by wrapping up nf with the transformers b2h and h2b.

```
evalB :: (Cat a) ⇒ B a → B a
evalB x  | isClosedB x = (h2b .nf . b2h) x
evalB _ = Vb e
```

We can then lend the evaluator also to compressed de Bruijn terms.

```
evalX :: (Cat a) ⇒ X a → X a
evalX x = (b2x . evalB . x2b) x
```

Example 8. *Reduction to the identity* $I = \lambda x_0.x_0$ *of* $SKK = ((\lambda x_0. \lambda x_1. \lambda x_2.$ $((x_0\ x_2)\ (x_1\ x_2))\ \lambda x_3.\ \lambda x_4.x_3)\ \lambda x_5.\ \lambda x_6.x_5)$ *in compressed de Bruijn notation.*

```
*XDB> evalX (Ax 0 (Ax 0 (Ax 3 (Ax 0 (Vx 0 2) (Vx 0 0))
            (Ax 0 (Vx 0 1) (Vx 0 0))) (Vx 2 1)) (Vx 2 1))
Vx 1 0
```

4.5   Catalan Objects as Lambda Terms

Given the bijection between instances of the Catalan family, we can go one step further and extend the evaluator to binary trees.

```
evalT :: T→T
evalT = x2t . evalX . t2x
```

As we have also made the usual natural numbers members of the Catalan family, we can define normal order reduction of such "arithmetized" lambda terms as the arithmetic function evalN.

```
evalN :: N→N
evalN = x2t . evalX . t2x
```

Example 9. *Evaluation of binary trees and natural numbers seen as lambda terms.*

```
*XDB> evalT (C (C E (C E E)) (C (C E E) E))
C (C (C E E) E) E
*XDB> filter (>0) (map evalN [0..31])
[1,4,8,1,11,1,15,16,15,20,23,15,28,31]
```

As evaluation happens in a Turing-complete language, these functions are not total. For instance, evalN 318, corresponding to the lambda term $\omega = (\lambda x.(x\ x))(\lambda x.(x\ x))$, is non-terminating.

5   Generation of Catalan Objects and Lambda Terms

Given the size-proportionate bijection between open lambda terms and Catalan objects, we can use generators for the later to generate the former.

5.1   A Generator for Catalan Objects

The function genCat implements a simple generator for Catalan objects with a fixed number of internal nodes. Note that computations are expressed in terms of the arithmetic operations on type Cat. It uses the function nums (see [22]) that generates an initial segment of the set of natural numbers as a Haskell list.

```
genCat :: Cat t ⇒ t → [t]
genCat n | e_ n = [n]
genCat n | c_ n =
  [ c (x,y) | k←nums (s' n), x←genCat k, y←genCat (s' (sub n k))]
```

Example 10. *Generation of Catalan object with 3 internal nodes and their natural number encodings.*

```
*XDB> mapM_ print (genCat (t 3))
C E (C E (C E E))
C E (C (C E E) E)
C (C E E) (C E E)
C (C E (C E E)) E
C (C (C E E) E) E

*XDB> genCat 3
[5,6,4,7,15]
```

Given that closed terms have interesting uses in random testing [8], we derive generators for them in compressed de Bruijn and de Bruijn form.

```
genCatX :: Cat a ⇒ a → [X a]
genCatX = filter isClosedX . map t2x . genCat

genCatB :: Cat a ⇒ a → [B a]
genCatB = filter isClosedB . map t2b . genCat
```

Example 11. *Generation of closed compressed de Bruijn terms decoded from binary trees with 3 internal nodes.*

```
*XDB> mapM_ print (genCatX 4)
Ax 0 (Vx 1 0) (Vx 1 0)
Ax 1 (Vx 0 0) (Vx 1 0)
Ax 1 (Vx 1 0) (Vx 0 0)
Ax 2 (Vx 0 0) (Vx 0 0)
Ax 3 (Vx 0 0) (Vx 0 0)
Vx 3 0
Vx 4 0
Vx 8 0
```

5.2   Generation of Lambda Terms via Unranking

While direct enumeration of terms constrained by number of nodes or depth is straightforward in Haskell an unranking algorithm is also usable for generation of large terms, including generation of very large random terms.

Generating Open Terms in Compressed de Bruijn Form. Open terms are generated simply by iterating over an initial segment of $\mathbb{N}$ with the function t2x.

```
genOpenX :: Cat a ⇒ a → [X a]
genOpenX l = map t2x (nums l)
```

Reusing unranking-based open term generators for more constrained families of lambda terms works when their asymptotic density is relatively high. Fortunately we know from the extensive quantitative analysis available in the literature [6,7,11] when this is the case.

The function `genClosedX` generates closed terms by filtering the results of `genOpenX` with the predicate `isClosedX`.

```
genClosedX l = filter isClosedX (genOpenX l)
```

Example 12. *Generation of closed compressed de Bruijn terms. Note the more than* 50 % *closed terms among the first* 10000 *open terms.*

```
*XDB> genClosedX 8
[Vx 1 0,Ax 1 (Vx 0 0) (Vx 0 0),Ax 2 (Vx 0 0) (Vx 0 0)]

*XDB> map x2t (genClosedX 30)
[1,4,8,9,11,12,15,16,19,20,23,24,28]

*XDB> length (genClosedX (t 10000))
5375
```

6   Random Generation of Lambda Terms

As the ranking bijection of the compressed de Bruijn lambda terms maps them to Catalan objects, we can use unranking of uniformly generated random binary trees to generate random terms.

6.1   Generating Random Binary Trees

We will rely on the Haskell library `Math.Combinat.Trees` to generate binary trees uniformly, using a variant of Rémy's algorithm described in [14], as well as Haskell's built-in random generator from package `System.Random`. This will allow generation of random lambda terms corresponding to super-exponentially sized numbers of type N, but size-proportionate when natural numbers are represented by the binary trees of type T.

The function ranCat is parametrized by the function `tf` that picks a type for a leaf among the instances of `Cat`, to be propagated as the type of tree, as well as the size of the tree and the random generator g.

```
ranCat :: (Cat t, RandomGen g) ⇒ (N →t) → Int → g → (t, g)
ranCat tf size g = (bt2c bt,g') where
  (bt,g') = randomBinaryTree size g
  bt2c (Leaf ()) = tf 0
  bt2c (Branch l r) = c (bt2c l,bt2c r)
```

The function `ranCat1` allows getting a random tree of a given size and type, by giving a seed that initializes the random generator g.

```
ranCat1 tf size seed = fst (ranCat tf size (mkStdGen seed))
```

6.2 Generating Random Compressed de Bruijn Terms

We will use the bijection t2x from Catalan objects to open compressed de Bruijn trees, parameterized by the function tf that picks the type of the instance of Cat to be used.

The function ranOpenX generates random terms in a way similar to the function ranCat.

```
ranOpenX tf size g = (t2x r,g') where(r,g') = ranCat tf size g
```

The function ranOpen1X generates random terms given a seed for the random generator.

```
ranOpen1X tf size seed = t2x (ranCat1 tf size seed)
```

The function ranClosedX filters the generated terms until a closed one is found.

```
ranClosedX tf size g =
  if isClosedX x then x else ranClosedX tf size g' where
    (a,g') = ranCat tf size g
    x = t2x a
```

The function ranClosed1X works in a similar way, except for providing a seed instead of a random generator.

```
ranClosed1X tf size seed = ranClosedX tf size g where g = mkStdGen seed
```

Example 13. *Generation of some random lambda terms (including very large ones) in compressed de Bruijn form.*

```
*XDB> ranClosed1X n 3 9
Ax 1 (Vx 0 0) (Vx 0 0)
*XDB> ranClosed1X t 3 9
Ax (C E E) (Vx E E) (Vx E E)
*XDB> n (sizeX (ranClosed1X t 100 9))
96
*XDB>  n (sizeX (ranOpen1X t 50000 42))
50001
```

7 Related Work

Originally introduced in [4], the de Bruijn notation makes terms equivalent up to α-conversion and facilitates their normalization [13]. As indices replace variable names by their stack-order relative positioning to their binders, they are already more compact than standard lambda terms. However as iteration of their lambda binders can be seen as a form of unary Peano arithmetic, it made sense to further compress them by counting the binders more efficiently. This mechanism, is first described in [24] where in combination with the generalized Cantor bijection between $\mathbb{N}^k \to \mathbb{N}$ it is used to provide a bijective Gödel numbering scheme. However, as the $\mathbb{N} \to \mathbb{N}^k$ side of this bijection is only computable using a binary search algorithm, it is limited to relatively small terms, by contrast to the one described in this paper that works in time proportional to the size of both the terms and their tree-based number encodings.

In [23] a binary tree-arithmetic encoding is introduced, that can be seen as an instance of the generic Catalan-object arithmetic used in this paper. However, as it describes computations in terms of ordinary arithmetic, it is size-proportionate only under the assumption that variables fit in word-represented integers.

Combinatorics of lambda terms, including enumeration, random generation and asymptotic behavior has seen an increased interest recently (see for instance [3,6,7,10,11]), partly motivated by applications to software testing [8,17] given the widespread use of lambda terms as an intermediate language in compilers for functional languages and proof assistants.

Ranking and unranking of lambda terms can be seen as a building block for bijective serialization of practical data types [15,26] as well as for Gödel numbering schemes of theoretical relevance. In fact, ranking functions for sequences can be traced back to Gödel numberings [9,12] associated to formulas.

8   Conclusions and Future Work

We have provided a fresh look at several aspects of the representation and encoding of lambda terms with focus on their de Bruijn form and a compressed variant of it. Our computations have used a type class defining generic arithmetic operations on members of the Catalan family of combinatorial objects, described in detail in [25]. They have served to implement bijections between representations of terms and conversion to/from HOAS-like form used for normalization of lambda terms. Some interesting synergies have been triggered by this combination of apparently heterogeneous techniques:

- we have provided a simple size-proportionate bijective encoding of compressed De Bruijn terms to our tree-based "natural numbers"
- the same "natural numbers" (actually operated on through a binary tree perspective on Catalan objects), have served to do routine arithmetic operations, with average complexity comparable to the usual binary numbers
- the use of tree-based numbers, a target for ranking/unranking of lambda terms and a uniform random generation algorithm for binary trees, have enabled generation of (possibly very large) random open lambda terms

Note also that our size-proportional encodings as arithmetic-endowed Catalan objects can be easily adapted to other tree representations widely used in computer science and computational sciences, like expression trees, recursive data types, directory structures, parse trees for programming and natural languages, phylogenetic trees, etc.

We have not approached yet some of the remaining hard problems related to uniform random generation of more "realistic" lambda terms appearing in compilers and proof assistants e.g. well-typed and closed terms, for which no linear-time algorithms are known. The techniques, involving binary search, based on ordinary binary numbers for either term algebras in [21] or closed lambda terms in [11] will require more work to adapt to possibly linear algorithms based on our size-proportionate encodings in a tree-based numbering system. Also, an empirical study of the shapes and distribution of frequent lambda term patterns appearing in written and generated code is likely to be useful to fine-tune ranking/unranking algorithms better suited for random generation of such terms.

Acknowledgement. This research has been supported by NSF grant 1423324. We thanks the reviewers of `PADL'16` for their constructive suggestions and comments.

References

1. Ackermann, W.F.: Die Widerspruchsfreiheit der allgemeinen Mengenlhere. Mathematische Annalen **114**, 305–315 (1937)
2. Barendregt, H.P.: The Lambda Calculus Its Syntax and Semantics, vol. 103, 2, revised edn. Elsevier, North Holland (1984)
3. Bodini, O., Gardy, D., Gittenberger, B.: Lambda-terms of bounded unary height. In: ANALCO, pp. 23–32. SIAM (2011)
4. de Bruijn, N.G.: Lambda calculus notation with nameless dummies, a tool for automatic formula manipulation, with application to the Church-Rosser theorem. Indagationes Mathematicae **34**, 381–392 (1972)
5. Cegielski, P., Richard, D.: On arithmetical first-order theories allowing encoding and decoding of lists. Theor. Comput. Sci. **222**(1–2), 55–75 (1999)
6. David, R., Grygiel, K., Kozik, J., Raffalli, C., Theyssier, G., Zaionc, M.: Asymptotically almost all λ-terms are strongly normalizing (2010). Preprint: arXiv:math.LO/0903.5505v3
7. David, R., Raffalli, C., Theyssier, G., Grygiel, K., Kozik, J., Zaionc, M.: Some properties of random lambda terms. Logical Methods Comput. Sci., 9(1) (2009)
8. Fetscher, B., Claessen, K., Pałka, M., Hughes, J., Findler, R.B.: Making random judgments: automatically generating well-typed terms from the definition of a typesystem. In: Vitek, J. (ed.) ESOP 2015. LNCS, vol. 9032, pp. 383–405. Springer, Heidelberg (2015)
9. Gödel, K.: Über formal unentscheidbare Sätze der principia mathematica und verwandter systeme I. Monatshefte für Mathematik und Physik **38**, 173–198 (1931)
10. Grygiel, K., Idziak, P.M., Zaionc, M.: How big is BCI fragment of BCK logic. J. Log. Comput. **23**(3), 673–691 (2013)
11. Grygiel, K., Lescanne, P.: Counting and generating lambda terms. J. Funct. Program. **23**(5), 594–628 (2013)
12. Hartmanis, J., Baker, T.P.: On simple Goedel numberings and translations. In: Loeckx, J. (ed.) ICALP. Lecture Notes in Computer Science, vol. 14, pp. 301–316. Springer, Berlin Heidelberg (1974)
13. Kamareddine, F.: Reviewing the classical and the de Bruijn notation for calculus and pure type systems. J. Logic Comput. **11**(3), 363–394 (2001)
14. Knuth, D.E.: The Art of Computer Programming, Volume 4, Fascicle 4: Generating All Trees-History of Combinatorial Generation (Art of Computer Programming). Addison-Wesley Professional, Boston (2006)
15. Kobayashi, N., Matsuda, K., Shinohara, A.: Functional programs as compressed data. In: ACM SIGPLAN 2012 Workshop on Partial Evaluation and Program Manipulation, ACM Press, January 2012

16. Lisi, M.: Some remarks on the Cantor pairing function. Le Matematiche **62**(1), 55–65 (2007). http://www.dmi.unict.it/ojs/index.php/lematematiche/article/view/14
17. Palka, M.H., Claessen, K., Russo, A., Hughes, J.: Testing an optimising compiler by generating random lambda terms. In: Proceedings of the 6th International Workshop on Automation of Software Test, AST 2011, pp. 91–97. ACM, New York, NY, USA (2011)
18. Pfenning, F., Elliot, C.: Higher-order abstract syntax. In: Proceedings of the ACM SIGPLAN 1988 Conference on Programming Language Design and Implementation, PLDI 1988, pp. 199–208. ACM, New York, NY, USA (1988)
19. Sestoft, P.: Demonstrating lambda calculus reduction. In: Mogensen, T.Æ., Schmidt, D.A., Sudborough, I.H. (eds.) The Essence of Computation. LNCS, vol. 2566, pp. 420–435. Springer, Heidelberg (2002)
20. Stanley, R.P.: Enumerative Combinatorics. Wadsworth Publishing Co., Belmont (1986)
21. Tarau, P.: Compact serialization of prolog terms (with catalan skeletons, cantor tupling and gödel numberings). Theor. Pract. Logic Program. **13**(4–5), 847–861 (2013)
22. Tarau, P.: A generic numbering system based on catalan families of combinatorial objects. CoRR abs/1406.1796 (2014)
23. Tarau, P.: On a uniform representation of combinators, arithmetic, Lambda terms and types. In: Albert, E. (ed.) PPDP 2015: Proceedings of the 17th international ACM SIGPLAN Symposium on Principles and Practice of Declarative Programming, pp. 244–255. ACM, New York, NY, USA, July 2015
24. Tarau, P.: Ranking/unranking of Lambda terms with compressed de Bruijn Indices. In: Kerber, M., Carette, J., Kaliszyk, C., Rabe, F., Sorge, V. (eds.) CICM 2015. LNCS, vol. 9150, pp. 118–133. Springer, Heidelberg (2015)
25. Tarau, P.: Computing with catalan families, generically. In: Gavanelli, M., Reppy, J. (eds.) PADL'16. LNCS. Springer, St. Petersburg, Florida, USA (2016)
26. Vytiniotis, D., Kennedy, A.: Functional pearl: every bit counts. ICFP 2010 : The 15th ACM SIGPLAN International Conference on Functional Programming, ACM Press, September 2010

Computing with Catalan Families, Generically

Paul Tarau[✉]

Department of Computer Science and Engineering,
University of North Texas, Denton, USA
paul.tarau@unt.edu

Abstract. We describe arithmetic algorithms on a canonical number representation based on the Catalan family of combinatorial objects specified as a Haskell type class.

Our algorithms work on a *generic* representation that we illustrate on instances members of the Catalan family, like ordered binary and multiway trees. We validate the correctness of our algorithms by defining an instance of the same type class based the usual bitstring-based natural numbers.

While their average and worst case complexity is within constant factors of their traditional counterparts, our algorithms provide superexponential gains for numbers corresponding to Catalan objects of low representation size.

Keywords: Tree-based numbering systems · Cross-validation with type classes · Arithmetic with combinatorial objects · Catalan families · Generic functional programming algorithms

1 Introduction

This paper generalizes the results of [12,13], where special instances of the Catalan family [5,7] of combinatorial objects (the language of balanced parentheses and the set ordered rooted trees with empty leaves, respectively) have been endowed with basic arithmetic operations corresponding to those on bitstring-represented natural numbers.

The main contribution of this paper is a *generic* Catalan family based numbering system that supports computations with numbers comparable in size with Knuth's "arrow-up" notation. These computations have an average and worst case and complexity that is comparable or better than the traditional binary numbers, while on neighborhoods of iterated powers of two they outperform binary numbers by an arbitrary tower of exponents factor.

As the Catalan family contains a large number of computationally isomorphic but structurally distinct combinatorial objects, we will describe our arithmetic computations generically, using Haskell's *type classes* [16], of which typical members of the Catalan family, like binary trees and multiway trees will be described as instances.

© Springer International Publishing Switzerland 2016
M. Gavanelli and J. Reppy (Eds.): PADL 2016, LNCS 9585, pp. 117–134, 2016.
DOI: 10.1007/978-3-319-28228-2_8

At the same time, an *atypical instance* will be derived, representing the set of *natural numbers* $\mathbb{N}$, which will be used to cross-validate the correctness of our generically defined arithmetic operations.

The paper is organized as follows. Section 2 discusses related work. Section 3 introduces a generic view of Catalan families as a Haskell type class, with Subsect. 3.4 embedding the set of natural numbers as an instance of the family. Section 4 introduces basic algorithms for arithmetic operations taking advantage of our number representation, with Subsect. 4.2 focusing on constant time successor and predecessor operations. Section 5 describes arithmetic operations that favor operands of low representation complexity including computations with giant numbers. Section 6 concludes the paper.

We have adopted a *literate programming* style, i.e. the code described in the paper forms a self-contained Haskell module (tested with ghc 7.10.2). It is available at http://www.cse.unt.edu/~tarau/research/2014/GCat.hs.

2   Related Work

The first instance of a *hereditary number system* representing natural numbers as multiway trees occurs in the proof of Goodstein's theorem [1], where replacement of finite numbers on a tree's branches by the ordinal ω allows him to prove that a "hailstone sequence", after visiting arbitrarily large numbers, eventually turns around and terminates.

Another hereditary number system is Knuth's TCALC program [4] that decomposes $n = 2^a + b$ with $0 \leq b < 2^a$ and then recurses on a and b with the same decomposition. Given the constraint on a and b, while hereditary, the TCALC system is not based on a bijection between $\mathbb{N}$ and $\mathbb{N} \times \mathbb{N}$ and therefore the representation is not a bijection. Moreover, the literate C-program that defines it only implements successor, addition, comparison and multiplication, and does not provide a constant time power of 2 and low complexity leftshift / rightshift operations.

Several notations for very large numbers have been invented in the past. Examples include Knuth's *up-arrow* notation [3], covering operations like the *tetration* (a notation for towers of exponents). In contrast to the tree-based natural numbers we describe in this paper, such notations are not closed under addition and multiplication, and consequently they cannot be used as a replacement for ordinary binary or decimal numbers.

While combinatorial enumeration and combinatorial generation, for which a vast literature exists (see for instance [5–7]) can be seen as providing unary Peano arithmetic operations implicitly, like in [12,13], the algorithms in this paper enable arithmetic computations of efficiency comparable to the usual binary numbers (or better) using combinatorial families.

Providing a *generic mechanism* for efficient arithmetic computations with *arbitrary members of the Catalan family* is the main motivation and the most significant contribution of this paper. It is notationally similar to the type class

mechanism sketched in [2]. Unfortunately, the simpler binary tree-based computation of [2] does not support the $O(log^*(n))$ successor and predecessor operations described in this paper, that facilitate size proportionate encodings of data
types. Such encodings are the critical component of the companion paper [14],
which describes their application to lambda terms.

3   The Catalan Family of Combinatorial Objects

The Haskell data type T representing ordered rooted binary trees with empty
leaves E and branches provided by the constructor C is a typical member of the
Catalan family of combinatorial objects [7].

```
data T = E | C T T deriving (Eq,Show,Read)
```

Note the use of the type classes Eq, Show and Read to derive structural equality
and respectively human readable output and input for this data type.

The data type M is another well-known member of the Catalan family, defining
multiway ordered rooted trees with empty leaves.

```
data M = F [M] deriving (Eq,Show,Read)
```

3.1   A Generic View of Catalan Families as a Haskell Type Class

We will work through the paper with a generic data type ranging over instances of
the type class Cat, representing a member of the Catalan family of combinatorial
objects [7].

```
class (Show a,Read a,Eq a) ⇒ Cat a where
  e :: a

  c  :: (a,a) → a
  c' :: a → (a,a)
```

The zero element is denoted e and we inherit from classes Read and Show which
ensure derivation of input and output functions for members of type class Cat
as well as from type class Eq that ensures derivation of the structural equality
predicate == and its negation /=.

We will also define the corresponding recognizer predicates e_ and c_, relying
on the derived equality relation inherited from the Haskell type class Eq.

```
e_ :: a → Bool
e_ a = a == e

c_ :: a → Bool
c_ a = a /= e
```

For each instance, we assume that c and c' are inverses on their respective
domains Cat × Cat and Cat - {e}, and e is distinct from objects constructed
with c, more precisely that the following hold:

$$\forall x.\ c'(c\ x) = x \wedge \forall y.\ (c_-\ y \Rightarrow c\ (c'\ y) = y) \tag{1}$$

$$\forall x. \ (e_- \ x \lor c_- \ x) \land \neg(e_- \ x \land c_- \ x.) \tag{2}$$

When talking about "objects of type `Cat`" we will actually mean an instance a of the polymorphic type `Cat a` that verifies Eqs. (1) and (2).

3.2 The Instance T of Ordered Rooted Binary Trees

The operations defined in type class `Cat` correspond naturally to the ordered rooted binary tree view of the Catalan family, materialized as the data type T.

```
instance Cat T where
  e = E

  c (x,y) = C x y

  c' (C x y) = (x,y)
```

Note that adding and removing the constructor C trivially verifies the assumption that our generic operations c and c' are inverses[1].

3.3 The Instance M of Ordered Rooted Multiway Trees

The alternative view of the Catalan family as multiway trees is materialized as the data type M.

```
instance Cat M where
  e = F []
  c (x,F xs) = F (x:xs)
  c' (F (x:xs)) = (x,F xs)
```

Note that the assumption that our generic operations c and c' are inverses is easily verified in this case as well, given the bijection between binary and multiway trees. Moreover, note that operations on types T and M, expressed in terms of their generic type class `Cat` counterparts, result in a constant extra effort. Therefore, we will safely ignore it when discussing the complexity of different operations.

3.4 An Unusual Member of the Catalan Family: The Set of Natural Numbers ℕ

The (big-endian) binary representation of a natural number can be written as a concatenation of binary digits of the form

$$n = b_0^{k_0} b_1^{k_1} \dots b_i^{k_i} \dots b_m^{k_m} \tag{3}$$

with $b_i \in \{0, 1\}$, $b_i \neq b_{i+1}$ and the highest digit $b_m = 1$. The following hold.

---

[1] In fact, one can see the functions e, e_ , c, c', c_ as a generic API abstracting away the essential properties of the constructors E and C.

Proposition 1. *An even number of the form $0^i j$ corresponds to the operation $2^i j$ and an odd number of the form $1^i j$ corresponds to the operation $2^i(j+1)-1$.*

Proof. It is clearly the case that $0^i j$ corresponds to multiplication by a power of 2. If $f(i) = 2i + 1$ then it is shown by induction (see [15]) that the i-th iterate of f, f^i is computed as in the Eq. (4)

$$f^i(j) = 2^i(j+1) - 1 \tag{4}$$

Observe that each block 1^i in n, represented as $1^i j$ in Eq. (3), corresponds to the iterated application of f, i times, $n = f^i(j)$.

Proposition 2. *A number n is even if and only if it contains an even number of blocks of the form $b_i^{k_i}$ in Eq. (3). A number n is odd if and only if it contains an odd number of blocks of the form $b_i^{k_i}$ in Eq. (3).*

Proof. It follows from the fact that the highest digit (and therefore the last block in big-endian representation) is 1 and the parity of the blocks alternate.

This suggests defining the c operation of type class `Cat` as follows.

$$c(i, j) = \begin{cases} 2^{i+1} j & \text{if } j \text{ is odd,} \\ 2^{i+1}(j + 1) - 1 & \text{if } j \text{ is even.} \end{cases} \tag{5}$$

Note that the exponents are $i + 1$ instead of i as we start counting at 0. Note also that $c(i, j)$ will be even when j is odd and odd when j is even.

Proposition 3. *The Eq. (5) defines a bijection $c : \mathbb{N} \times \mathbb{N} \to \mathbb{N}^+ = \mathbb{N} - \{0\}$.*

Therefore c has an inverse c', that we will constructively define together with c. The following Haskell code defines the instance of the Catalan family corresponding to $\mathbb{N}$.

```
type N = Integer
instance Cat Integer where
  e = 0

  c (i,j) | i≥0 && j≥0 = 2^(i+1)*(j+b)-b where b = mod (j+1) 2
```

The definition of the inverse c' relies on the *dyadic valuation* of a number n, $\nu_2(n)$, defined as the largest exponent of 2 dividing n, implemented as the helper function `dyadicVal`. Note that $\nu_2(n)$ could also be computed slightly faster, by using Haskell's bit operations, as n .&. (-n).

```
  c' k | k>0 = (max 0 (i-1),j-b) where
    b = mod k 2
    (i,j) = dyadicVal (k+b)

  dyadicVal k | even k = (1+i,j) where (i,j) = dyadicVal (div k 2)
  dyadicVal k = (0,k)
```

Note the use of the parity b in both definitions, which differentiates between the computations for *even* and *odd* numbers.

The following examples illustrate the use of c and c' on this instance.

```
*GCat> c (100,200)
5095955412917482194016746885611151
*GCat> c' it
(100,200)
*GCat> map c' [1..10]
[(0,0),(0,1),(1,0),(1,1),(0,2),(0,3),(2,0),(2,1),(0,4),(0,5)]
*GCat> map c it
[1,2,3,4,5,6,7,8,9,10]
```

Figure 1 illustrates the DAG obtained by applying the operation c' repeatedly and merging identical subtrees for three consecutive numbers. The order of the edges is marked with 0 and 1.

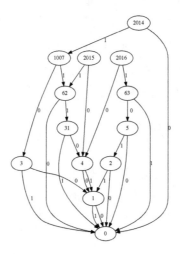

Fig. 1. DAG representing 2014, 2015 and 2016

3.5   The Transformers: Morphing Between Instances of the Catalan Family

As all our instances implement the bijection c and its inverse c', a generic transformer from an instance to another is defined by the function view:

```
view :: (Cat a, Cat b) ⇒ a → b
view z | e_ z = e
view z | c_ z = c (view x,view y) where (x,y) = c' z
```

To obtain transformers defining bijections with ℕ, T and M as ranges, we will simply provide specialized type declarations for them:

```
n :: Cat a ⇒ a→N
n = view

t :: Cat a ⇒ a→T
t = view

m :: Cat a ⇒ a→M
m = view
```

The following examples illustrate the resulting specialized conversion functions:

```
*GCat> t 42
C E (C E (C E (C E (C E (C E E)))))
*GCat> m it
F [F [],F [],F [],F [],F [],F []]
*GCat> n it
42
```

A list view of an instance of type class `Cat` is obtained by iterating the constructor `c` and its inverse `c'`.

```
to_list :: Cat a ⇒ a → [a]
to_list x | e_ x = []
to_list x | c_ x = h:hs where
    (h,t) = c' x
    hs = to_list t

from_list :: Cat a ⇒ [a] → a
from_list [] = e
from_list (x:xs) = c (x,from_list xs)
```

They work as follows:

```
*GCat> to_list 2014
[0,3,0,4]
*GCat> from_list it
2014
```

The function `to_list` corresponds to the children of a node in the multiway tree view provided by instance M. Along the lines of [9,10] one can use `to_list` and `from_list` to define size-proportionate bijective encodings of sets, multisets and data types built from them.

The function `catShow` provides a view as a string of balanced parentheses, an instance of the Catalan family for which arithmetic computations are introduced in [12].

```
catShow :: Cat a ⇒ a → [Char]
catShow x | e_ x ="()"
catShow x | c_ x = r where
    xs = to_list x
    r = "(" ++ (concatMap catShow xs) ++ ")"
```

It is illustrated below.

```
*GCat> catShow 0
"()"
*GCat> catShow 1
"(())"
*GCat> catShow 12345
"(()(())(()())(()()())(()))"
```

4   Generic Arithmetic Operations on Members of the Catalan Family

We will now implement arithmetic operations on Catalan families, generically, in terms of the operations on type class Cat.

4.1   Basic Utilities

We start with some simple functions to be used later.

Inferring Even and Odd. As we know for sure that the instance $\mathbb{N}$, corresponding to natural numbers supports arithmetic operations, we will mimic their behavior at the level of the type class Cat.

The operations even_ and odd_ implement the observation following from of Proposition 2 that parity (staring with 1 at the highest block) alternates with each block of distinct 0 or 1 digits.

```
even_ :: Cat a ⇒ a → Bool
even_ x | e_ x = True
even_ z | c_ z = odd_ y where (_,y)=c' z

odd_ :: Cat a ⇒ a → Bool
odd_ x | e_ x = False
odd_ z | c_ z = even_ y where (_,y)=c' z
```

One. We also provide a constant u and a recognizer predicate u_ for 1.

```
u :: Cat a ⇒ a
u = c (e,e)

u_ :: Cat a ⇒ a→ Bool
u_ z = c_ z && e_ x && e_ y where (x,y) = c' z
```

4.2   Average Constant Time Successor and Predecessor.

We will now specify successor and predecessor on the family of data types Cat through two mutually recursive functions, s and s'. They are based on arithmetic observations about the behavior of these blocks when incrementing or decrementing a binary number by 1, derived from Eq. (5).

They first decompose their arguments using c'. Then, after transforming them as a result of adding or subtracting 1, they place back the results with the c operation.

Note that the two functions work *on a block of* 0 *or* 1 *digits at a time*. The main intuition is that as adding or subtracting 1 changes the parity of a number and as carry-ons propagate over a block of 1s in the case of addition and over a block of 0s in the case of subtraction, *blocks* of contiguous 0 and 1 digits will be flipped as a result of applying s or s'.

```
s :: Cat a ⇒ a → a
s x | e_ x = u -- 1
s z | c_ z && e_ y = c (x,u) where -- 2
   (x,y) = c' z
```

For the general case, the successor function s delegates the transformation of the blocks of 0 and 1 digits to functions f and g handling even_ and respectively odd_ cases.

```
s a | c_ a = if even_ a then f a else g a where

   f k | c_ w && e_ v = c (s x,y) where -- 3
   (v,w) = c' k
   (x,y) = c' w
   f k = c (e, c (s' x,y)) where -- 4
     (x,y) = c' k

   g k | c_ w && c_ n && e_ m = c (x, c (s y,z)) where -- 5
   (x,w) = c' k
   (m,n) = c' w
   (y,z) = c' n
   g k | c_ v = c (x, c (e, c (s' y, z))) where -- 6
   (x,v) = c' k
   (y,z) = c' v
```

The predecessor function s' inverts the work of s as marked by a comment of the form k --, for k ranging from 1 to 6.

```
s' :: Cat a ⇒ a → a
s' k | u_ k = e where -- 1
   (x,y) = c' k
s' k | c_ k && u_ v = c (x,e) where -- 2
   (x,v) = c' k
```

For the general case, s' delegates the transformation of the blocks of 0 and 1 digits to functions g and f handling even_ and respectively odd_ cases.

```
s' a | c_ a = if even_ a then g' a else f' a where

   g' k | c_ v && c_ w && e_ r = c (x, c (s y,z)) where -- 6
   (x,v) = c' k
   (r,w) = c' v
   (y,z) = c' w
```

```
g' k  | c_ v = c (x,c (e, c (s' y, z))) where -- 5
    (x,v) = c' k
    (y,z) = c' v

f' k  | c_ v && e_ r = c (s x,z) where -- 4
    (r,v) = c' k
    (x,z) = c' v
f' k =  c (e, c (s' x,y)) where -- 3
    (x,y) = c' k
```

One can see that their use matches successor and predecessor on instance N:

```
*GCat> map s [0..15]
[1,2,3,4,5,6,7,8,9,10,11,12,13,14,15,16]
*GCat> map s' it
[0,1,2,3,4,5,6,7,8,9,10,11,12,13,14,15]
```

Proposition 4. *Denote* $Cat^+ = Cat - \{e\}$. *The functions* $s : Cat \rightarrow Cat^+$ *and* $s' : Cat^+ \rightarrow Cat$ *are inverses.*

Proof. For each instance of Cat, it follows by structural induction after observing that patterns for rules marked with the number -- k in s correspond one by one to patterns marked by -- k in s' and vice versa.

More generally, it can be shown that Peano's axioms hold and as a result $< Cat, e, s >$ is a *Peano algebra*. This is expected, as s provides a combinatorial enumeration of the infinite stream of Catalan objects, as illustrated below on instance T:

```
Cats> s E
C E E
*GCat> s it
C E (C E E)
*GCat> s it
C (C E E) E
```

The function nums generates an initial segment of the "natural numbers" defined by an instance of Cat.

```
nums :: Cat a ⇒ a → [a]
nums x = f x [] where
  f x xs | e_ x = e:xs
  f x xs = f (s' x) (x:xs)
```

Note that if parity information is kept explicitly, the calls to odd_ *and* even_ *are constant time, as we will assume in the rest of the paper. We will also assume, that when complexity is discussed, a representation like the tree data types* T *or* M *are used, making the operations* c *and* c' *constant time.* Note also that this is clearly not the case for the instance N using the traditional bitstring representation where effort proportional to the length of the bitstring may be involved.

Proposition 5. *The worst case time complexity of the* s *and* s' *operations on a input n is given by the* iterated logarithm $O(log_2^*(n))$.

Proof. Note that calls to s,s' in s or s' happen on terms at most logarithmic in the bitsize of their operands. The recurrence relation counting the worst case number of calls to s or s' is: $T(n) = T(log_2(n)) + O(1)$, which solves to $T(n) = O(log_2^*(n))$.

Note that this is much better than the logarithmic worst case for binary numbers (when computing, for instance, binary 111...111+1=1000...000).

Proposition 6. s *and* s' *are constant time, on the average.*

Proof. When computing the successor or predecessor of a number of bitsize n, calls to s,s' in s or s' happen on at most one subterm. Observe that the average size of a contiguous block of 0s or 1s in a number of bitsize n has the upper bound 2 as $\sum_{k=0}^{n} \frac{1}{2^k} = 2 - \frac{1}{2^n} < 2$. As on 2-bit numbers we have an average of 0.25 more calls, we can conclude that the total average number of calls is constant, with upper bound $2 + 0.25 = 2.25$.

A quick empirical evaluation confirms this. When computing the successor on the first $2^{30} = 1073741824$ natural numbers, there are in total 2381889348 calls to s and s', averaging to 2.2183 per computation. The same average for 100 successor computations on 5000 bit random numbers oscillates around 2.22.

4.3   A Few Other Average Constant Time, $O(log^*)$ Worst Case Operations

We will derive a few operations that inherit their complexity from s and s'.

Double and Half. Doubling a number db and reversing the db operation (hf) are quite simple. For instance, db proceeds by adding a new counter for odd numbers and incrementing the first counter for even ones.

```
db :: Cat a ⇒ a → a
db x | e_ x  = e
db x | odd_ x = c (e,x)
db z = c (s x,y) where (x,y) = c' z
```

```
hf :: Cat a ⇒ a → a
hf x | e_ x = e
hf z | e_ x = y where (x,y) = c' z
hf z  = c (s' x,y) where (x,y) = c' z
```

Power of 2 and its Left Inverse. Note that such efficient implementations follow directly from simple number theoretic observations.

For instance, exp2, computing an power of 2, has the following definition in terms of c and s' from which it inherits its complexity up to a constant factor.

```
exp2 :: Cat a ⇒ a → a
exp2 x | e_ x = u
exp2 x = c (s' x, u)
```

The same applies to its left inverse log2:

```
log2 :: Cat a ⇒ a → a
log2 x | u_ x = e
log2 x | u_ z = s y where (y,z) = c' x
```

Proposition 7. *The operations* db, hf, exp2 *and* log2 *are average constant time and are* log^* *in the worst case.*

Proof. At most one call to s,s' is made in each definition. Therefore these operations have the same worst and average complexity as s and s'.

We illustrate their work on instances N:

```
*GCat> map exp2 [0..14]
[1,2,4,8,16,32,64,128,256,512,1024,2048,4096,8192,16384]
*GCat> map log2 it
[0,1,2,3,4,5,6,7,8,9,10,11,12,13,14]
```

More interestingly, a tall tower of exponents that would overflow memory on instance N, is easily supported on instances T and M as shown below:

```
*GCat> exp2 (exp2 (exp2 (exp2 (exp2 (exp2 (exp2 E))))))
C (C (C (C (C (C E E) E) E) E) E) (C E E)
*GCat> m it
F [F [F [F [F [F [F []]]]]],F []]
*GCat> log2 (log2 (log2 (log2 (log2 (log2 (log2 it))))))
F []
```

This example illustrates the main motivation for defining arithmetic computation with the "typical" members of the Catalan family: their ability to deal with giant numbers.

Another average constant time / worst case log^* algorithm is counting the trailing 0s of a number (on instance T):

```
trailingZeros x | e_ x = e
trailingZeros x | odd_ x = e
trailingZeros x = s (fst (c' x))
```

This contrasts with the O(log(n)) worst case performance to count them with a bitstring representation.

5   Addition, Subtraction and Their Mutually Recursive Helpers

We will derive in this section efficient addition and subtraction that *work on one run-length compressed block at a time*, rather than by individual 0 and 1 digit steps.

5.1   Multiplication by a Power of 2

We start with the functions `leftshiftBy`, `leftshiftBy'` and `leftshiftBy"` corresponding respectively to $(\lambda x.2x)^n(k)$, $(\lambda x.2x+1)^n(k)$ and $(\lambda x.2x+2)^n(k)$.

The function `leftshiftBy` prefixes an odd number with a block of 1s and extends a block of 0s by incrementing their count.

```
leftshiftBy :: Cat a ⇒ a → a → a
leftshiftBy x y | e_ x = y
leftshiftBy _ y | e_ y = e
leftshiftBy x y | odd_ y = c (s' x, y)
leftshiftBy x v = c (add x y, z) where (y,z) = c' v
```

The function `leftshiftBy'` is based on Eq. (6).

$$(\lambda x.2x + 1)^n(k) = 2^n(k + 1) - 1 \qquad (6)$$

```
leftshiftBy' :: Cat a ⇒ a → a → a
leftshiftBy' x k = s' (leftshiftBy x (s k))
```

The function `leftshiftBy'` is based on Eq. (7) (see [15] for a direct proof by induction).

$$(\lambda x.2x + 2)^n(k) = 2^n(k + 2) - 2 \qquad (7)$$

```
leftshiftBy'' :: Cat a ⇒ a → a → a
leftshiftBy'' x k = s' (s' (leftshiftBy x (s (s k))))
```

They are part of a *chain of mutually recursive functions* as they are already referring to the `add` function. Note also that instead of naively iterating, they implement a more efficient algorithm, working "one block at a time". For instance, when detecting that its argument counts a number of 1s, `leftshiftBy'` just increments that count. As a result, the algorithm favors numbers with relatively few large blocks of 0 and 1 digits.

While not directly used in the addition operation it is interesting to observe that division by a power of 2 can also be computed efficiently.

5.2   An Inverse Operation: Division by a Power of 2

The function `rightshiftBy` goes over its argument y one block at a time, by comparing the size of the block and its argument x that is decremented after each block by the size of the block. The local function f handles the details, irrespectively of the nature of the block, and stops when the argument is exhausted. More precisely, based on the result `EQ, LT, GT` of the comparison, f either stops or, calls `rightshiftBy` on the value of x reduced by the size of the block a' = s a.

```
rightshiftBy :: Cat a ⇒ a → a → a
rightshiftBy x y | e_ x = y
rightshiftBy _ y | e_ y = e
rightshiftBy x y = f (cmp x a')  where
```

```
(a,b) = c' y
a' = s a
f LT = c (sub a x,b)
f EQ = b
f GT = rightshiftBy (sub  x a') b
```

5.3 Addition Optimized for Numbers Built from a Few Large Blocks of 0s and 1s

We are now ready to define addition. The base cases are

```
add :: Cat a ⇒ a → a → a
add x y | e_ x = y
add x y | e_ y = x
```

In the case when both terms represent even numbers, the two blocks add up to an even block of the same size. Note the use of cmp and sub in helper function f to trim off the larger block such that we can operate on two blocks of equal size.

```
add x y |even_ x && even_ y = f (cmp a b) where
  (a,as) = c' x
  (b,bs) = c' y
  f EQ = leftshiftBy (s a) (add as bs)
  f GT = leftshiftBy (s b) (add (leftshiftBy (sub a b) as) bs)
  f LT = leftshiftBy (s a) (add as (leftshiftBy (sub b a) bs))
```

In the case when the first term is even and the second odd, the two blocks add up to an odd block of the same size.

```
add x y |even_ x && odd_ y = f (cmp a b) where
  (a,as) = c' x
  (b,bs) = c' y
  f EQ = leftshiftBy' (s a) (add as bs)
  f GT = leftshiftBy' (s b) (add (leftshiftBy (sub a b) as) bs)
  f LT = leftshiftBy' (s a) (add as (leftshiftBy' (sub b a) bs))
```

In the case when the second term is even and the first odd the two blocks also add up to an odd block of the same size.

```
add x y |odd_ x && even_ y = add y x
```

In the case when both terms represent odd numbers, we use the identity (8):

$$(\lambda x.2x + 1)^k(x) + (\lambda x.2x + 1)^k(y) = (\lambda x.2x + 2)^k(x + y) \tag{8}$$

```
add x y | odd_ x && odd_ y = f (cmp a b) where
  (a,as) = c' x
  (b,bs) = c' y
  f EQ =  leftshiftBy'' (s a) (add as bs)
  f GT =  leftshiftBy'' (s b) (add (leftshiftBy' (sub a b) as) bs)
  f LT =  leftshiftBy'' (s a) (add as (leftshiftBy' (sub b a) bs))
```

Note the presence of the comparison operation `cmp` also part of our chain of mutually recursive operations. Note also the local function `f` that in each case ensures that a block of the same size is extracted, depending on which of the two operands `a` or `b` is larger.

Details of implementation for subtraction are quite similar to those of the addition. The curious reader can find the implementation and the literate programming explanations of the complete set of arithmetic operations with the type class `Cat` in our arxiv draft at [11].

Comparison

The comparison operation `cmp` provides a total order (isomorphic to that on $\mathbb{N}$) on our generic type `Cat`. It relies on `bitsize` computing the number of binary digits constructing a term in `Cat`, also part of our mutually recursive functions, to be defined later.

We first observe that only terms of the same bitsize need detailed comparison, otherwise the relation between their bitsizes is enough, *recursively*. More precisely, the following holds:

Proposition 8. *Let* `bitsize` *count the number of digits of a base-2 number, with the convention that it is* 0 *for* 0*. Then* `bitsize`(x) `<bitsize`$(y) \Rightarrow x < y$.

Proof. Observe that their lexicographic enumeration ensures that the bitsize of base-2 numbers is a non-decreasing function.

The comparison operation also proceeds one block at a time, and it also takes some inferential shortcuts, when possible.

```
cmp :: Cat a⇒ a→a→Ordering
cmp x y | e_ x && e_ y = EQ
cmp x _ | e_ x = LT
cmp _ y | e_ y = GT
cmp x y | u_ x && u_ (s' y) = LT
cmp x y | u_ y && u_ (s' x) = GT
```

For instance, it is easy to see that comparison of `x` and `y` can be reduced to comparison of bitsizes when they are distinct. Note that `bitsize`, to be defined later, is part of the chain of our mutually recursive functions.

```
cmp x y | x' /= y'  = cmp x' y' where
  x' = bitsize x
  y' = bitsize y
```

When bitsizes are equal, a more elaborate comparison needs to be done, delegated to function `compBigFirst`.

```
cmp xs ys =  compBigFirst True True (rev xs) (rev ys) where
  rev = from_list . reverse . to_list
```

The function `compBigFirst` compares two terms known to have the same `bitsize`. It works on reversed (highest order digit first) variants, computed by `reverse` and it takes advantage of the block structure using the following proposition:

Proposition 9. *Assuming two terms of the same bitsizes, the one with 1 as its first before the highest order digit, is larger than the one with 0 as its first before the highest order digit.*

Proof. Observe that little-endian numbers obtained by applying the function rev are lexicographically ordered with $0 < 1$.

As a consequence, cmp only recurses when *identical* blocks lead the sequence of blocks, otherwise it infers the LT or GT relation.

```
compBigFirst _ _ x y | e_ x && e_ y = EQ
compBigFirst False False x y = f (cmp a b) where
  (a,as) = c' x
  (b,bs) = c' y
  f EQ = compBigFirst True True as bs
  f LT = GT
  f GT = LT
compBigFirst True True x y = f (cmp a b) where
  (a,as) = c' x
  (b,bs) = c' y
  f EQ = compBigFirst False False as bs
  f LT = LT
  f GT = GT
compBigFirst False True x y = LT
compBigFirst True False x y = GT
```

The following examples illustrate the agreement of cmp with the usual order relation on $\mathbb{N}$.

```
*Cats> cmp 5 10
LT
*Cats> cmp 10 10
EQ
*Cats> cmp 10 5
GT
```

Note that the complexity of the comparison operation is proportional to the size of the (smaller) of the two trees.

The function bitsize, last in our chain of mutually recursive functions, computes the number of digits, except that we define it as e for constant function e (corresponding to 0). It works by summing up the counts of 0 and 1 digit blocks composing a tree-represented natural number.

```
bitsize :: Cat a ⇒ a → a
bitsize z | e_ z = z
bitsize   z = s (add x (bitsize y)) where (x,y) = c' z
```

It follows that the base-2 integer logarithm is computed as

```
ilog2 :: Cat a ⇒ a→a
ilog2 = s' . bitsize
```

6   Conclusion

We have described through a type class mechanism an arithmetic system working on members of the Catalan family of combinatorial objects, that takes advantage of compact representations of some giant numbers and can perform interesting computations intractable with their bitstring-based counterparts.

This ability comes from the fact that tree representation, in contrast to the traditional binary representation, supports constant average time and space application of exponentials.

The resulting numbering system is *canonical* - each natural number is represented as a unique object. Besides unique decoding, canonical representations allow testing for *syntactic equality*. It is also *generic* – no commitment is made to a particular member of the Catalan family – our type class provides all the arithmetic operations to several instances, including typical members of the Catalan family together with the usual natural numbers.

While these algorithms share similar complexity with those described in [13], which focuses on instance M of our type class Cat, the generic implementation in this paper enables one to perform efficient arithmetic operations with any of the 58 known instances of the Catalan family described in [7,8], some of them with geometric, combinatorial, algebraic, formal languages, number and set theoretical or physical flavor. Therefore, we believe that this generalization is significant and it opens the door to new and possibly unexpected applications.

Acknowledgement. This research has been supported by NSF grant 1423324. We thanks the reviewers of PADL'16 for their constructive suggestions and comments.

References

1. Goodstein, R.: On the restricted ordinal theorem. J. Symbolic Logic **9**, 33–41 (1944)
2. Haraburda, D., Tarau, P.: Binary trees as a computational framework. Comput. Lang. Syst. Struct. **39**(4), 163–181 (2013)
3. Knuth, D.E.: Mathematics and computer science: coping with finiteness. Science **194**(4271), 1235–1242 (1976)
4. Knuth, D.E.: TCALC (1994). http://math.mit.edu/~rstan/ec/catadd.pdf
5. Knuth, D.E.: The Art of Computer Programming, Volume 4, Fascicle 4: Generating All Trees-History of Combinatorial Generation (Art of Computer Programming). Addison-Wesley Professional (2006)
6. Kreher, D.L., Stinson, D.: Combinatorial Algorithms: Generation, Enumeration, and Search. The CRC Press Series on Discrete Mathematics and its Applications, CRC PressINC (1999)
7. Stanley, R.P.: Enumerative Combinatorics. Wadsworth Publ. Co., Belmont (1986).http://www-cs-faculty.stanford.edu/~uno/programs/tcalc.w.gz
8. Stanley, R.P.: Catalan Addendum (2013). http://www-math.mit.edu/rstan/ec/catadd.pdf
9. Tarau, P.: A groupoid of isomorphic data transformations. In: Carette, J., Dixon, L., Coen, C.S., Watt, S.M. (eds.) MKM 2009, Held as Part of CICM 2009. LNCS, vol. 5625, pp. 170–185. Springer, Heidelberg (2009)

10. Tarau, P.: Bijective collection encodings and boolean operations with hereditarily binary natural numbers. In: Proceedings of the 16th international ACM SIGPLAN Symposium on Principles and Practice of Declarative Programming, PPDP 2014. ACM, New York (2014)
11. Tarau, P.: A Generic Numbering System based on Catalan Families of Combinatorial Objects (2014). CoRR abs/1406.1796
12. Tarau, P.: Computing with Catalan families. In: Dediu, A.-H., Martín-Vide, C., Sierra-Rodríguez, J.-L., Truthe, B. (eds.) LATA 2014. LNCS, vol. 8370, pp. 565–575. Springer, Heidelberg (2014)
13. Tarau, P.: The arithmetic of recursively run-length compressed natural numbers. In: Ciobanu, G., Méry, D. (eds.) ICTAC 2014. LNCS, vol. 8687, pp. 406–423. Springer, Heidelberg (2014)
14. Tarau, P.: A Size-proportionate Bijective Encoding of Lambda Terms as Catalan Objects endowed with Arithmetic Operations. In: Gavanelli, M., Reppy, J. (eds.) PADL 2016. LNCS, vol. 9585, pp. 99–116. Springer (2016)
15. Tarau, P., Buckles, B.: Arithmetic algorithms for hereditarily binary natural numbers. In: Proceedings of SAC 2014, ACM Symposium on Applied Computing, PL track. ACM, Gyeongju, March 2014
16. Wadler, P., Blott, S.: How to make ad-hoc polymorphism less ad-hoc. In: POPL, pp. 60–76 (1989)

Simplifying Probabilistic Programs Using Computer Algebra

Jacques Carette[1]([⊠]) and Chung-chieh Shan[2]

[1] McMaster University, Hamilton, Canada
carette@mcmaster.ca
[2] Indiana University, Bloomington, USA
ccshan@indiana.edu

Abstract. We transform probabilistic programs to run more efficiently and read more easily, by composing three semantics-preserving transformations: (1) apply the denotational semantics; (2) improve the resulting integral; then (3) invert the denotational semantics. Whereas step 1 is a straightforward transformation from monadic to continuation-passing style, the rest builds on computer algebra: step 2 reorders and performs integrals, and step 3 represents density functions as differential operators.

Keywords: Probabilistic programming · Computer algebra · Integrating continuous distributions

1 Introduction

The success of machine learning has made it clear that computing with probability distributions is very useful. Given a distribution, we might want a simpler representation of it or to generate random samples from it. These two computations go hand in hand: If we are lucky, we can find a simple representation, maybe even an exact one, that renders all further calculation trivial. If not, we would likely want to generate random samples, a process that can be made dramatically more efficient and accurate by any simplification we manage to perform.

1.1 Contributions

We introduce a way to simplify probabilistic programs: starting with a monadic representation of a distribution (Sect. 2), we transform it to an integral (Sect. 4),

---

Thanks to Mike Kucera, Praveen Narayanan, Natalie Perna, and Robert Zinkov for developing the Hakaru probabilistic programming system, the home of our research. Thanks also to the anonymous referees for many comments, which improved this paper. This research was supported by DARPA grant FA8750-14-2-0007, NSF grant CNS-0723054, Lilly Endowment, Inc. (through its support for the Indiana University Pervasive Technology Institute), and the Indiana METACyt Initiative. The Indiana METACyt Initiative at IU is also supported in part by Lilly Endowment, Inc.

M. Gavanelli and J. Reppy (Eds.): PADL 2016, LNCS 9585, pp. 135–152, 2016.
DOI: 10.1007/978-3-319-28228-2_9

improve the integral by controlled use of computer algebra (Sect. 6), then transform back (Sect. 5). Whereas the denotational semantics that maps probabilistic programs to integrals is straightforward and well known (Sect. 3), we put it to work and show how to turn integrals into simpler programs. In particular, we identify necessary transformations on mathematical and integral expressions that direct an existing computer algebra system (CAS) to simplify the kind of multidimensional integrals that probabilistic programs tend to mean. We also apply computer algebra to convert integrals back to programs robustly. The CAS we use is Maple, but other systems such as Mathematica are similar.

1.2   Three Examples

We showcase our approach using three natural (if small) examples.

A Discrete Distribution. Start with the following sampling procedure: choose two real numbers x, y independently from the uniform distribution between 0 and 1, then return whether $x < y$. The corresponding term in our language

$$\mathsf{Bind}(\mathsf{Uniform}(0,1), x, \mathsf{Bind}(\mathsf{Uniform}(0,1), y, \mathsf{If}(x < y, \mathsf{Ret}(\mathsf{true}), \mathsf{Ret}(\mathsf{false})))) \quad (1)$$

denotes a measure over Booleans ($\mathbb{B}$). As explained in Sect. 3, a measure is equivalent to a linear operator. This equivalence means that we can integrate with respect to this distribution an arbitrary function $h : \mathbb{B} \to \mathbb{R}^+$, and the result completely determines the denotation of the term (1). That result is the number

$$\int_0^1 \int_0^1 \left(\begin{cases} h(\mathsf{true}) & \text{if } x < y \\ h(\mathsf{false}) & \text{otherwise} \end{cases} \right) dy \, dx. \quad (2)$$

Off the shelf, a CAS like Maple can simplify this integral expression to $\frac{1}{2} \cdot h(\mathsf{true}) + \frac{1}{2} \cdot h(\mathsf{false})$. From this integral, we read off the simpler term in our language

$$\mathsf{Msum}(\mathsf{Weight}(1/2, \mathsf{Ret}(\mathsf{true})), \mathsf{Weight}(1/2, \mathsf{Ret}(\mathsf{false}))). \quad (3)$$

This term expresses a linear combination of measures, namely the average of the two measures $\mathsf{Ret}(\mathsf{true})$ and $\mathsf{Ret}(\mathsf{false})$. So this term denotes the same measure as (1), but it is more efficient as a sampling procedure: instead of drawing two numbers from a uniform distribution, just flip one fair coin and return either true or false accordingly. This term is also easier for humans to understand. Indeed, this representation amounts to a compact table that lists the outcomes (true and false) alongside their exact probabilities (1/2 each). Nothing could be better.

A Continuous Distribution. Let us take two steps on a one-dimensional random walk: first choose x from the Gaussian distribution with mean 0 and standard deviation 1, then choose y from the Gaussian distribution with mean x and standard deviation 1. If we only care about the final point y, then the corresponding term

$$\mathsf{Bind}(\mathsf{Gaussian}(0,1), x, \mathsf{Bind}(\mathsf{Gaussian}(x,1), y, \mathsf{Ret}(y))) \quad (4)$$

denotes a measure over $\mathbb{R}$. In other words, we can integrate with respect to this distribution any function h from $\mathbb{R}$ to $\mathbb{R}^+$. The result is the number

$$\int_{-\infty}^{\infty} \frac{\exp\left(-\frac{x^2}{2}\right)}{\sqrt{2 \cdot \pi}} \cdot \int_{-\infty}^{\infty} \frac{\exp\left(-\frac{(y-x)^2}{2}\right)}{\sqrt{2 \cdot \pi}} \cdot h(y) \, dy \, dx. \tag{5}$$

With Maple's help, we can simplify this integral expression to

$$\int_{-\infty}^{\infty} \frac{\exp\left(-\frac{y^2}{4}\right)}{2 \cdot \sqrt{\pi}} \cdot h(y) \, dy. \tag{6}$$

From this, we read off the much simpler term in our language $\mathsf{Gaussian}(0, \sqrt{2})$, which expresses the fact that taking two steps on a random walk with standard deviation 1 is equivalent to taking one step on a random walk with standard deviation $\sqrt{2}$. This term denotes the same measure over $\mathbb{R}$ as (4), but it is more efficient as a sampling procedure: instead of drawing two numbers from Gaussian distributions, just draw one number from a third Gaussian. This term is also easier for humans to understand (for instance, easier to visualize as a bell curve).

A Conditional Distribution. What if, instead of caring about the second step y and throwing away x, we *observe* y from an actual walk and want to use that information to *infer* the first step x? One way to express the observation is to replace the random choice of y in (4) by a *probability density* $\mathcal{D}$:

$$\mathsf{Bind}(\mathsf{Gaussian}(0, 1), x, \mathsf{Weight}(\mathcal{D}(\mathsf{Gaussian}(x, 1), y), \mathsf{Ret}(x))) \tag{7}$$

This term denotes a measure over $\mathbb{R}$. As a sampling procedure, it means to draw x from $\mathsf{Gaussian}(0, 1)$ then return x with the *weight* $\mathcal{D}(\mathsf{Gaussian}(x, 1), y)$. This weight, defined in Table 1, is a positive real number that reaches its maximum when $x = y$ and decreases as x moves farther from y.

The integral of h with respect to the distribution (7) is similar to (5),

$$\int_{-\infty}^{\infty} \frac{\exp\left(-\frac{x^2}{2}\right)}{\sqrt{2 \cdot \pi}} \cdot \frac{\exp\left(-\frac{(y-x)^2}{2}\right)}{\sqrt{2 \cdot \pi}} \cdot h(x) \, dx. \tag{8}$$

From this integral, we read off the term

$$\mathsf{Weight}\left(\frac{\exp\left(-\frac{y^2}{4}\right)}{2 \cdot \sqrt{\pi}}, \mathsf{Gaussian}\left(\frac{y}{2}, \frac{1}{\sqrt{2}}\right)\right) \tag{9}$$

for the *conditional* distribution of x *given* the observation y. This term tells us that this distribution is proportional to a Gaussian with mean $y/2$ and standard deviation $1/\sqrt{2}$. It denotes the same measure over $\mathbb{R}$ as (7), but it is more efficient as a sampling procedure because every sample of x is returned with the same weight, depending only on y. Statisticians call the equivalence between (7) and (9) a *conjugacy* between the two Gaussians in (7). This simplification underpins the popular *Kalman filter* (Mayback 1979).

2 Adding Measures to a Mathematical Language

Instead of building our own language from scratch, we start with a CAS whose language already expresses integral calculus. For example, Maple represents the integral (2) internally as the term

$$\mathsf{Int}\big(\mathsf{Int}\big(\mathsf{If}(x < y, h(\mathsf{true}), h(\mathsf{false})), y = 0..1\big), x = 0..1\big) \tag{10}$$

using the syntax constructors Int If true false $<$ $=$ $..$ (the last three of which are written infix) and the variables x y and h.

We add to this language a handful of constructors that amount to an abstract data type of measures. These constructors are summarized in Fig. 1, using informal "typing rules" even though Maple is not statically typed. If A is a type, then $\mathbb{M}A$ is our informal type of measures over A. In particular, the top two rows of Fig. 1 show several primitive measures of types $\mathbb{M}\mathbb{R}$ and $\mathbb{M}\mathbb{R}^+$, where $\mathbb{R}$ is the type of reals and $\mathbb{R}^+$ is the type of non-negative reals (including $+\infty$).

Moving on in Fig. 1, the constructors Ret and Bind represent the unit and bind operations of the measure monad. In $\mathsf{Bind}(m, x, m')$, the variable x takes scope over the measure term m'. Here we write x as a metavariable that ranges over variables in the syntax; whereas for terms we use a variety of metavariables, including $e, a, b, k, \alpha, \beta, \gamma, \mu, \nu, \sigma, \theta$, and especially m for a measure term, and g for an integral term.

The next two constructors express non-negative linear combinations of measures. The term $\mathsf{Msum}(m_1, \ldots, m_n)$ represents the sum of n measures, so $\mathsf{Msum}()$ is the zero measure. The term $\mathsf{Weight}(e, m)$ represents multiplying a measure m by a non-negative scalar factor e.

We use the conditional If in measure terms as well as in ordinary expressions denoting numbers. Thus $\mathsf{If}(x < y, \mathsf{Ret}(\mathsf{true}), \mathsf{Ret}(\mathsf{false}))$ is a measure term, whereas the expression $\mathsf{If}(x<y, h(\mathsf{true}), h(\mathsf{false}))$ denotes a number. In our Maple

$$\frac{a : \mathbb{R} \quad b : \mathbb{R}}{\mathsf{Uniform}(a, b) : \mathbb{M}\mathbb{R}} \qquad \frac{\mu : \mathbb{R} \quad \sigma : \mathbb{R}^+}{\mathsf{Gaussian}(\mu, \sigma) : \mathbb{M}\mathbb{R}} \qquad \frac{\mu : \mathbb{R} \quad \gamma : \mathbb{R}^+}{\mathsf{Cauchy}(\mu, \gamma) : \mathbb{M}\mathbb{R}}$$

$$\frac{\nu : \mathbb{R} \quad \mu : \mathbb{R} \quad \gamma : \mathbb{R}^+}{\mathsf{StudentT}(\nu, \mu, \gamma) : \mathbb{M}\mathbb{R}} \qquad \frac{\alpha : \mathbb{R}^+ \quad \beta : \mathbb{R}^+}{\mathsf{Beta}(\alpha, \beta) : \mathbb{M}\mathbb{R}^+} \qquad \frac{k : \mathbb{R}^+ \quad \theta : \mathbb{R}^+}{\mathsf{Gamma}(k, \theta) : \mathbb{M}\mathbb{R}^+}$$

$$\frac{e : A}{\mathsf{Ret}(e) : \mathbb{M}A} \qquad \frac{m : \mathbb{M}A \quad m' : \mathbb{M}B}{\mathsf{Bind}(m, x, m') : \mathbb{M}B} \qquad \frac{\forall i \leq n, \, m_i : \mathbb{M}A}{\mathsf{Msum}(m_1, \ldots, m_n) : \mathbb{M}A}$$

$$\frac{e : \mathbb{R}^+ \quad m : \mathbb{M}A}{\mathsf{Weight}(e, m) : \mathbb{M}A} \qquad \frac{e : \mathbb{B} \quad m : \mathbb{M}A \quad m' : \mathbb{M}A}{\mathsf{If}(e, m, m') : \mathbb{M}A} \qquad \frac{g : \mathbb{R}^+}{\mathsf{LO}(\hbar, g) : \mathbb{M}A}$$

where the Bind rule has hypothesis $[x : A]$, the LO rule has hypothesis $[\hbar : A \to \mathbb{R}^+]$.

Fig. 1. Informal typing rules for how we represent measures

implementation, we actually handle the multiway conditional construct piecewise (Carette 2007), but we describe only if-then-else in this paper to keep the notation simple.

The last constructor is LO, short for "linear operator". In LO($ħ, g$), the metavariable $ħ$ stands for an *integrand* variable, like h in Eq. (2). As the typing rule indicates, $ħ$ takes scope over g. We use LO to name a measure by specifying how it integrates a function: LO($ħ, g$) means the measure m such that the integral of a measurable non-negative function $ħ$ with respect to m is g.

An operational way to interpret a measure term is to run it as an *importance sampler*, which generates a random outcome along with a weight. Interpreted thus, Gaussian means to draw a number from a Gaussian distribution, Ret means to produce the given outcome, and Bind means to sequence two importance samplers. As Eq. (3) exemplifies, a non-negative linear combination of measures

$$\mathsf{Msum}\big(\mathsf{Weight}(e_1, m_1), \ldots, \mathsf{Weight}(e_n, m_n)\big) \tag{11}$$

is an n-way random choice: we choose one of the subterms m_i with probability proportional to e_i, and at the same time multiply the current weight (which starts at 1) by $\sum_{i=1}^{n} e_i$. In particular, if $m_1 = \cdots = m_n = 1/n$ then we choose m_i uniformly and leave the weight unaffected. If an immediate subterm m_i of $\mathsf{Msum}(m_1, \ldots, m_n)$ is not built with Weight, then we treat m_i like $\mathsf{Weight}(1, m_i)$. And if the term $\mathsf{Weight}(e, m)$ occurs in isolation, then its sampling interpretation is as with $\mathsf{Msum}(\mathsf{Weight}(e, m))$: scale the weight by e and continue with m.

We can also interpret each measure term denotationally—as a measure. To do this, we specify the integral of a function with respect to the measure. Our approach to simplification starts with this definition, so we turn to it next.

3 Connecting Abstract and Concrete Integration

A fundamental result of measure theory is that measures can be viewed in two equivalent ways (Theorems ⟨12⟩ and ⟨13⟩ in Pollard 2001).

On one hand, we can view a measure as a function that maps sets to their sizes in $\mathbb{R}^+$, by *measuring* the sets' length or volume.

On this view, the uniform distribution on the unit interval (Uniform$(0, 1)$ in our language) is a function that maps the interval $[2/3, 2]$ to the number $1/3$, because $[0, 1] \cap [2/3, 2]$ has length $1/3$. In other words, the probability is $1/3$ for a point randomly drawn from Uniform$(0, 1)$ to lie in $[2/3, 2]$. The same function maps the singleton set $\{1/2\}$ to the number 0, which is the probability for a point randomly drawn from Uniform$(0, 1)$ to be exactly $1/2$. Similarly, the *Dirac distribution* at $1/2$ (which we write Ret$(1/2)$) is a function that maps each set S to 1 if $1/2 \in S$, and to 0 otherwise. So it maps the interval $[2/3, 1]$ to 0 and the singleton $\{1/2\}$ to 1. After all, if we draw the point $1/2$ deterministically, then the probability that the point lies in $[2/3, 1]$ is 0, and the probability that the point is exactly $1/2$ is 1.

On the other hand, we can view a measure as a function that maps functions to their integrals in $\mathbb{R}^+$, with higher-order type $(\cdots \to \mathbb{R}^+) \to \mathbb{R}^+$, so mathematicians call it an *operator*. On this view, Uniform$(0,1)$ is a function that maps h to $\int_0^1 h(x)\,dx$. For example, it maps $\lambda x.x$ to $\int_0^1 x\,dx = 1/2$. In other words, the expected value of a random draw from Uniform$(0,1)$ is $1/2$. We can view the Dirac distribution Ret$(1/2)$ as a function as well. It maps h to the number $h(1/2)$. And lo and behold, the expected value of drawing the number $1/2$ deterministically is $1/2$.

It may seem strange to call the application $h(1/2)$ an integral of h, but it satisfies the important properties of integration that we use. To start with, if h is non-negative, then so is $h(1/2)$, just like the integral $\int_0^1 h(x)\,dx$. Moreover, application is *linear*: for example, we have

$$\big(\lambda x.a \cdot h(x) + b \cdot k(x)\big)(1/2) = a \cdot h(1/2) + b \cdot k(1/2) \tag{12}$$

for any functions $h, k : \mathbb{R} \to \mathbb{R}^+$ and weights $a, b : \mathbb{R}^+$. Thus the application of a measure m as a linear operator to a function h is called the *(abstract) integral* of the *integrand* h with respect to m. We represent it by integrate(m, h).

These two views are equivalent, as mentioned above. Specifically, the size of a set S with respect to a measure m is the integral integrate(m, χ_S) of its *characteristic function* χ_S, defined by $\chi_S(x) = 1$ if $x \in S$ and $\chi_S(x) = 0$ otherwise.

Despite this correspondence, we need to view a measure as an integrator, for three reasons. First, abstract integration is required to define the Bind operation of the measure monad (Giry 1982; Ramsey and Pfeffer 2002), and Bind is essential in the probabilistic programs we seek to simplify. Second, existing CASes can handle concrete integrals, as demonstrated in the introduction. Third, existing CASes are weak at representing and measuring sets.

The ability to compute integrals is useful to us in the common cases where abstract integration involves concrete integration, like with Uniform and Gaussian. But to take advantage of this ability, we need to relate concrete integration to abstract integration, which CASes off the shelf do not even represent. For example, Maple has plenty of facilities we covet for simplifying and transforming concrete integrals $\int$, sums $\sum$, function applications, and their iterated combinations, but the facilities for integration, for summation, and for function application are separate, and there is no single way to represent, say, a product measure.

Hence, our plan is to simplify measure terms in three steps:

1. View the given measure term as a linear operator, which specifies the abstract integral of an arbitrary integrand.
2. Improve the integral using computer algebra, keeping the integrand arbitrary.
3. Read off a new measure term from the improved linear operator.

A major contribution of this paper is to automate not only step 1 (Sect. 4) but also step 3 (Sect. 5), so that the task of simplifying probabilistic programs reduces to the task of improving integrals. This reduction leads to another major contribution of this paper, namely to improve integrals using the building blocks provided by an existing CAS (Sect. 6).

4   From Measure Term to Linear Operator

Step 1 is to convert a given measure term m to a term of the form $\mathsf{LO}(\hbar, g)$. Recall that the $\hbar$ in $\mathsf{LO}(\hbar, g)$ represents an arbitrary function to be integrated, so we set $\hbar$ to a fresh name. Then, to preserve the meaning of m, the g in $\mathsf{LO}(\hbar, g)$ should be the abstract integral of $\hbar$ with respect to m, so we set g to $\mathsf{integrate}(m, \hbar)$, defined in Fig. 2.

Figure 2 defines $\mathsf{integrate}(m, h)$ by structural induction on measure term m, so our definition serves as a compositional denotational semantics of measure terms, and a standard one at that. The integrand h is an accumulator argument that may not just be a name $\hbar$, as can be seen in the right-hand side of the Bind case. Actually, h amounts to a continuation, so step 1 amounts to a one-pass transform from monadic to continuation-passing style (CPS) (Hatcliff and Danvy 1994)(more precisely, to continuation-composing style (Danvy and Filinski 1990).

$$\mathsf{integrate}\big(m, \qquad\qquad h\big) = \int_{\mathcal{L}(m)}^{\mathcal{U}(m)} \mathcal{D}(m, x) \cdot h(x)\, dx$$
$$\text{where } m \text{ is a primitive measure term and } x \text{ is fresh}$$
$$\mathsf{integrate}\big(\mathsf{Ret}(e), \qquad h\big) = h(e)$$
$$\mathsf{integrate}\big(\mathsf{Bind}(m, x, m'), h\big) = \mathsf{integrate}\big(m, \lambda x.\, \mathsf{integrate}(m', h)\big)$$
$$\mathsf{integrate}\big(\mathsf{Msum}(m, \dots), \ h\big) = \mathsf{integrate}(m, h) + \cdots$$
$$\mathsf{integrate}\big(\mathsf{Weight}(e, m), \ h\big) = e \cdot \mathsf{integrate}(m, h)$$
$$\mathsf{integrate}\big(\mathsf{If}(e, m, m'), \quad h\big) = \mathsf{If}\big(e, \mathsf{integrate}(m, h), \mathsf{integrate}(m', h)\big)$$
$$\mathsf{integrate}\big(\mathsf{LO}(\hbar, g), \qquad h\big) = g\{\hbar \mapsto h\}$$
$$\mathsf{integrate}\big(m, \qquad\qquad h\big) = \mathsf{Integrate}(m, h) \qquad\qquad\qquad \text{otherwise}$$

Fig. 2. Translating a measure term m to a linear operator $\mathsf{LO}(\hbar, \mathsf{integrate}(m, \hbar))$, where $\hbar$ is fresh

When m is primitive, $\mathsf{integrate}$ produces a concrete integral using the standard properties of m listed in Table 1. In this paper, all primitive measures range over real intervals. The properties we use from Table 1 are

- $\mathcal{L}(m)$, the lower bound of the interval, possibly $-\infty$;
- $\mathcal{U}(m)$, the upper bound of the interval, possibly $+\infty$; and
- $\mathcal{D}(m, x)$, the *density* of m with respect to the Lebesgue measure.

Many more measures could be added to Table 1, but some measures cannot be so represented, such as $\mathsf{Ret}(0)$ and the logistic distribution.

The last line in Fig. 2 handles the case where m is a free variable representing an unknown measure. The result is a residual term $\mathsf{Integrate}(m, h)$.

For the example (1), step 1 produces the term

$$\mathsf{LO}\left(h, \int_0^1 \frac{1}{1 - 0} \cdot \int_0^1 \frac{1}{1 - 0} \cdot \left(\begin{cases} h(\mathsf{true}) & \text{if } x < y \\ h(\mathsf{false}) & \text{otherwise} \end{cases} \right) dy\, dx \right), \tag{13}$$

Table 1. Defining properties of primitive measures

Measure term m	Bounds $\mathcal{L}(m)$ $\mathcal{U}(m)$	Density $\mathcal{D}(m,x)$	Holonomic representation $\frac{p_0(x)}{p_1(x)} = -\frac{\frac{d}{dx}\mathcal{D}(m,x)}{\mathcal{D}(m,x)}$
Uniform(a,b)	a $\quad$ b	$\frac{1}{b-a}$	0
Gaussian(μ,σ)	$-\infty$ $\quad$ $+\infty$	$\frac{\exp\left(-\frac{1}{2}\cdot(\frac{x-\mu}{\sigma})^2\right)}{\sqrt{2\cdot\pi}\cdot\sigma}$	$\frac{x-\mu}{\sigma^2}$
Cauchy(μ,γ)	$-\infty$ $\quad$ $+\infty$	$\frac{\left(1+(\frac{x-\mu}{\gamma})^2\right)^{-1}}{\pi\cdot\gamma}$	$\frac{2\cdot(x-\mu)}{(x-\mu)^2+\gamma^2}$
StudentT(ν,μ,γ)	$-\infty$ $\quad$ $+\infty$	$\frac{\left(1+(\frac{x-\mu}{\gamma})^2\nu\right)^{-(\nu+1)/2}}{\frac{\Gamma(\nu/2)}{\Gamma((\nu+1)/2)}\cdot\sqrt{\pi\cdot\nu}\cdot\gamma}$	$\frac{(\nu+1)\cdot(x-\mu)}{(x-\mu)^2+\gamma^2\cdot\nu}$
Beta(α,β)	0 $\quad$ 1	$\frac{x^{\alpha-1}\cdot(1-x)^{\beta-1}}{B(\alpha,\beta)}$	$\frac{(\alpha+\beta-2)\cdot x-(\alpha-1)}{x\cdot(1-x)}$
Gamma(k,θ)	0 $\quad$ $+\infty$	$\frac{x^{k-1}\cdot\exp(-\frac{x}{\theta})}{\Gamma(k)\cdot\theta^k}$	$\frac{\frac{x}{\theta}+1-k}{x}$

in which we notate the conditional If with a curly left brace. Maple immediately removes the factor $\frac{1}{1-0}$, yielding Eq. (2).

As Eq. (13) illustrates, the output of this integrate step is patently a linear operator. In other words, just by examining the integral produced syntactically, without any deep reasoning, we can tell that it is linear in the integrand $\hbar$. Formally, we say that g is *patently linear in $\hbar$* iff g is generated by the grammar

$$g ::= \hbar(e) \mid g_1 + \cdots + g_n \mid \int_a^b g\,dx \mid e\cdot g \mid \mathsf{If}(e,g,g') \mid \mathsf{Integrate}(m,\lambda x.g) \quad (14)$$

where a,b,e,m do not contain $\hbar$ free, and $x \neq \hbar$. (For simplicity, this grammar omits $\sum_a^b g\,dx$, and this paper omits measures over $\mathbb{Z}$.)

Of course, patent linearity entails linearity, but the converse is not the case. For example, the term $\sin(h(a))^2+\cos(h(a))^2-1$ is linear in h (because it is zero) but not patently linear. Still, the right-hand sides in Fig. 2 all maintain patent linearity, so step 1 produces a patently linear integral, which we then subject to algebraic manipulations in step 2. As long as our manipulations of the integral preserve patent linearity, the result can be turned back to a measure term. That is the job of step 3, which we present next.

5   From Linear Operator Back to Measure Term

Figure 3 defines unintegrate$(\hbar,g,c)$, whose goal is to find a measure term m (built without LO) such that integrate$(m,\hbar) = g$. If we think of step 1 above as a transform from monadic style to CPS, then step 3 inverts this.

Like integrate, unintegrate proceeds by structural induction on the input term. Most lines of this definition just handle a case in the grammar (14) by inverting a corresponding line defining integrate in Fig. 2. The main deviations from this pattern are three, described in the three subsections below.

$$\text{unintegrate}\big(\hbar, \textstyle\int_a^b g\,dx, \qquad\qquad c\big) = \text{weight}\big(e_1, \text{bind}(m, x, \text{weight}(e_2, m'))\big)$$
$$\text{where } x \neq \hbar \text{ and } (e, m') = \text{unweight}\big(\text{unintegrate}(\hbar, g, c \wedge a < x < b)\big)$$
$$(m, e') = \text{recognize}(e, x, a, b, c)$$
$$e_1 \cdot e_2 = e' \qquad \text{where } e_1 \text{ does not contain } x \text{ free}$$

$$\text{unintegrate}\big(\hbar, \hbar(e), \qquad\quad c\big) = \text{Ret}(e)$$
$$\text{unintegrate}\big(\hbar, g + \cdots, \qquad c\big) = \text{Msum}\big(\text{unintegrate}(\hbar, g, c), \ldots\big)$$
$$\text{unintegrate}\big(\hbar, e \cdot g, \qquad\quad c\big) = \text{weight}\big(e, \text{unintegrate}(\hbar, g, c)\big)$$
$$\text{where } e \text{ does not contain } \hbar \text{ free}$$

$$\text{unintegrate}\big(\hbar, \text{If}(e, g, g'), \quad c\big) = \text{If}\big(e, \text{unintegrate}(\hbar, g, c \wedge e), \text{unintegrate}(\hbar, g', c \wedge \neg e)\big)$$
$$\text{unintegrate}\big(\hbar, \text{Integrate}(m, h), c\big) = \text{bind}\big(m, x, \text{unintegrate}(\hbar, h(x), c)\big) \quad \text{where } x \text{ is fresh}$$
$$\text{unintegrate}\big(\hbar, g, \qquad\qquad c\big) = \text{LO}(\hbar, g) \qquad\qquad\qquad\qquad\qquad \text{otherwise}$$

$$\text{bind}(m, \quad x, \text{Ret}(x)) = m \qquad\qquad\quad \text{weight}(1, m) \qquad\quad = m$$
$$\text{bind}(\text{Ret}(e), x, m) \quad = m\{x \mapsto e\} \qquad\quad \text{weight}(0, m) \qquad\quad = \text{Msum}()$$
$$\text{bind}(m, \quad x, m') \quad = \text{Bind}(m, x, m') \qquad \text{weight}(e, \text{Weight}(e', m)) = \text{weight}(e \cdot e', m)$$
$$\text{otherwise} \qquad\quad \text{weight}(e, m) \qquad\quad = \text{Weight}(e, m)$$
$$\text{otherwise}$$

$$\text{unweight}\big(\text{Weight}(e, m)\big) \qquad = \big(e, m\big)$$
$$\text{unweight}\big(\text{Msum}(m_1, \ldots, m_n)\big) = \big(e, \text{Msum}(\text{weight}(\tfrac{1}{e}, m_1), \ldots, \text{weight}(\tfrac{1}{e}, m_n))\big)$$
$$\text{where } e = e_1 + \cdots + e_n \text{ and } (e_i, \_) = \text{unweight}(m_i)$$
$$\text{unweight}\big(m\big) \qquad\qquad\qquad = \big(1, m\big) \qquad\qquad\qquad\qquad\qquad\qquad\quad \text{otherwise}$$

Fig. 3. Translating a linear operator $\text{LO}(\hbar, g)$ to a measure term $\text{unintegrate}(\hbar, g, \text{true})$

5.1 Peephole Optimizations

As unintegrate builds a measure term, it invokes the smart constructors bind and weight, defined in Fig. 3. They are semantically equivalent to Bind and Weight but perform peephole optimizations using algebraic laws: bind uses the right and left monad identity laws to eliminate Bind, and weight uses linearity to eliminate Weight. We wait until step 3 to perform these optimizations, so that they apply to terms produced by density recognition (Sect. 5.3).

5.2 Assumption Context

As unintegrate traverses the input integral g, it maintains a *context* of assumptions about the variables in g.

For example, when unintegrate processes $\text{If}(e, g, g')$, it conjoins the condition e onto the current context c while processing the then-case g, and it conjoins $\neg e$ onto c while processing the else-case g'. So if e is the condition $x > 0$, then the recursive call to $\text{unintegrate}(\hbar, g, c \wedge e)$ can simplify any occurrence of $\sqrt{x^2}$ to x, and sgn x to 1. These simplifications are performed by the call to recognize and benefit later calls to recognize, as explained near the end of Sect. 5.3 below.

Similarly, when unintegrate processes $\int_a^b g\, dx$, it conjoins $a < x < b$ onto the current context c. (Actually, that recursive call to unintegrate$(\hbar, g, c \wedge a < x < b)$ is free to ignore any countable number of points in the interval $[a, b]$, but unintegrate does not currently exercise that freedom.)

5.3 Density Recognition

When unintegrate processes $\int_a^b g\, dx$, it tries to recognize a concrete integral that belongs to a primitive measure. For example, when unintegrate processes the concrete integral in Eq. (2), it recognizes $\int_0^1 \ldots dx$ as belonging to Uniform$(0, 1)$ and so produces a term of the form Bind(Uniform$(0, 1), x, \ldots)$. This requires nontrivial computer algebra because there is a gulf between the body of that integral, namely the integral $\int_0^1 \left(\left\{ \begin{smallmatrix} h(\text{true}) & \text{if } x < y \\ h(\text{false}) & \text{otherwise} \end{smallmatrix} \right. \right) dy$, and $\mathcal{D}(m, x) \cdot h(x)$ at the top of Eq. (2), namely the product $\frac{1}{b-a} \cdot h(x)$. These terms do not unify syntactically.

For recognizing primitive measures other than Uniform, the gulf is even wider, and syntactic matching is even more futile. For example, how can an *algorithm* recognize that the density in (8) is proportional to a certain Gaussian distribution and read off the measure term (9)? When unintegrate processes the integral (8), the recursive call to unintegrate$(\hbar, g, c')$ returns the measure term

$$\text{Weight}\left(\frac{\exp\left(-\frac{x^2}{2}\right)}{\sqrt{2 \cdot \pi}} \cdot \frac{\exp\left(-\frac{(y-x)^2}{2}\right)}{\sqrt{2 \cdot \pi}}, \text{Ret}(x) \right), \tag{15}$$

and the call to unweight (defined in Fig. 3) decomposes this term into its two subterms, the weight

$$f(x) = \frac{\exp\left(-\frac{x^2}{2}\right)}{\sqrt{2 \cdot \pi}} \cdot \frac{\exp\left(-\frac{(y-x)^2}{2}\right)}{\sqrt{2 \cdot \pi}} \tag{16}$$

and the measure Ret(x). The weight is a function in the integration variable x. We call this function the *target density*. We need an algorithm to recognize that it is proportional to $\mathcal{D}(\text{Gaussian}(\mu, \sigma))$ and not, say, $\mathcal{D}(\text{Cauchy}(\mu, \gamma))$.

Holonomic Representation. We solve this density recognition problem in one fell swoop for *all* our primitive measures, by treating the target density f as a *holonomic*[1] expression (Wilf and Zeilberger 1992; Chyzak and Salvy 1998. A good tutorial on holonomicity is provided by Kauers (2013). In short, it means we find a *homogeneous linear differential equation*

$$p_n(x) \cdot f^{(n)}(x) + \cdots + p_1(x) \cdot f'(x) + p_0(x) \cdot f(x) = 0 \tag{17}$$

---

[1] More precisely, a *D-finite* expression. We speak of holonomicity, which encompasses D-finite functions and *P-recursive* sequences, because we foresee recognizing discrete measures using P-recursive equations. Those are almost as effective as D-finite equations, modulo the issue of *accurate summation* (Abramov and Petkovšek 2005).

that defines $f(x)$ up to a constant factor, in which each $p_i(x)$ is a polynomial in x. For example, the density (16) is defined up to a constant factor by

$$1 \cdot f'(x) + (2 \cdot x - y) \cdot f(x) = 0, \tag{18}$$

so $n = 1$, $p_1(x) = 1$, and $p_0(x) = 2 \cdot x - y$.

The general algorithm for finding a differential Eq. (17) from a closed-form expression $f(x)$ is well established and efficiently implemented by the Maple function `gfun[holexprtodiffeq]`[2] (Salvy and Zimmermann 1994). Such differential equations are only determined up to scaling by a polynomial in x. For example, scaling (18) by x yields another differential equation

$$x \cdot f'(x) + (2 \cdot x^2 - y \cdot x) \cdot f(x) = 0, \tag{19}$$

which is also satisfied by (16), as well as by some new but singular solutions (which can be found by Laplace-transform methods). To reduce this degree of freedom and eliminate such spurious solutions, we divide the differential equation by the leading coefficient $p_n(x)$, so that the coefficients become the rational functions $1, p_{n-1}(x)/p_n(x), \ldots, p_0(x)/p_n(x)$. We then use the non-leading coefficients to identify the primitive measure.

For all our primitive measures (listed in Table 1), it turns out that $n = 1$, so we have to consider just one ratio $p_0(x)/p_1(x)$, which is $2 \cdot x - y$ for the density (16). In general, when $n = 1$, this ratio is equal to $-f'(x)/f(x)$, but the algorithm that computes this ratio is completely different from differentiating f then dividing by f and hoping that the factors that do not form a rational function cancel out. Rather, the algorithm achieves efficiency and robustness by performing linear algebra on *Ore algebra* elements, which represent linear differential operators and enjoy many closure properties that are efficiently computable (Salvy 2005).

Rational-Function Matching. Thanks to existing efficient algorithms for normalizing rational functions (such as Euclid's algorithm), we can easily and robustly match rational functions against each other, and thus recognize all our primitive measures in the same way. For example, given that $n = 1$ and the ratio $p_0(x)/p_1(x) = 2 \cdot x - y$ is linear in x for our target density (16), we look through the rightmost column of Table 1 for a rational function whose numerator's degree in x is one higher than its denominator's.[3] The only candidate is $m = \mathsf{Gaussian}(\mu, \sigma)$, and its integration bounds match those of (8), so we equate corresponding coefficients ($2 = 1/\sigma^2$ and $-y = -\mu/\sigma^2$) and solve to get $\mu = y/2$ and $\sigma = 1/\sqrt{2}$. This solving step can be done by calling Maple's `solve` or by designing a custom matcher for each primitive measure. We prefer the latter as it is more efficient.

---

[2] The version of `gfun` shipped with Maple has several important bugs, fixed in the version at http://perso.ens-lyon.fr/bruno.salvy/software/the-gfun-package/.

[3] We only consider the difference between the two degrees, because the numerator and denominator may not be relatively prime, like for $\mathsf{Beta}(1, \beta)$ and $\mathsf{Beta}(\alpha, 1)$.

The recognize *algorithm.* In general, unintegrate in Fig. 3 tries to recognize a target density e by invoking recognize(e, x, a, b, c). Here the density expression e may contain the integration variable x free, a and b are the bounds on x, and c is the context. The goal of recognize is to robustly satisfy the equation

$$\text{recognize}\big(\mathcal{D}(m, x) \cdot e', x, \mathcal{L}(m), \mathcal{U}(m), c\big) = (m, e'), \tag{20}$$

where m is a primitive measure term and e' does not contain x free. To do so, recognize proceeds through four steps:

1. Convert e as a function of x to a holonomic representation.
2. Find the primitive measure m by rational-function matching under the assumption context c. Thus new measures can be added by extending Table 1.
3. Solve for the constant factor e', by equating the target e and the matched $\mathcal{D}(m, x) \cdot e'$ at certain points x. To choose x, either use initial conditions returned by gfun[holexprtodiffeq], if any, or default to $x \in \{0, 1/2, 1\}$.
4. Simplify e' using the assumption context c. Often the e' returned by one call to $(m, e') = \text{recognize}(e, x, a, b, c)$ is then passed to the next call as part of e, so it helps if we can eliminate tricky constructs such as sgn from e'.

If any step above fails, then recognize resorts to the following:

- if $-\infty < a < b < \infty$, then return $\big(\text{Uniform}(a, b), e_1 \cdot (b - a)\big)$;
- otherwise, return $\big(\text{LO}(\hbar', \int_a^b \hbar'(x)\, dx), e_1\big)$, where $\hbar'$ is fresh;

even though e_1 may contain x free. Returning LO is our unobtrusive way to admit failure, which is also done in the the catch-all case at the bottom of Fig. 3 when g is not patently linear.

This approach to density recognition is general and modular enough so that it took one of us only a couple of hours to add each primitive measure in Table 1, once we had implemented the general infrastructure.

6   Improving Linear Operators Algebraically

The previous two sections established a two-way bridge between measure terms and patently linear expressions. Patently linear expressions are real-valued expressions, and computer algebra gives us many more tools for these than for measure terms. We now put these tools to work.

6.1   What Automatic Simplification Can and Cannot Do

To start with, every CAS incessantly performs so-called *automatic simplification* on every expression, using linear-time algorithms that are much faster than naive rewrite rules. Automatic simplification ensures that

- addition + and multiplication · are commutative and associative, with identities 0 and 1, so for example $e_1 \cdot (1 \cdot e_2 \cdot g)$ is equivalent to $(e_1 \cdot e_2) \cdot g$;

– repeated terms are collected, so for example $g_1 + (g_1 + g_2)$ becomes $2 \cdot g_1 + g_2$;
– arithmetic on rational numbers happens, so the factor $\frac{1}{1-0}$ in (13) disappears.

Our language of patently linear expressions take advantage of automatic simplification pervasively. In particular, in Figs. 3 and 4, we pattern-match against $+$ and $\cdot$ using commutativity and associativity. Hence just by composing step 1 and 3 (Figs. 2 and 3), we already simplify the measure term

$$\mathsf{Weight}(e_1, \mathsf{Weight}(1, \mathsf{Weight}(e_2, \mathsf{Msum}(m_1, \mathsf{Msum}(m_1, m_2))))) \qquad (21)$$

to $\mathsf{Weight}(e_1 \cdot e_2, \mathsf{Msum}(\mathsf{Weight}(2, m_1), m_2))$.

This immediate success of automatic simplification might embolden us to feed patently linear expressions to Maple functions such as `value`, which triggers symbolic integration, and `simplify`, whose behaviour is not precisely defined (Moses 1971; Carette 2004). But such optimism would be misplaced. First, CASes tend to be ineffective at multidimensional integrals, which are typical of probabilistic programs. For example, Maple's `value` can only simplify the double integral (5) (to (6)) if we reverse the order of integration between x and y. On the other hand, even though there is no hope to improve a nested integral of the form

$$\iiint \exp(x \cdot y \cdot z) \cdot h(x, y, z)\, dz\, dy\, dx \qquad (22)$$

because h is arbitrary, the amount of time Maple's `value` takes to return the integral unimproved explodes as the nesting depth increases.

Second, the nebulous notion of simplification that CASes use can wreck havoc on patently linear expressions. For example, consider this probabilistic program, which draws a number from a Gaussian then returns its absolute value:

$$\mathsf{Bind}(\mathsf{Gaussian}(0, 1), x, \mathsf{If}(x < 0, \mathsf{Ret}(-x), \mathsf{Ret}(x))) \qquad (23)$$

In step 1, we compute the corresponding linear operator

$$\mathsf{LO}\left(h, \int_{-\infty}^{\infty} \frac{\exp\left(-\frac{x^2}{2}\right)}{\sqrt{2 \cdot \pi}} \cdot \left(\begin{cases} h(-x) & \text{if } x < 0 \\ h(x) & \text{otherwise} \end{cases}\right) dx\right). \qquad (24)$$

If we feed this linear operator straight to step 3, then we recover the measure term (23) unchanged. But if we feed it to Maple's `simplify` or `value`, the Gaussian density becomes duplicated and unrecognized: we get the linear operators

$$\mathsf{LO}\left(h, \int_{-\infty}^{\infty} \left(\begin{cases} \frac{\exp\left(-\frac{x^2}{2}\right)}{\sqrt{2 \cdot \pi}} \cdot h(-x) & \text{if } x < 0 \\ \frac{\exp\left(-\frac{x^2}{2}\right)}{\sqrt{2 \cdot \pi}} \cdot h(x) & \text{otherwise} \end{cases}\right) dx\right) \qquad (25)$$

$$\mathsf{LO}\left(h, \int_{-\infty}^{0} \frac{\exp\left(-\frac{x^2}{2}\right)}{\sqrt{2 \cdot \pi}} \cdot h(-x)\, dx + \int_{0}^{\infty} \frac{\exp\left(-\frac{x^2}{2}\right)}{\sqrt{2 \cdot \pi}} \cdot h(x)\, dx\right), \qquad (26)$$

which step 3 cannot express as measure terms without LO. Therefore, trying to improve a patently linear expression by feeding it willy-nilly to symbolic integration or simplification can be not only ineffective but even counter-productive.

$$\text{reduce}\Big(\hbar, \int_a^b g\,dx, \quad c\Big) = \begin{cases} \text{reduce}(\hbar, g', c) \\ \quad \text{if no argument to } \hbar \text{ in } g \text{ contains } x \text{ free} \\ \quad\quad \hbar' \text{ is fresh} \\ \quad\quad g' = \text{banish}\big(\text{LO}(\hbar', \int_a^b \hbar'(x)\,dx), x, \hbar, g\big) \\ \quad\quad g' \text{ contains fewer } \int \text{ signs than } \int_a^b g\,dx \text{ does} \\ 0 \quad \text{if } c' \text{ is inconsistent} \\ \text{if}\big(c_1', \cdot \int_{a'}^{b'} \text{if}(c_2', g', 0)\,dx, 0\big) \\ \quad \text{if } c_1' \wedge c_2' \wedge a' < x < b' \text{ is equivalent to } c' \\ \quad\quad c_1' \text{ does not contain } x \text{ free} \end{cases}$$

$$\text{where } x \neq \hbar \text{ and } \text{Indicator}(c_1) \cdots \text{Indicator}(c_n) \cdot g' = \text{reduce}(\hbar, g, c \wedge a < x < b)$$
$$c' = c_1 \wedge \cdots \wedge c_n \wedge a < x < b$$

$$\text{reduce}\big(\hbar, g + \cdots, \quad c\big) = \text{reduce}(\hbar, g, c) + \cdots$$
$$\text{reduce}\big(\hbar, e \cdot g, \quad c\big) = \text{simplifyIf}\big(\text{simplify}(e, c)\big) \cdot \text{reduce}(\hbar, g, c)$$
$$\text{where } e \text{ does not contain } \hbar \text{ free}$$
$$\text{reduce}\big(\hbar, \text{If}(e, g, g'), \quad c\big) = \text{if}\big(\text{simplify}(e, c), \text{reduce}(\hbar, g, c \wedge e), \text{reduce}(\hbar, g', c \wedge \neg e)\big)$$
$$\text{reduce}\big(\hbar, \text{Integrate}(m, h), c\big) = \text{Integrate}\big(m, \lambda x. \text{reduce}(\hbar, h(x), c)\big) \quad \text{where } x \text{ is fresh}$$
$$\text{reduce}\big(\hbar, g, \quad c\big) = \text{simplify}(g, c) \qquad\qquad\qquad\qquad \text{otherwise}$$

$$\text{banish}\big(m, x, \hbar, g\big) = \big(\text{do the integral in } \text{integrate}(m, \lambda x.\, 1)\big) \cdot g$$
$$\text{if } g \text{ does not contain } x \text{ free}$$
$$\text{banish}\big(m, x, \hbar, \int_a^b g\,dy\big) = \int_a^b \text{banish}(m, x, \hbar, g)\,dy$$
$$\text{if } a, b \text{ do not contain } x, \hbar \text{ free and } x \neq \hbar$$
$$\text{where } m \text{ does not contain } y \text{ free and } x \neq y$$
$$\text{banish}\big(m, x, \hbar, g + \cdots\big) = \text{banish}(m, x, \hbar, g) + \cdots$$
$$\text{banish}\big(m, x, \hbar, e \cdot g\big) = \text{banish}\big(\text{Bind}(m, x, \text{Weight}(e, \text{Ret}(x))), x, \hbar, g\big)$$
$$\text{where } e \text{ does not contain } \hbar \text{ free}$$

$$\text{banish}\big(m, x, \hbar, \text{If}(e, g, g')\big) = \begin{cases} \text{banish}\big(\text{Bind}(m, x, \text{If}(e, \text{Ret}(x), \text{Msum}())), x, \hbar, g\big) + \\ \text{banish}\big(\text{Bind}(m, x, \text{If}(e, \text{Msum}(), \text{Ret}(x))), x, \hbar, g'\big) \\ \qquad\qquad \text{if } e \text{ contains } x \text{ free} \\ \text{If}\big(e, \text{banish}(m, x, \hbar, g), \\ \qquad\quad \text{banish}(m, x, \hbar, g')\big) \quad \text{otherwise} \end{cases}$$

$$\text{banish}\big(m, x, \hbar, \text{Integrate}(n, h)\big) = \text{Integrate}\big(n, \lambda y. \text{banish}(m, x, \hbar, h(y))\big)$$
$$\text{if } n \text{ does not contain } x \text{ free}$$
$$\text{where } m \text{ does not contain } \hbar \text{ free and } y \text{ is fresh}$$

$$\text{simplifyIf}(\text{If}(c, e, e')) = \text{if}(c, \text{simplifyIf}(e), \text{simplifyIf}(e')) \quad \text{if}(c, e, 0) = \text{Indicator}(c) \cdot e$$
$$\text{simplifyIf}(e) \qquad = e \qquad\qquad\qquad \text{otherwise} \quad \text{if}(c, e, e') = \text{If}(c, e, e') \text{ otherwise}$$

Fig. 4. Improving a linear operator $\text{LO}(\hbar, g)$ to $\text{LO}(\hbar, \text{reduce}(\hbar, g, \text{true}))$ Some cases of banish and if are relegated to Fig. 5 in our technical report (Carette and Shan 2015).

6.2 Following the Grammar of Patently Linear Expressions

We achieve effective improvement by *controlled* application of symbolic integration and algebraic simplification. Informally, our idea is to apply these CAS facilities throughout a patently linear expression *except* where the grammar (14) calls for a patently linear subexpression. Intuitively, these places form the control-flow tree of a probabilistic program. For example, in (24) we withhold the conditional If subexpression from CAS facilities, and in (5) we withhold $h(y)$.

Our workhorse is the reduce function defined in Fig. 4. Starting with a linear operator $LO(\hbar, g)$, the goal of $reduce(\hbar, g, c)$ is to improve g under the assumption context c (initially true, as in Sect. 5.2). The reduce function exercises control over CAS facilities by following the grammar (14). To start with, reduce only invokes $simplify(e, c)$ in three places, namely where the grammar (14) calls for a general e rather than some patently linear g. The call $simplify(e, c)$ means to simplify the expression e under the context c (using Maple's `simplify`).

When reduce encounters an integral $\int_a^b g \, dx$, it first checks if the integration variable x is used in any call to the arbitrary integrand $\hbar$ (in other words, if x is used to Return any outcome). If not, then the variable x could be *eliminated* (Dechter 1998) or *integrated out*. An example is the variable x in (5). To perform the integral over x, we push it in past the integral over y, to form the expression

$$\int_{-\infty}^{\infty} \left(\int_{-\infty}^{\infty} \frac{\exp\left(-\frac{x^2}{2}\right)}{\sqrt{2 \cdot \pi}} \cdot \frac{\exp\left(-\frac{(y-x)^2}{2}\right)}{\sqrt{2 \cdot \pi}} \, dx \right) \cdot h(y) \, dy, \tag{27}$$

then ask Maple to do just the inner integral over x, which no longer contains any call to h. In general, we push the integral to be eliminated all the way in, so that it becomes the innermost integral and does not contain any call to $\hbar$, then ask Maple to do just that integral. This pushing and symbolic integration is performed by banish. The specification of banish is that $LO(\hbar, banish(m, x, \hbar, g))$ should mean the same measure as $Bind(m, x, LO(\hbar, g))$ but integrate over x innermost rather than outermost. Achieving this specification requires doubling the work when g is an If. The upshot of this improvement is that we manage to simplify the measure term (4) to $Gaussian(0, \sqrt{2})$.

If the integral $\int_a^b g \, dx$ cannot be eliminated altogether, then reduce tries to shrink the integral's bounds a, b by checking g to see if it looks like $If(a' < x < b', g', 0)$ or $If(a' < x < b', 1, 0) \cdot g'$. If it does, then the recursive call to $reduce(\hbar, g, c \wedge a < x < b)$ would return a product like $Indicator(a' < x < b') \cdot g'$. The meaning of $Indicator(\ldots)$ is same as $If(\ldots, 1, 0)$, but we introduce a separate constructor Indicator for this particular use of If to encode a domain restriction that reduce should incorporate into the integration bounds. The constructor Indicator is called in the appropriate cases by the smart constructor if. Any domain restriction so gathered is then used by reduce to shrink the integration bounds. The upshot of this improvement is that we manage to simplify the measure terms

$$Bind(Uniform(0, 1), x, If(0 < x < 1/2, Ret(x), Msum())) \tag{28}$$
$$Bind(Uniform(0, 1), x, Weight(If(0 < x < 1/2, 1, 0), Ret(x))) \tag{29}$$

both to $Weight(1/2, Uniform(0, 1/2))$.

Besides these improvements that constitute reduce, we have found two other operations on patently linear expressions to be sometimes useful: pushing an integral inward but not all the way in; and reparameterizing an integral so that the integration variable is what's passed to the arbitrary integrand h. These operations are not always beneficial, so reduce does not perform them automatically; rather, human or heuristic guidance is required to invoke them for now.

7   Evaluation

Through our work on probabilistic programming, we have assembled a test suite with 66 input-output pairs of measure terms, including probabilistic models and inference procedures that arise in practice. Our simplifier passes all of these tests. A referee asked if some heuristics had crept in; they had, in droves, in a previous simplifier. We present a rational reconstruction, where the only heuristics are the ones documented in Sect. 5.

Many tests have the same input and output, because our simplifier should not degrade any term, especially one that is already as simple as can be. As explained in Sect. 6, this requirement—although basic—is not trivial to satisfy. Indeed, if we only apply step 1 followed by step 3, 42 of our tests still pass.

Our test suite can be seen online[4] alongside our implementation.[5] The following ablation results give a sense of our tests' coverage and variety. If we remove banish, 14 tests fail. If we remove assumption contexts, 8 tests fail. If we remove calls to Maple's simplify, 8 tests fail. If we remove shrinking integration bounds, 9 tests fail. If we remove density recognition from step 3, fully 53 tests fail.

8   Related Work

Statisticians have long used CASes to analyze the expected values, densities, moments, and other properties of particular distributions (Andrews and Stafford 2000). For modularity, however, we need to express distributions by *composing* building blocks, especially using monadic Bind. Researchers handling such distributions have long acknowledged that tasks like exact inference (Dechter 1998), lifted inference (de Salvo Braz et al. 2005), and sampler code generation (Tristan et al. 2014) amount to computer algebra. By bringing an off-the-shelf CAS to bear on these tasks, and by producing output in the same language as the input, we hope to have laid the groundwork for more robustness and reuse. For example, once we defined the densities and density recognition for Gaussian and Gamma, the handful of conjugacies among those distributions all fall out from the CAS.

Compared to our earlier (unpublished) attempts at simplifying probabilistic programs using a CAS, this version is quite compact: 775 lines of Maple code (including comments and testing infrastructure). More importantly, the design of

---

[4] https://github.com/hakaru-dev/hakaru/blob/master/maple/NewSLOTests.mpl.

[5] https://github.com/hakaru-dev/hakaru/blob/master/maple/NewSLO.mpl.

this version can be explained. Especially effective and robust are our conversion between measure terms and linear operators, and our use of differential equations for density recognition. These techniques pave the way for two pressing tasks:

- Add arrays. This will let us express many more distributions in wide use. However, it is a wide-open problem how to deal with product measures and their linear-operator counterparts, especially when their length is symbolic.
- Recover domain restrictions from more advanced uses of If, such as multivariate conditions. Potential solutions include SMT solvers and methods based on normal forms for inequalities.

References

Abramov, S.A., Petkovšek, M.: Gosper's algorithm, accurate summation, and the discrete Newton-Leibniz formula. In: Proceedings of the International Symposium on Symbolic and Algebraic Computation (ISSAC), pp. 5–12. ACM Press (2005)

Andrews, D.F., Stafford, J.E.H.: Symbolic Computation for Statistical Inference. Oxford University Press, Oxford (2000)

Carette, J.: Understanding expression simplification. In: Proceedings of the International Symposium on Symbolic and Algebraic Computation (ISSAC), pp. 72–79. ACM Press (2004)

Carette, J.: A canonical form for piecewise defined functions. In: Proceedings of the International Symposium on Symbolic and Algebraic Computation (ISSAC), pp. 77–84. ACM Press (2007)

Carette, J., Shan, C.: Simplifying probabilistic programs using computer algebra. Technical report 719, Indiana University (2015). http://www.cs.indiana.edu/cgi-bin/techreports/TRNNN.cgi?trnum=TR719

Chyzak, F., Salvy, B.: Non-commutative elimination in ore algebras proves multivariate holonomic identities. J. Symb. Comput. **26**(2), 187–227 (1998)

Danvy, O., Filinski, A.: Abstracting control. In: Proceedings of the Conference on LISP and Functional Programming, pp. 151–160. ACM Press (1990)

de Salvo Braz, R., Amir, E., Roth, D.: Lifted first-order probabilistic inference. In: Proceedings of the 19th International Joint Conference on Artificial Intelligence, pp. 1319–1325 (2005)

Dechter, R.: Bucket elimination: a unifying framework for probabilistic inference. In: Jordan, M.I., (ed.) Learning and Inference in Graphical Models. Kluwer, Dordrecht, Paperback: Learning in Graphical Models. MIT Press (1998)

Giry, M.: A categorical approach to probability theory. In: Banaschewski, B. (ed.) Categorical Aspects of Topology and Analysis. Lecture Notes in Mathematics, vol. 915, pp. 68–85. Springer, Heidelberg (1981)

Hatcliff, J., Danvy, O.: A generic account of continuation-passing styles. In: Proceedings of the 21st Symposium on Principles of Programming Languages (POPL), pp. 458–471. ACM Press (1994)

Kauers, M.: The holonomic toolkit. In: Schneider, C., Blümlein, J. (eds.) Computer Algebra in Quantum Field Theory. Texts and Monographs in Symbolic Computation, pp. 119–144. Springer, Vienna (2013)

Maybeck, P.S.: Stochastic Models, Estimation, and Control. Academic Press, New York (1979)

Moses, J.: Algebraic simplification: a guide for the perplexed. Commun. ACM **14**(8), 548–560 (1971)

Pollard, D.: A User's Guide to Measure Theoretic Probability. Cambridge University Press, Cambridge (2001)

Ramsey, N., Pfeffer, A.: Stochastic lambda calculus and monads of probability distributions. In: Proceedings of the 29th Symposium on Principles of Programming Languages (POPL), pp. 154–165. ACM Press (2002)

Salvy, B.: D-finiteness: Algorithms and applications. In: Proceedings of the International Symposium on Symbolic and Algebraic Computation (ISSAC), pp. 2–3 (2005)

Salvy, B., Zimmermann, P.: Gfun: a Maple package for the manipulation of generating and holonomic functions in one variable. ACM Trans. Math. Softw. **20**(2), 163–177 (1994)

Tristan, J.B., Huang, D., Tassarotti, J., Pocock, A.C., Green, S.J., Steele, G.L., Jr.: Augur: Data-parallel probabilistic modeling. In: Advances in Neural Information Processing Systems, pp. 2600–2608 (2014)

Wilf, H.S., Zeilberger, D.: An algorithmic proof theory for hypergeometric (ordinary and "q") multisum/integral identities. Inventiones mathematicae **108**, 557–633 (1992)

Haskino: A Remote Monad for Programming the Arduino

Mark Grebe$^{(\boxtimes)}$ and Andy Gill

Information and Telecommunication Technology Center,
The University of Kansas, Lawrence, KS, USA
{mark.grebe,andy.gill}@ittc.ku.edu

Abstract. The Haskino library provides a mechanism for programming the Arduino microcontroller boards in high level, strongly typed Haskell instead of the low level C language normally used. Haskino builds on previous libraries for Haskell based Arduino programming by utilizing the recently developed remote monad design pattern. This paper presents the design and implementation of the two-level Haskino library. This first level of Haskino requires communication from the host running the Haskell program and the target Arduino over a serial link. We then investigate extending the initial version of the library with a deep embedding allowing us to cut the cable, and run the Arduino as an independent system.

Keywords: Haskell · Arduino · Remote monad · Embedded systems

1 Introduction

The Arduino line of microcontroller boards provide a versatile, low cost and popular platform for development of embedded control systems. Arduino boards have extremely limited resources that make running a high level functional language natively on the boards infeasible. Instead, the standard way of developing software for these systems is to use a C/C++ environment that is distributed with the boards. This paper documents our efforts to advance the use of Haskell to program the Arduino systems, starting with executing remote commands over a tethered serial port, towards supporting complete standalone systems.

To be specific, the most popular Arduino, the Arduino Uno, has a 16 MHz clock rate, 2 KB of RAM, 32 KB of Flash, and 1 KB of EEPROM. This is cripplingly small by modern standards, but at a few dollars per unit and built-in A-to-D convertors and PWM support, many projects can be prototyped quickly and cheaply with careful programming. Using the Arduino itself as a testbed, we are interested in investigating how Haskell can contribute towards programming such small devices.

Programming the Arduino is, for the most part, straightforward imperative programming. There are side-effecting functions for reading and writing pins, supporting both analog voltages and digital logic. Furthermore, there are

© Springer International Publishing Switzerland 2016
M. Gavanelli and J. Reppy (Eds.): PADL 2016, LNCS 9585, pp. 153–168, 2016.
DOI: 10.1007/978-3-319-28228-2_10

libraries for protocols like I^{2}C, and controlling peripherals, such as LCD displays. We want to retain these APIs by providing an Arduino monad, which supports the low-level Arduino API, and allows programming in Haskell. Ideally, we want to cross-compile arbitrary Haskell code; the reality is we can get close using deeply embedded domain specific languages.

1.1   Outline

To make programming an Arduino accessible to functional programmers, we provide two complementary ways of programming a specific Arduino board.

- First, we provide a way of programming a *tethered* Arduino board, from directly inside Haskell, with the Arduino being a remote service. We start with the work of Levent Erkök, and his hArduino package [1], building on and generalizing the system by using a more efficient way of communicating, and generalizing the controls over the remote execution. We discuss this in Sect. 4.
- Second, we provide a way of out-sourcing entire groups of commands and control-flow idioms. This allows a user's Haskell program to program a board, then step back and let it run. It is this step – taming any allocation by using staging – that we want to be better able to understand, and later partially automate. We discuss this embedding in Sect. 6.

These two complimentarily ways provide a gentler way of programming Arduinos, first using an API to prototype an idea, but with the full power of Haskell, then adjusting control flow and resource usage, to allow the exportation of the program. Both these methods use the remote monad design pattern [2] to provide the key capabilities.

In both systems, we build on the Firmata protocol and firmware [3], and provide a customizable interpreter that runs on the Arduino, written in C. In Sect. 5 we discuss our runtime system, and compare it to previous works.

Our thesis is that structuring remote services in the manner outlined above allows for access to productive and powerful capabilities directly in Haskell, with a useable path to offshoring the entire remote computation. In Sect. 8 we describe our most recent version of Haskino which extends the second API, and this is able to create a stored program on the Arduino which will run without being connected to the host.

2   Programming the Arduino in C

Programming the Arduino in C/C++ consists of defining two top level functions, `setup()`, which specifies the steps necessary to initialize the program, and `loop()`, which defines the main loop of the program. The Arduino environment provides a base set of APIs for controlling digital and analog input pins on the board, as well as standard libraries for other standard interfaces such as I^{2}C.

We present the following simple example of programming the Arduino in C/C++, and we will carry this example through the paper to demonstrate programming in several versions of our Haskino environment. This example has one

Fig. 1. Tethered Arduino Uni with breadboard

digital input from a button, and two LED's for digital output. When the button is not pressed, LED1 will be off, and LED2 will be on. When the button is pressed, their states will be reversed. Figure 1 illustrates an Arduino Uno connected to two LEDs and a button running the example program. The constants 2, 6, and 7 in the program identify the numbers of the Arduino pins to which the button and LED's are connected.

```
int button = 2;
int led1 = 6;
int led2 = 7;

void setup() {
  pinMode(button, INPUT);
  pinMode(led1, OUTPUT);
  pinMode(led2, OUTPUT);
}

void loop() {
  int x;
  x = digitalRead(button);
  digitalWrite(led1, x);
  digitalWrite(led2, !x);
  delay(100);
}
```

3   The Remote Monad

A **remote monad** [2] is a monad that has its evaluation function in a remote location, outside the local runtime system. The key idea is to have a natural transformation, often called **send**, between *Remote* effect and *Local* effect.

$$\text{send} :: \forall a . \; Remote \; a \rightarrow Local \; a$$

The *Remote* monad encodes, via its primitives, the functionality of what can be done remotely, then the **send** command can be used to execute the remote commands. The **send** command is polymorphic, so it can be used to run individual commands, for their result, or to batch commands together. For example, Blank Canvas, our library for accessing HTML5 web-based graphics, uses the remote monad to provide a batchable remote service. Specifically, three representative functions from the API are:

```
send          :: Device -> Canvas a -> IO a
lineWidth     :: Double           -> Canvas ()
isPointInPath :: (Double,Double)  -> Canvas Bool
```

The `Canvas` is the remote monad, and there are three remote primitives given here, as well as bind and return. To use the remote monad, we use **send**:

```
send device $ do
    inside <- isPointInPath (0,0)
    lineWidth (if inside then 10 else 2)
```

The remote monad design pattern splits remote primitives into commands, where there is no interesting result value or temporal consequence, and procedures, which have a result value or temporal consequence. The design pattern then proposes different bundling strategies, based on the distinction between commands and procedures.

A *weak* remote monad is a remote monad that sends both commands and procedures one at a time, to be remotely executed. The design pattern is a way of structuring remote procedure calls, but has no performance advantage. A *strong* remote monad, however, bundles together chains of commands, terminated by an optional procedure, which has the interesting result. There are also other bundling strategies.

We have built a number of libraries using the remote monad design pattern. Blank Canvas is our Haskell library that provides the complete HTML5 Canvas API, using a strong remote monad that remotely calls JavaScript, and is fast enough to write small games. We have also built a general JSON-RPC framework in Haskell. In particular, the JSON-RPC protocol supports multiple batched calls, as well as individual calls, and our implementation uses monads and applicative functors to notate batching. We have also reimplemented the Minecraft API found in `mcpi`, adding a strong remote monad. We see many other applications for the remote monad, beyond the topic of this paper, a remote Arduino monad.

4   The Arduino Remote Monad

The hArduino package, written by Levent Erkök, allows programmers to control Arduino boards through a serial connection. The serial protocol used between the host computer and the Arduino, and the firmware which runs on the Arduino, are together known as Firmata. Firmata was originally intended as a generic protocol for controlling microcontrollers from a host computer. It has become popular in the Arduino community, and programming interfaces for many programming languages have been developed for it. The hArduino library, using our terminology, uses a *weak* remote monad, and does not have a polymorphic send. Instead, once send is called, the function never terminates or returns values. This is our starting point.

Our first step in developing Haskino was to extend the hArduino library using the strong remote monad design pattern. The monad passed in hArduino represents the whole computation to be executed, which is then executed piecemeal by many individual remote calls. In contrast, Haskino's send function is able to send one or more commands terminated by a procedure which may return a value. This bundling of commands increases the efficiency of the communication, not requiring host interaction until a value is returned from the remote microcontroller.

With Haskino, to open a connection to an Arduino, `openArduino` is called passing a boolean flag for debugging mode, a file path to the serial port, and returns an ArduinoConnection data structure:

```
openArduino :: Bool -> FilePath -> IO ArduinoConnection
```

Once the connection is open, the `send` function may be called, passing an Arduino monad representing the computation to be performed remotely, and possibly returning a result.

```
send :: ArduinoConnection -> Arduino a -> IO a
```

The Arduino strong remote monad, like our other remote monad implementations, contains two types of monadic primitives, commands and procedures. An example of a command primitive is writing a digital value to a pin on the Arduino. In the strong version of Haskino, this has the following signature:

```
digitalWrite :: Pin -> Bool -> Arduino ()
```

The function takes the pin to write to and the boolean value to write, and returns a monad which returns unit. An example of a procedure primitive is reading the number of milliseconds since boot from the Arduino. The type signature of that procedure looks like:

```
millis :: Arduino Word32
```

Due to the nature of the Firmata protocol, the initial version of Haskino required a third type of monadic primitive. The Firmata protocol is not strictly a command and response protocol. Reads of analog and digital values from the Arduino are accomplished by issuing a command to start the reading process. Firmata will then send a message to the host at a set interval with the current requested value. In hArduino, and the initial version of Haskino, a background thread is used to read these returned values and store them in a local structure. To allow monadic computations to include reading of digital and analog values, the monadic primitive *local* is defined. A *local* is treated like a procedure from a bundling perspective, in that the send function sends any queued commands when the local is reached. However, unlike the procedure, the local is executed on the host, returning the digital or analog pin value that was stored by the background thread. Haskino also makes use of the these local type monadic primitives to provide a debug mechanism, allowing the language user to insert debug strings that will be printed when the they are reached during the send function processing.

The Arduino monad used in Haskino is defined using a GADT:

```
data Arduino :: * -> * where
    Command     :: Command                          -> Arduino ()
    Procedure   :: Procedure a                       -> Arduino a
    Local       :: Local a                           -> Arduino a
    Bind        :: Arduino a -> (a -> Arduino b)      -> Arduino b
    Return      :: a                                  -> Arduino a

instance Monad Arduino where
        return = Return
        (>>=) = Bind
```

The instance definition for the Monad type class is shown above, but similar definitions are also defined for the Applicative, Functor, and Monoid type classes as well. Each of the types of monadic primitives described earlier in this section is encoded as a sub data type, Command, Procedure, and Local. The data types for Command, Procedure and Local are shown below, with only a subset of their actual constructors as examples.

```
data Command =
    DigitalWrite Pin Bool
    | AnalogWrite Pin Word16

data Procedure :: * -> * where
    Millis      :: Procedure Word32
    | Micros     :: Procedure Word32

data Local :: * -> * where
    DigitalRead    :: Pin -> Local Bool
    | AnalogRead    :: Pin -> Local Word16
```

Finally, the API functions which are exposed to the programmer are defined in terms of these constructors, as shown for the example of `digitalWrite` below:

```
digitalWrite :: Pin -> Bool -> Arduino ()
digitalWrite p b = Command $ DigitalWrite p b
```

hArduino used the original version of Firmata, known as Standard Firmata. The initial version of Haskino used a newer version of Firmata, called Configurable Firmata, adding the ability to control additional Arduino libraries, such as I^2C, OneWire and others. In addition to providing control of new interfaces, it introduces a basic scheduling system. Firmata commands are able to be combined into tasks, which then can be executed at a specified time in the future. Haskino makes use of this capability to specify a monadic computation which is run at a future time. The strong version is limited in what it can do with the capability, as it has no concept of storing results of computations on the remote system for later use, or of conditionals. However, we will return to this basic scheduling capability in Sects. 5 and 6, when we describe enhancements that are made in our deep version of Haskino.

To demonstrate the use of Haskino, we return to the simple example presented in Sect. 2, this time written in the strong version of the Haskino language.

```
example :: IO ()
example = withArduino False "/dev/cu.usbmodem1421" $ do
          let button = 2
          let led1 = 6
          let led2 = 7
          setPinMode button INPUT
          setPinMode led1 OUTPUT
          setPinMode led2 OUTPUT
          loop $ do
              x <- digitalRead button
              digitalWrite led1 x
              digitalWrite led2 (not x)
              delayMillis 100
```

This example uses the Haskino convenience function, `withArduino`, which calls `openArduino`, and then calls `send` with the passed monad:

```
withArduino :: Bool -> FilePath -> Arduino () -> IO ()
```

The `setPinMode` commands configure the Arduino pins for the proper mode, and will be sent as one sequence by the underlying send function. The `loop` primitive is similar to the forever construct in Control.Monad, and executes the sequence of commands and procedures following it indefinitely. The `digitalRead` function is a procedure, so it will be sent individually by the `send` function. The two `digitalWrite` commands following the `digitalRead` will be bundled with the `delayMillis` procedure.

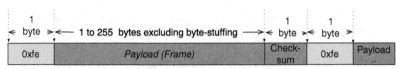

Payload and Payload checksum are byte-stuffed for 0x7e
with 0x7d 0x5e, and byte-stuffed for 0x7d with 0x7d 0x5d,
and checksum is over payload only

Fig. 2. Haskino framing

5   Haskino Firmware and Protocol

We want to move from sending bundles of commands to our Arduino, to sending entire control-flow idioms, even whole programs, as large bundles. We do this by using deep embedding technology, embedding both a small expressing language, and deeper Arduino primitives.

Specifically, to move Haskino from a straightforward use of the strong remote monad to a deeper embedding, required extending the protocol used for communication with the Arduino to handle expressions and conditionals. The Firmata protocol, while somewhat expandable, would have required extensive changes to accommodate expressions. Also, since it was developed to be compatible with MIDI, it uses a 7 bit encoding which added complexity to the implementation on both the host and Arduino sides of the protocol. As we had no requirement to maintain MIDI compatibility, we determined that it would be easier to develop our own protocol specifically for Haskino.

Like Firmata, the Haskino protocol sends frames of data between the host and Arduino. Commands are sent to the Arduino from the host, with no response expected. Procedures are sent to the Arduino as a frame, and then the host waits for a frame from the Arduino in reply to indicated completion, returning the value from procedure computation.

Instead of 7 bit encoding, the frames are encoded with an HDLC (High-level Data Link Control) type framing mechanism. Frames are separated by a hex 0x7E frame flag. If a 0x7E appears in the frame data itself, it is replaced by an escape character (0x7D) followed by a 0x5E. If the escape character appears in the frame data, it is replaced by a 0x7D 0x5D sequence. The last byte of the frame before the frame flag is a checksum byte. Currently, this checksum is an additive checksum, since the error rate on the USB based serial connection is relatively low, and the cost of a CRC computation on the resource limited Arduino is relatively high. However, for a noisier, higher error rate environment, a CRC could easily replace the additive checksum. Figure 2 illustrates the framing structure used.

The new Haskino protocol also makes another departure from the Firmata style of handling procedures which input data from the Arduino. With the deep embedded language being developed, results of one computation may be used in another computation on the remote Arduino. Therefore, the continuous, periodic style of receiving digital and analog input data used by Firmata does not make sense for our application. Instead, digital and analog inputs are requested each time they are required for a computation. Although, this increases the communication overhead for the strong remote monad implementation, it enables the deep implementation, and allows a common protocol to be used by both.

The final design decision required for the protocol was to determine if the frame size should have a maximum limit. As the memory resources on the Arduino are limited, the frame size of the protocol a maximum frame size of 256 bytes was chosen to minimize the amount of RAM required to store a partially received frame on the Arduino.

The basic scheduling concept of Firmata was retained in the new protocol as well. The CreateTask command creates a task structure of a specific size. The AddToTask command adds monadic commands and procedures to a task. Multiple AddToTask commands may be used for a task, such that the task size is not limited by the maximum packet size, but only by the amount of free memory on the Arduino. The ScheduleTask command specifies the future time offset to start running a task. Multiple tasks may be defined, and they run till completion, or until they delay. A delay as the last action in a task causes it to restart. Commands and procedures within a task message use the same format as the command sent in a individual frame, however, the command is proceeded by a byte which specifies the length of the command.

The new protocol was implemented in both Arduino firmware and the strong remote monad version of the Haskell host software, producing the second version of Haskino.

6 Deep EDSL

To move towards our end goal of writing an Arduino program in Haskell that may be run on the Arduino without the need of a host computer and serial interface, we needed to move from the strong remote monad used in the first two versions of the library. A deep embedding of the Haskino language allows us to deal not just with literal values, but with complex expressions, and to define bindings that are used to retain results of computations remotely.

To accomplish this goal, we have extended the command and procedure monadic primitives to take expressions as parameters, as opposed to simple values. For example, the `digitalWrite` command described earlier now becomes the `digitalWriteE` command:

```
digitalWriteE :: Expr Word8 -> Expr Bool -> Arduino ()
```

Procedure primitives now also return Expr values, so the `millis` procedure described earlier now becomes the `millisE` procedure defined as:

```
millisE :: Arduino (Expr Word32)
```

The Expr data type is used to express arithmetic and logical operations on both literal values of a data type, as well as results of remote computations of the same data type. Expr is currently defined over boolean and unsigned integers of length 8, 16 and 32, as these are the types used by the builtin Arduino API. It could be easily extended to handle signed types as well. For booleans, the standard logical operations of not, and, and or are defined. Integer operations include addition, subtraction, multiplication and division, standard bitwise operations, and comparison operators which return a boolean. Type classes and type families are defined using the Data.Boolean [4] package such that operations used in expressions may be written in same manner that operations on similar data types are written in native Haskell. For example, the following defines two expressions of type Word8, and then defines a boolean expression which determines if the first expression is less than the second.

```
a :: Expr Word8
a = 4 + 5 * 9

a :: Expr Word8
b = 6 * 7

c :: Expr Bool
c = a <* b
```

Strong remote monad commands may be defined in terms of their deep counterparts, allowing both to coexist in the deep embedded version. For example:

```
digitalWrite :: Word8 -> Bool -> Arduino ()
digitalWrite p b = digitalWriteE (lit p) (lit b)
```

The second component of the deep embedding is the ability to define remote bindings which allow us to use the results of one remote computation in another. For this, we define a RemoteReference typeclass, with an API that is similar to Haskell's IORef. With this API, remote references may be created and easily read and written to.

```
class RemoteReference a where
    newRemoteRef    :: Expr a -> Arduino (RemoteRef a)
    readRemoteRef   :: RemoteRef a -> Arduino (Expr a)
    writeRemoteRef  :: RemoteRef a -> Expr a -> Arduino ()
    modifyRemoteRef :: RemoteRef a -> (Expr a -> Expr a) ->
                       Arduino ()
```

The final component of the deep embedding is adding conditionals to the language. Haskino defines three types of conditional monadic structures, an If-Then-Else structure, and a While structure, and a LoopE structure. The while structure emulates while loops, and it takes a RemoteRef, a function returning a boolean expression to determine if the loop terminates, a function which updates the remote reference at the end of each loop, and a Arduino () monad which specifies the loop body. The loopE structure provides a deep analog of the loop structure used in the strong remote monad version.

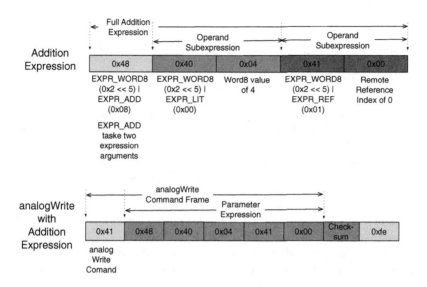

Fig. 3. Example of expression encoding

```
ifThenElse :: Expr Bool -> Arduino () -> Arduino () -> Arduino ()
while :: RemoteRef a -> (Expr a -> Expr Bool) ->
        (Expr a -> Expr a) -> Arduino () -> Arduino ()
loopE :: Arduino () -> Arudino ()
```

Changes to the Haskino protocol and firmware were also required to implement expressions, conditionals and remote references. Expressions are transmitted over the wire using a bytecode representation. Each operation is encoded as a byte with two fields. The upper 3 bits indicate the type of expression (currently Bool, Word8, Word16, or Word32) and the lower 5 bits indicate the operation type (literal, remote reference, addition, etc.). Expression operations may take one, two, or three parameters determined by the operation type, and each of the parameters is again an expression. Evaluation of the expression occurs recursively, until a terminating expression type of a literal, remote reference, or remote bind is reached. Figure 3 shows an example of encoding the addition of Word8 literal value of 4 the first remote reference defined on the board, as well as a diagram of that expression being used in an analogWrite command.

Conditionals are packaged in a similar manner to the way tasks are packaged, with the commands and procedures packaged into a code block. Two code blocks are used for the IfThenElse conditional (one block for the then branch, and one block for the else branch), and one code block is used for the While loop. In addition, a byte is used for each code block to indicate the size of the block. A current limitation of conditionals in the protocol is that the entire conditional and code blocks must fit within a single Haskino protocol frame. However, if the conditional is part of a task, this limitation does not apply, as a task body

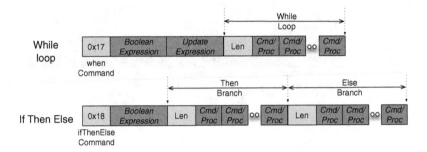

Fig. 4. Protocol packing of conditionals

may span multiple Haskino protocol frames. Figure 4 shows the encoding of both conditional types.

Now that we have described the components of the deeply embedded version of Haskino, we can return to a deep version of the simple example we used earlier.

```
exampleE :: IO ()
exampleE = withArduino True "/dev/cu.usbmodem1421" $ do
          let button = 2
          let led1 = 6
          let led2 = 7
          x <- newRemoteRef false
          setPinModeE button INPUT
          setPinModeE led1 OUTPUT
          setPinModeE led2 OUTPUT
          loopE $ do
              writeRemoteRef x  =<< digitalReadE button
              ex <- readRemoteRef x
              digitalWriteE led1 ex
              digitalWriteE led2 (notB ex)
              delayMillis 100
```

This deep example looks very similar to the strong example in structure. The binding x, which was previously stored on the host, is now kept on the Arduino, and created by the `newRemoteRef` function. The `writeRemoteRef` function updates the remote reference and is passed an expression, which in this case is the result of a remote computation using the `=<<` operator. The remote binds represented in this `writeRemoteRef` example, and the bind to `ex` with the value returned from `readRemoteRef` in the following line require implicit allocation on the Arduino. The Haskino firmware currently implements this allocation by storing the result of a procedure computation that would normally be sent across the serial interface to a local buffer associated with that bind instance instead. The expression bytecode language includes an `EXPR_BIND` operator, which takes it's input from this local buffer. Determining the best method of dealing with these allocations is still an open issue in our research.

In this example, since the computation results that are stored in the remote reference are used only within one iteration of the loop, the RemoteRef is not strictly required, but is used to demonstrate the RemoteRef API. The loop body could have been written using only binds as shown below.

```
loopE $ do
        ex <- digitalReadE button
        digitalWriteE led1 ex
        digitalWriteE led2 (notB ex)
        delayMillis 100
```

The tasks discussed in Sect. 4 become much more useful with the deeply embedded implementation. In the strong implementation, they were limited to sequences of commands and delays, as the remote language had no method of either binding computations together, or storing the result of a computation for future use. However, with the deep implementation, tasks may use the procedure primitives as well, and with the addition of conditionals, full programs may be stored for execution at a later time.

7   Comparing Runtime-Tethered Strong to Deeply Embedded Strong Remote Monad

Table 1 summarizes the major differences we found between the strong and deep implementations. In the strong version, all values are stored on the host, and passing values between computations requires communication with the host. With the deep version, values may be stored on the Arduino and passed between computations on the Arduino, eliminating the need for intermediate host communications. The basic task scheduling mechanism is able to use the full power of the language in the deep version, where it is limited to only commands with the strong version. One limiting factor of the deep version, is that the size of the program that may be written is limited by the available Arduino memory, while the strong version, due to the host interaction, is only limited by the larger host memory.

8   Cutting the Cord

One final addition to the firmware and Haskino language has allowed us to reach our goal of executing a stored Haskino program on the Arduino without requiring a connection to the host. The addition of the bootTaskE primitive allows the programer to write one previously defined task to EEPROM storage on the Haskino. The Haskino firmware checks for the presence of a boot task during the boot process, and if it is present, copies the task from EEPROM to RAM, and starts it's execution.

The following example illustrates how a programmer would create a boot task on the Arduino. The functionality of the program is the same as our other

Table 1. Comparison of strong and deep embedding

	Runtime-tethered	Deeply-embedded
Values stored on	Host	Arduino
Binds occur on	Host	Arduino
Conditionals on target	No	Yes
Tasks can use procedures	No	Yes
Maximum program size	Limited by host memory	Limited by Arduino memory
Communication overhead	Higher	Lower

button and 2 LED examples. In this case, the `createTaskE` primitive is used to create the task in RAM on the Arduino, using the program stored in the example monad. The `bootTaskE` function is then called to write the task from RAM to EEPROM. On the next power on, the interpreter will start execution of the task. The `scheduleReset` primitive may be used to clear a previously written program from EEPROM.

```
example :: Arduino ()
example = do let button = 2
             let led1 = 6
             let led2 = 7
             x <- newRemoteRef (lit False)
             setPinModeE button INPUT
             setPinModeE led1 OUTPUT
             setPinModeE led2 OUTPUT
             loopE $ do
                 writeRemoteRef x  =<< digitalReadE button
                 ex <- readRemoteRef x
                 digitalWriteE led1 ex
                 digitalWriteE led2 (notB ex)
                 delayMillis 100

exampleProg :: IO ()
exampleProg = withArduino False "/dev/cu.usbmodem1421" $ do
              let tid = 1
              createTaskE tid example
              bootTaskE tid
```

We have achieved our original goal of programming a stand alone Arduino, using Haskell. The remote monad design pattern served us well by providing a path to this stand alone solution. There is however, much more that can be done. Having the ability to generate code from a DSL opens many possibilities. For example, recompiling to bake in timing, security constraints, or robustness concerns are possible paths forward.

9   Related Work

There is other ongoing work on using functional languages to program embedded systems in general, and the Arduino in specific. An early use of deep embeddings for remote execution was in the domain of graphics [5,6]. A recent example is the Ivory language [7] provides a deeply embedded DSL for use in programming high assurance systems, but does not make use of the strong remote monad design pattern, and generates C rather than use a remote interpreter.

The Feldspar project [8,9,13] is Haskell embedding of a monadic interface that targets C, and focuses on high-performance. Interestingly, this work also attempt to make use of both deep and shallow embeddings inside a single implementation. Both Feldspar and Haskino use some form of monadic reification technology [10,11,14].

There is ongoing, and as yet unpublished, work by Pieter Koopman and Rinus Plasmeijer at Radboud University Institute for Computing and Information Sciences to develop a deep embedding around a Clean-based deep DSL. Their work also does not use the remote monad, and generates C rather that use a remote interpreter. Also, Kiwamu Okabe of Metasepi Design and Hongwei Xi of Boston University, in an as yet unpublished work, use a direct language implementation of ATS, as opposed to a DSL, to program the Arduino.

10   Conclusion and Future Work

Our two ways of structuring remote computations, provide complimentary but effective ways of using Haskell as a development environment for Arduino software. The strong Haskino provides a method for quick prototyping of software in a tethered environment. The deep version of Haskino allows the programmer to bring the full power of Haskell to developing standalone software for the Arduino. The connected version need not be limited to serial connections, as the Arduino Stream class would allow Arduino Ethernet connections to be used in a similar manner.

In the future, we plan to add a third way to our methodology, and directly generate C programs from our Arduino Monad. This will allow us to bootstrap the system. We also want to extend the scheduling mechanisms in Haskino, using the task structure for interrupt processing, and adding mechanism for communications between tasks in the system. Finally, we also plan on investigating using HERMIT [12] to semi-automatically translate from programs written in the tethered strong remote monad into programs written using the deep embedding. This will improve the applicability of the library.

This material is based upon work supported by the National Science Foundation under Grant No. 1350901.

References

1. Erkok, L.: Hackage package hArduino-0.9 (2014)
2. Gill, A., Sculthorpe, N., Dawson, J., Eskilson, A., Farmer, A., Grebe, M., Rosenbluth, J., Scott, R., Stanton, J.: The remote monad design pattern. In: Proceedings of the 8th ACM SIGPLAN Symposium on Haskell, pp. 59–70. ACM (2015)
3. Steiner, H.C.: Firmata: Towards making microcontrollers act like extensions of the computer, pp. 125–130 (2009)
4. Elliott, C.: Hackage package boolean-0.2.3 (2013)
5. Elliott, C., Hudak, P.: Functional reactive animation. In: International Conference on Functional Programming (1997)
6. Elliott, C., Finne, S., de Moor, O.: Compiling embedded languages. J. Funct. Program. **13**(2), 455–481 (2003)
7. Elliott, T., Pike, L., Winwood, S., Hickey, P., Bielman, J., Sharp, J., Seidel, E., Launchbury, J.: Guilt free ivory. In: Proceedings of the 8th ACM SIGPLAN Symposium on Haskell, pp. 189–200. ACM (2015)
8. Axelsson, E., Claessen, K., Dévai, G., Horváth, Z., Keijzer, K., Lyckegård, B., Persson, A., Sheeran, M., Svenningsson, J., Vajdax, A.: Feldspar: a domain specific language for digital signal processing algorithms. In: MEMOCODE 2010, pp. 169–178 (2010)
9. Axelsson, E., Claessen, K., Sheeran, M., Svenningsson, J., Engdal, D., Persson, A.: The design and implementation of feldspar. In: Hage, J., Morazán, M.T. (eds.) IFL 2010. LNCS, vol. 6647, pp. 121–136. Springer, Heidelberg (2011)
10. Persson, A., Axelsson, E., Svenningsson, J.: Generic monadic constructs for embedded languages. In: Gill, A., Hage, J. (eds.) IFL 2011. LNCS, vol. 7257, pp. 85–99. Springer, Heidelberg (2012)
11. Sculthorpe, N., Bracker, J., Giorgidze, G., Gill, A.: The constrained-monad problem. In: Proceedings of the 18th ACM SIGPLAN International Conference on Functional Programming, pp. 287–298. ACM (2013)
12. Farmer, A., Sculthorpe, N., Gill, A.: Reasoning with the HERMIT: tool support for equational reasoning on GHC core programs. In: Proceedings of the 8th ACM SIGPLAN Symposium on Haskell, pp. 23–34. ACM (2015)
13. Svenningsson, J., Axelsson, E.: Combining deep and shallow embedding for EDSL. In: Loidl, H.-W., Peña, R. (eds.) TFP 2012. LNCS, vol. 7829, pp. 21–36. Springer, Heidelberg (2013)
14. Svenningsson, J.D., Svensson, B.J.: Simple and compositional reification of monadic embedded languages. In: Proceedings of the 18th International Conference on Functional Programming, pp. 299–304. ACM (2013)

From Monads to Effects and Back

Niki Vazou[1][(✉)] and Daan Leijen[2]

[1] UC San Diego, San Diego, USA
nvazou@cs.ucsd.edu
[2] Microsoft Research, Redmond, USA

Abstract. The combination of monads and effects leads to a clean and easy to reason about programming paradigm. Monadic programming is easy to reason about, but can be cumbersome, as it requires explicit lifting and binding. In this paper, we combine monads and effects within a single programming paradigm: we use monads to *define* the semantics of effect types, and then, use the effects to *program* with those monads. We implemented an extension to the effect type system of Koka [15] with *user defined effects*. We use a type-directed translation to automatically lift effectful into monadic programs, by inserting bind - and unit operations.

1 Introduction

Monads (proposed by Moggi and others [17,29]) are used in programming languages to wrap effectful computations, but they can be cumbersome to program with as they require explicit lifting and binding. In this paper, we combine *monads* and *effect typing* (proposed by Gifford and others [9,26]) within a single programming paradigm: we use monads to *define* the semantics of effect types, and then, use the effect types to *program* with those monads.

We implemented these ideas as an extension of the effect type system of Koka [15] – a strict, JavaScript-like, strongly typed programming language that automatically infers the type and *effect* of functions. Koka has a type inference system for a set of standard effects like divergence, exceptions, heap operations, input/output, etc. Here we extend the effect system with *monadic user defined effects*, where we can define our own effect in terms of any monad. As an example, we define an *amb* effect for ambiguous computations [13]. In particular we would like to have ambiguous operations that return *one* of many potential values, but in the end get a list of *all* possible outcomes of the ambiguous computation. Using our new **effect** declaration we can define the semantics of the *amb* effect in terms of a concrete list monad:

```
effect amb⟨a⟩ = list⟨a⟩ {
  function unit( x )    { [x] }
  function bind( xs, f ) { xs.concatMap(f) }
}
```

where the *unit* and *bind* are the usual list-monad definitions.

© Springer International Publishing Switzerland 2016
M. Gavanelli and J. Reppy (Eds.): PADL 2016, LNCS 9585, pp. 169–186, 2016.
DOI: 10.1007/978-3-319-28228-2_11

Using the above effect definition we can write functions that have the *amb*iguous effect. For example we can write a *flip* primitive that returns either true or false and use it to compute the truth table of *xor*:

function *flip* : () → *amb bool*

```
function xor() : amb bool {
  val p = flip()
  val q = flip()
  (p || q) && not(p&&q)     // p,q : bool
}
```

Note how the result of *flip* is just typed as *bool* (even though *amb* computations internally use a list monad of *all* possible results). Furthermore, unlike languages like Haskell, we do not need to explicitly lift expressions into a monad, or explicitly bind computations using *do* notation.

Translation. Koka uses an *automatic type directed translation* that translates a program with user-defined effect types into a corresponding monadic program. Internally, the previous example gets translated into:

```
function xor() : list⟨bool⟩ {
  bind( flip(), fun(p) {
  bind( flip(), fun(q) {
    unit( (p || q) && not(p&&q) )
})})}
```

Here we see how the *unit* and *bind* of the effect declaration are used: *bind* is inserted when a monadic value is returned and passed the current continuation.

The capture of the continuation at every *bind* makes monadic effects very expressive. For example, the *amb* effect can cause subsequent statements to be executed multiple times, i.e. once for every possible result. This is somewhat dual to the built-in exception effect which can cause subsequent statements to not be executed at all, i.e. when an exception is thrown. As such, this kind of expressiveness effectively let us take "control of the semi-colon".

Our *contributions* are summarized as follows:

- Using the correspondence between monads and effects [30], we propose a novel system where you *define* the semantics of an effect in terms of a first-class monadic value, but you *use* the monad using a first-class effect type. We build on the existing Koka type system [15] to incorporate monadic effects with full polymorphic and higher-order effect inference.
- We propose (Sect. 3) a sound *type directed monadic translation* that transforms a program with effect types into one with corresponding monadic types. This translation builds on our earlier work on monadic programming in ML [25] and automatically lifts and binds computations.
- In contrast to programming with monads directly (as in Haskell), programming with monadic effects integrates seamlessly with built-in effects where there is no need for families of functions like *map*, and *mapM*, or other special monadic syntax, as we further explain in Sect. 2.2.1.

2 Overview

Types tell us about the behavior of functions. For example, the ML type $int{\rightarrow}int$ of a function tells us that the function is well defined on inputs of type int and returns values of type int. But that is only *one* part of the story, the ML type tells us nothing about all *other* behaviors: i.e. if it accesses the file system perhaps, or throws exceptions, or never returns a result at all.

Koka is a strict programming language with a type system that tracks effects. The type of a function in Koka is of the form $\tau{\rightarrow}\epsilon\ \tau'$ signifying a function that takes an argument of type τ, returns a result of type τ' *and may* have a side effect ϵ. We can leave out the effect and write $\tau{\rightarrow}\tau'$ as a shorthand for the total function without any side effect: $\tau{\rightarrow}\langle\rangle\ \tau'$. A key observation on Moggi's early work on monads [17] was that *values* and *computations* should be assigned a different type. Koka applies that principle where effect types only occur on function types; and any other type, like int, truly designates an evaluated value that cannot have any effect.

In contrast to many other effect systems, the effect types are not just labels that are propagated but they truly describe the semantics of each function. As such, it is essential that the basic effects include exceptions (exn) and divergence (div). The deep connection between the effect types and the semantics leads to strong reasoning principles. For example, Koka's soundness theorem [15] implies that if the final program does not have an exn effect, then its execution *never* results in an exception (and similarly for divergence and state).

The main contribution of this paper is how we extend Koka so that the user can define her own effects, by specifying the type and meaning of new effects and defining primitive operations on them.

2.1 The Ambiguous Effect

In the introduction we saw how one can define and use the ambiguous *amb* effect with *flip* and *xor* operations. We now discuss the definition and translation in more detail. The *amb* effect is defined using an `effect` declaration:

```
effect amb⟨a⟩ = list⟨a⟩ {
  function unit( x : a ) : list⟨a⟩ { [x] }
  function bind( xs : list⟨a⟩, f : a → e list⟨b⟩ ) : e list⟨b⟩ {
    xs.concatMap(f)
  }
}
```

Defining the *amb* effect amounts to defining the standard list monad, which can be further simplified by removing the *optional* type annotations. Given the above definition, a new effect type *amb* is introduced, and we know:

1. how to *represent* (internally) ambiguous computations of a values: as a $list\langle a\rangle$
2. how to *lift* plain values into ambiguous ones: using *unit*, and
3. how to *combine* ambiguous computations: using *bind*.

Moreover, with the above definition Koka *automatically* generates the *to_amb* and *from_amb* primitives, and a monadic type alias:

function *to_amb*   (*xs* : *list⟨a⟩*)   : *amb a*
function *from_amb* (*action* : () → *amb a*) : *list⟨a⟩*
alias *M_amb⟨a⟩* = *list⟨a⟩*

that allow us to go from monadic values to effect types and vice versa. These are typed versions of the *reify* and *reflect* methods of Filinski's embedding [6].

We use the above primitives to define *flip* that creates the *amb*iguous effect and *main* that evaluates the effectful computation:

function *flip*() : *amb bool* { *to_amb*([*False, True*]) }

function *main*() : *console* () { *print*(*from_amb*(*xor*)) }

When we evaluate *main* we get a list of *all* possible output values: [*False, True, True, False*]. One can extend such mechanism to, for example, return a histogram of the results, or to general probabilistic results [13,25].

2.2   Translating Effects

Koka uses a *type directed* translation to internally translate effectful to monadic code. As shown in the introduction, the *xor* function is translated as:

```
function xor() : amb bool                function xor() : list⟨bool⟩
{                                        {
  val p = flip()                           bind( flip(), fun(p) {
  val q = flip()              ⤳             bind( flip(), fun(q) {
                                              unit(
  (p || q) && not(p&&q)                         (p || q) && not(p&&q) )
}                                        })})}
```

In particular, *bind* is inserted at every point where a monadic value is returned, and passed the current continuation at that point. Since *flip* has an ambiguous result, our type-directed translation binds its result to a function that takes p as an argument and similarly for q. Finally, the last line returns a pure boolean value, but *xor*'s result type is ambiguous. We use *unit* to lift the pure value to the ambiguous monad. We note that in Koka's actual translation, *xor* is translated more efficiently using a single *map* instead of a *unit* and *bind*.

The translation to monadic code is quite subtle and relies crucially on type information provided by type inference. In particular, the intermediate core language is explicitly typed à la System F (Sect. 3.1). This way, we compute effects precisely and determine where *bind* and *unit* get inserted (Sect. 3.3). Moreover, we rely on the user to ensure that the *unit* and *bind* operations satisfy the monad laws [29], i.e. that *unit* is a left- and right identity for *bind*, and that *bind* is associative. This is usually the case though; in particular because the effect typing discipline ensures that both *unit* and *bind* are *total* and cannot have any side-effect (which makes the translation semantically robust against rewrites).

```
// source effectful code                    // translated monadic code
function map(xs, f) {                        function map(d : dict⟨e⟩, xs, f) {
  match(xs) {                                  match(xs) {
    Nil → Nil                                    Nil → d.unit(Nil)
    Cons(y, ys) →                                Cons(y, ys) →
      val z  = f(y)                                d.bind( f(y), fun(z) {
      val zs = map(ys, f)                          d.bind( map(ys, f),
      Cons(z, zs)                                    fun(zs) {
                                                       d.unit(Cons(z, zs)
  }                                              })})}
}                                            }

function xor() {                             function xor() {
  val [p,q] =                                  dict_amb.bind(
    map( [1,2],                                  map( dict_amb, [1,2],
      fun(_) { flip() })                           fun(_) { flip() }),
                                               fun([p,q]) {
                                                 dict_amb.unit(
  (p || q) && not(p&&q)                            (p || q) && not(p&&q))
                                               })
}                                            }
```

Fig. 1. Dictionary translation of *map* and *xor*

2.2.1   Translating Polymorphic Effects

One of the crucial features of Koka is effect polymorphism. Consider the function
map

```
function map(xs : list⟨a⟩, f : (a) → e b) : e list⟨b⟩ {
  match(xs) {
    Nil → Nil
    Cons(y, ys) → Cons( f(y), map(ys,f) )
}}
```

The function *map* takes as input a function f with some effect e. Since it calls
f, *map* can itself produce the effect e, *for any* effect e. This means that we can
use such existing abstractions on user defined effects too:

```
function xor() {
  val [p,q] = map( [1,2], fun(_) { flip() } )
  (p || q) && not(p&&q)
}
```

Unfortunately, this leads to trouble when doing a type directed translation: since
the function passed to *map* has a monadic effect, we need to *bind* the call $f(y)$
inside the *map* function! Moreover, since we can apply *map* to *any* monadic
effect, we need to dynamically call the right *bind* function.

The remedy is to pass Haskell-like *dictionaries* or monad interfaces to effect
polymorphic functions. In our case, a dictionary is a structure that wraps the

monadic operators *bind* and *unit*. The dictionaries are transparent to the user and are automatically generated and inserted. During the translation, every effect polymorphic function takes a dictionary as an additional first argument. Figure 1 shows how the *map* function gets translated.

Now that internally every effect polymorphic function gets an extra dictionary argument, we need to ensure the corresponding dictionary is supplied at every call-site. Once again, dictionary instantiation is type-directed and builds upon Koka's explicitly typed intermediate core language. Whenever a polymorphic effect function is instantiated with a specific effect, the type directed translation automatically inserts the corresponding dictionary argument. Figure 1 shows this in action when we call *map* inside the *xor* function. We can still use *map* with code that has a non-monadic effect and in that case the translation will use the dictionary of the primitive identity monad, e.g. *map*(*dict_id*, [1,2], *sqr*).

Being able to reuse any previous abstractions when using monadic effects is very powerful. If we insert user-defined effects to a function, only the type of the function changes. Contrast this to Haskell: when inserting a monad, we need to do a non-trivial conversion of the syntax to *do* notation, but also we need to define and use monadic counterparts of standard functions, like *mapM* for *map*.

Koka allows combination of user defined effects. Consider a behavior user defined effect, which represents computations whose value varies with time, as in functional reactive programs [5]. We encode the *beh* effect as a function from *time* to *a*. Since a *beh*aviour is a function, it may have effects itself: it can diverge or throw exceptions for example. This means that we need to parameterize the *beh* effect with two type parameters one for the value *a* and one for the effect *e*:

effect $beh\langle e, a\rangle = time \rightarrow e\ a\ \{\ ...\ \}$

With the above definition, Koka automatically creates a type alias for the behavioral monad and the respective *unit* and *bind* operators:

alias $M\_beh\langle e, a\rangle = time \rightarrow e\ a;$
$ub : a \rightarrow e\ M\_beh\langle e, a\rangle;$
$bb : (M\_beh\langle e, a\rangle, a \rightarrow e\ M\_beh\langle e, b\rangle) \rightarrow e\ M\_beh\langle e, b\rangle$

As with the *amb* effect, the user can define primitives that, for example, return the temperature and humidity over time:

$temp : () \rightarrow beh\ int;$
$hum : () \rightarrow beh\ int;$

We use these primitives to define a function that states that one goes out when temperature is more than 70°F and humidity less than 80%. Koka automatically translates the effectful function to its monadic version:

```
function go_out() : beh bool{              function go_out() : time → bool{
    val t = temp()                             bb( temp(), fun(t) {
    val h = hum()              ⤳               bb( hum(), fun(h) { ub(
    (t ≥ 70 && h ≤ 80)                              (t ≥ 70 && h ≤ 80)
}                                          })})}
```

Next, we want to insert ambiguity into the above function. Following Swamy et al. [25] we combine the ambiguous and behavioral effects by tupling them

effect $\langle amb, beh \rangle \langle e, a \rangle \; = \; time \rightarrow e \; list\langle a \rangle \; \{ \; ... \; \}$

and Koka creates the appropriate monadic operators

alias $M\_ab\langle e, a \rangle = time \rightarrow e \; list\langle a \rangle$;
$uab : a \rightarrow e \; M\_ab\langle e, a \rangle$;
$bab : (M\_ab\langle e, a \rangle, a \rightarrow e \; M\_ab\langle e, b \rangle) \rightarrow e \; M\_ab\langle e, b \rangle$;

Then, we define morphisms to lift from a single to the joined effect

morphism amb $\langle amb, beh \rangle\{$ fun$(xs)\{$ fun$(t)\{$ xs $\}\}$ $\}$
morphism beh $\langle amb, beh \rangle\{$ fun$(b)\{$ fun$(t)\{$ $[b(t)]$ $\}\}$ $\}$

With the above morphism definitions, Koka derives internal morphism functions

$a2ab :: M\_amb \; \langle e, a \rangle \rightarrow e \; M\_\langle amb, beh \rangle \langle e, a \rangle$;
$b2ab :: M\_beh \; \langle e, a \rangle \rightarrow e \; M\_\langle amb, beh \rangle \langle e, a \rangle$;

and use them to automatically translate our modified *go_out* function that combines the two user defined effects:

```
function go_out()
{
  val t = temp()
  val h = hum()
  val u = flip()

  (u || (t ≥ 70 && h ≤ 80))
}
```

$\rightsquigarrow$

```
function go_out()
{
  bab( b2ab(temp()), fun(t) {
   bab( b2ab(hum()), fun(h) {
    bab( a2ab(flip()), fun(u) {
     uab(
      (u || (t ≥ 70 && h ≤ 80))
  })})}
```

This technique for combining monads by tupling is taken from [25]. But, as further discussed in Sect. 4 our current work, though highly inspired, crucially differs from [25] in that the use of effect polymorphism (instead of effect subtyping that was previously used) makes types much simpler.

There are various language design aspects with regard to morphism declarations – here we highlight the most important ones and defer to [12,25] for a more in-depth discussion. First of all, since effect rows are equivalent up to re-ordering of labels, we can only declare one combined monad for a specific set of user-defined effects. For example, we can combine $\langle amb, beh \rangle$ in only one of the two possible ways (within the scope of a module), where the compiler rejects duplicate definitions. Finally, if we assume that the morphism laws hold, the compiler could derive morphisms from the existing ones, i.e. morphisms from ma to mb, and mb to mc can be combined to give rise to a morphism from ma to mc. Currently, we assume that the user provides all required morphisms explicitly, but we plan to implement automatic morphism derivation.

3   Formalism

In this section we formalize the type-directed translation using an explicitly typed effect calculus we call $\lambda^{\kappa u}$. First, we present the syntax (Sect. 3.1) and

expressions	e	::=	$x^\sigma \mid c^\sigma \mid e\,e$	
			$\mid \quad \lambda^\epsilon x : \sigma.\,e$	
			$\mid \quad \text{val } x^\sigma = e; e$	
			$\mid \quad \text{if } e \text{ then } e \text{ else } e$	
			$\mid \quad e\,[\sigma] \mid \Lambda\alpha^\kappa.\,e$	

| types | τ^κ | ::= | α^κ | type variable |
| | | | $\mid \quad c^{\kappa_0}\langle \tau_1^{\kappa_1}, ..., \tau_n^{\kappa_n}\rangle$ | $\kappa_0 = (\kappa_1,...,\kappa_n) \to \kappa$ |

kinds	κ	::=	$* \mid \text{e}$	values, effects
			$\mid \quad \text{k}$	effect constants
			$\mid \quad \text{u}$	user effects
			$\mid \quad (\kappa_1, ..., \kappa_n) \to \kappa$	type constructor

| type scheme | σ | ::= | $\forall\alpha^\kappa.\,\sigma \mid \tau^*$ | |

const	(), $bool$	::	$*$	unit, bool type
	$(\_ \to \_\_)$	::	$(*, \text{e}, *) \to *$	functions
	$\langle\rangle$	::	e	empty effect
	$\langle\_ \mid\_\rangle$	::	$(\text{k}, \text{e}) \to \text{e}$	effect extension
	user$\langle\_\rangle$	::	$\text{u} \to \text{k}$	user effects
	tdict$\langle\_\rangle$	::	$\text{e} \to *$	effect to universe

Syntactic sugar:

effects	ϵ	$\doteq$	τ^e
effect variables	μ	$\doteq$	α^e
closed effects	$\langle l_1, ..., l_n\rangle$	$\doteq$	$\langle l_1, ..., l_n \mid \langle\rangle\rangle$
single effect	l	$\doteq$	$\langle l\rangle$
user effects	l^u	$\doteq$	user$\langle l^\text{u}\rangle$

Fig. 2. Syntax of explicitly typed Koka, $\lambda^{\kappa u}$.

typing (Sect. 3.2) rules for $\lambda^{\kappa u}$. Then, we formalize our translation (Sect. 3.3) from effectful to monadic $\lambda^{\kappa u}$. Finally, we prove soundness (Sect. 3.4) by proving type preservation.

3.1   Syntax

Figure 2 defines the syntax of expressions and types of $\lambda^{\kappa u}$, a polymorphic explicitly typed λ-calculus. $\lambda^{\kappa u}$ is System F [10,22] extended with effect types.

Expressions. $\lambda^{\kappa u}$ expressions include typed variables x^σ, typed constants c^σ, λ-abstraction $\lambda^\epsilon x : \sigma.\,e$, application $e\,e$, value bindings val $x^\sigma = e; e$, if combinators if e then e else e, type application $e\,[\sigma]$ and type abstraction $\Lambda\alpha^\kappa.\,e$. Each value variable is annotated with its type and each type variable is annotated with its kind. Finally, each λ-abstraction $\lambda^\epsilon x : \sigma.\,e$ is annotated with its result effect ϵ which is necessary to check effect types.

Type and Effect Checking $\boxed{\vdash e \,:\, \sigma \,|\, \epsilon}$

$$\frac{}{\vdash c^\sigma \,:\, \sigma \,|\, \epsilon} \qquad \frac{\vdash e \,:\, \forall\alpha.\,\sigma \,|\, \epsilon}{\vdash e[\tau] \,:\, \sigma[\alpha \mapsto \tau] \,|\, \epsilon} \qquad \frac{\vdash e \,:\, \sigma \,|\, \langle\rangle}{\vdash \Lambda\alpha^\kappa.\,e \,:\, \forall\alpha^\kappa.\,\sigma \,|\, \epsilon}$$

$$\frac{}{\vdash x^\sigma \,:\, \sigma \,|\, \epsilon} \qquad \frac{\vdash e \,:\, \tau_2 \,|\, \epsilon}{\vdash \lambda^\epsilon x : \tau_1.\,e \,:\, \tau_1 \to \epsilon\, \tau_2 \,|\, \epsilon'} \qquad \frac{\vdash e_1 \,:\, \tau_1 \to \epsilon\, \tau_2 \,|\, \epsilon \quad \vdash e_2 \,:\, \tau_1 \,|\, \epsilon}{\vdash e_1\, e_2 \,:\, \tau_2 \,|\, \epsilon}$$

$$\frac{\vdash e_1 \,:\, \sigma_1 \,|\, \epsilon \quad \vdash e_2 \,:\, \sigma_2 \,|\, \epsilon}{\vdash \mathsf{val}\, x \,=\, e_1;\, e_2 \,:\, \sigma_2 \,|\, \epsilon} \qquad \frac{\vdash e \,:\, \mathsf{bool} \,|\, \epsilon \quad \vdash e_1 \,:\, \sigma \,|\, \epsilon \quad \vdash e_2 \,:\, \sigma \,|\, \epsilon}{\vdash \mathsf{if}\, e\, \mathsf{then}\, e_1\, \mathsf{else}\, e_2 \,:\, \sigma \,|\, \epsilon}$$

Type Checking $\boxed{\vdash e \,:\, \sigma}$

$$\frac{\vdash e \,:\, \sigma \,|\, \epsilon}{\vdash e \,:\, \sigma}$$

Fig. 3. Type rules for explicitly typed Koka.

Types and Type Schemes. Types consist of explicitly kinded type variables α^κ and application of constant type constructors $c^{\kappa_0}\langle\tau_1^{\kappa_1}, ..., \tau_n^{\kappa_n}\rangle$, where the type constructor c has the appropriate kind $\kappa_0 = (\kappa_1, ..., \kappa_n) \to \kappa$. We do not provide special syntax for function types, as they can be modeled by the constructor $(\_ \to \_ \_) :: (*, \mathsf{e}, *) \to *$ that, unlike the usual function type, explicitly reasons for the effect produced by the function. Finally, types can be qualified over type variables to yield type schemata.

Kinds. Well-formedness of types is guaranteed by a kind system. We annotate the type τ with its kind κ, as τ^κ. We have the kind of types $(*)$ and the kind of functions $\to$, kinds for effect rows (e), effect constants (k), and user-defined effects (u). We omit the kind κ of the type τ^κ, and write τ, when κ is immediately apparent or not relevant. For clarity, we use α for regular type variables and μ for effect type variables. Finally, we write ϵ for effects, i.e. types of kind e.

Effects. Effects *are* types. Effect types are defined as a row of effect labels l. Such effect row is either empty $\langle\rangle$, a polymorphic effect variable μ, or an extension of an effect row ϵ with an effect constant l, written as $\langle l | \epsilon\rangle$. Effect constants are either built-in Koka effects, i.e. anything that is interesting to our language like exceptions (exn), divergence (div) etc. or lifted user-defined monadic effects like the ambiguous effect $\mathsf{amb}^\mathsf{u} :: \mathsf{u}$. Note that for an effect row to be well-formed we use the user effect function to lift $\mathsf{user}\langle\mathsf{amb}^\mathsf{u}\rangle :: \mathsf{k}$ to the appropriate kind k. For simplicity, in the rest of this section we omit the explicit lifting and write amb^u to denote $\mathsf{user}\langle\mathsf{amb}^\mathsf{u}\rangle$ when a label of kind k is expected.

Finally, Fig. 2 includes definition of type constants and syntactic sugar required to simplify the rest of this section.

Type Rules. Figure 3 describes type rules for $\lambda^{\kappa\mathsf{u}}$ where the judgment $\vdash e \,:\, \sigma \,|\, \epsilon$ assigns type σ and effect ϵ to an expression e. All the rules are equivalent to the System F rules, except for rule (Lam) where the effect of the function in the type is drawn from the effect annotation in the λ-abstraction. $\lambda^{\kappa\mathsf{u}}$ is explicitly typed, in that variables are annotated with their type and functions with their

Declarations of User Effects and Morphisms $\boxed{\Gamma \vdash def : \Gamma}$

$$(\text{Eff}) \; \dfrac{\begin{array}{c} \Gamma, \mu^e, \alpha^* \vdash_k \tau :: *\quad \Gamma' = \Gamma,\; M_{eff}\langle \mu, \alpha \rangle = \tau \quad \Gamma' \vdash_k e_1 \; : \; \forall \alpha \mu.\, \alpha \to \mu\; M_{eff}\langle \mu, \alpha \rangle \\ \Gamma' \vdash_k e_2 \; : \; \forall \mu \alpha \beta.\, (M_{eff}\langle \mu, \alpha \rangle,\; \alpha \to \mu\; M_{eff}\langle \mu, \beta \rangle) \to \mu\; M_{eff}\langle \mu, \beta \rangle \end{array}}{\begin{array}{c} \Gamma \vdash \mathsf{effect}\; eff\langle \mu, \alpha \rangle \; = \; \tau \; \{\; unit \; = \; e_1;\; bind \; = \; e_2 \; \} \; : \\ \Gamma',\; eff^u,\; dict_{eff} \; : \; tdict\langle M_{eff}\rangle \\ to_{eff} \; : \; \forall \alpha \mu.\, (M_{eff}\langle \mu, \alpha \rangle) \to \langle eff | \mu \rangle\, \alpha, \\ from_{eff} \; : \; \forall \alpha \beta \mu.\, (() \to \langle eff | \mu \rangle\, \alpha) \to \mu\; M_{eff}\langle \mu, \alpha \rangle \end{array}}$$

$$(\text{Morph}) \; \dfrac{s \equiv \langle l_1, ..., l_n \rangle \quad t \equiv \langle l_1, ..., l_n, ..., l_m \rangle \quad \Gamma \vdash_k e \; : \; \forall \alpha \mu.\, M_s\langle \mu,\, \alpha \rangle \to \mu\; M_t\langle \mu,\, \alpha \rangle}{\Gamma \vdash \mathsf{morphism}\; s\; t\; \{\, e\, \} \; :\! \Gamma,\; s \rhd t \; : \; \forall \alpha \mu.\, M_s\langle \mu,\, \alpha \rangle \to \mu\; M_t\langle \mu,\, \alpha \rangle}$$

Fig. 4. Type rule for effect and morphism declarations.

effect, hence, type checking does not require an environment. By construction, the Koka type inference rules always produce well-formed $\lambda^{\kappa u}$. Soundness of $\lambda^{\kappa u}$ follows from soundness of Koka as described in [15]. Next, we write $\vdash e \; : \; \sigma$ if there exists a derivation $\vdash e \; : \; \sigma | \epsilon$ for some effect ϵ.

3.2 Type Inference for Effect and Morphism Declarations

In this subsection we present how Koka preprocesses the effect and morphism declarations provided by the user. Figure 4 summarizes the rules that the Koka compiler follows to desugar the user definitions to $\lambda^{\kappa u}$. After desugaring, Koka proceeds to effect- and type- inference as presented in previous work [14, 15].

3.2.1 Effect Declarations
Before we look at the general type inference rule for effect declarations we start with describing the identity effect uid:

```
effect uid⟨e,a⟩ = a {
  function unit(x) { x }
  function bind(x,f) { f(x) }
}
```

From the above effect definition, initially, Koka generates a type alias that relates the effect name with its monadic representation.

$\qquad$ alias $M_{uid}\langle \epsilon, \alpha \rangle \; = \; \alpha$

Then, Koka checks well-formedness of the effect definition, by (type-) checking that $unit$ and $bind$ are the appropriate monadic operators, i.e.:

$\qquad unit \; : \; \forall \alpha \mu.\, \alpha \to \mu\; M_{uid}\langle \mu, \alpha \rangle$
$\qquad bind \; : \; \forall \alpha \beta \mu.\, (M_{uid}\langle \mu, \alpha \rangle,\; \alpha \to \mu\; M_{uid}\langle \mu, \beta \rangle) \to \mu\; M_{uid}\langle \mu, \beta \rangle$

Given the definitions of $unit$ and $bind$, Koka *automatically* constructs the primitives required by the rest of the program to safely manipulate the identity effect:

- uid^u – the effect constant that can be used inside types,
- to_{uid} : $\forall \alpha \mu. (M_{uid}\langle \mu, \alpha \rangle) \rightarrow \langle uid | \mu \rangle \alpha$ – the function that converts monadic computations to effectful ones,
- $from_{uid}$: $\forall \alpha \beta \mu. (() \rightarrow \langle uid | \mu \rangle \alpha) \rightarrow \mu \ M_{uid}\langle \mu, \alpha \rangle$ – the dual function that converts effectful function to their monadic equivalent, and finally,
- $dict_{uid}$ – the (internal) effect dictionary that stores uid's monadic operators.

Dictionaries. The first three values are user-visible but the final dictionary value is only used internally during the monadic translation. The type of the effect dictionary (e.g. $dict_{uid}$), is a structure that contains the monadic operators *unit* and *bind* of the effect. It can also include the monadic *map* which will otherwise be automatically derived from *unit* and *bind*. Thus, we define the dictionary structure as a type that is polymorphic on the particular monad, represented as type variable $m :: (e, *) \rightarrow *$:

```
struct tdict⟨m⟩ {
    unit : ∀αμ. α→ μ m⟨μ, α⟩
    map  : ∀αβμ. (m⟨μ, α⟩, α→ β) → μ m⟨μ, β⟩
    bind : ∀αβμ. (m⟨μ, α⟩, α→ μ m⟨μ, β⟩) → μ m⟨μ, β⟩
```

With this we can type $dict_{uid}$: $tdict\langle M_{uid} \rangle$.

General User-defined Effects. Figure 4 generalizes the previous concrete example to any user-defined effect declaration. The judgment:

$$\Gamma \vdash \text{effect } eff\langle \mu, \alpha \rangle = \tau\langle \mu, \alpha \rangle \ \{ \ unit = e_1; \ bind = e_2 \ \} : \Gamma'$$

states that under a kind- and type- environment Γ, the effect declaration *eff* results in the type environment Γ' that is extended with the needed types and primitives implied by *eff*. As shown in Fig. 4, we first check well-formedness of the effect types, then check that *unit* and *bind* operations have the proper types. Finally, the environment is extended with these types and values.

3.2.2 Morphism Declarations

As a morphism example, we assume the existence of the two user defined effects from the Overview (Sect. 2), the *amb*iguous and the *beh*aviour. Moreover, we assume that the user appropriately defined their joined effect $\langle amb, beh \rangle$. These three effect definitions yield three aliases:

```
alias M_amb⟨ε, α⟩ = list⟨α⟩
alias M_beh⟨ε, α⟩ = time →ε α
alias M_⟨amb, beh⟩⟨ε, α⟩ = time →ε list⟨α⟩
```

The user can define morphisms that go from *amb* or *beh* to $\langle amb, beh \rangle$

```
morphism amb ⟨amb, beh⟩ {          morphism beh ⟨amb, beh⟩ {
  fun(xs : list⟨a⟩) : time → e list⟨a⟩{     fun(x : time → e a) : time → e list⟨a⟩{
    fun(t){xs}                               fun(t){[x(t)]}
}}                                         }}
```

From the above definitions, Koka will generate two morphism functions:

$$amb \rhd \langle amb, beh \rangle \; : \; \forall \alpha \mu. \, M_{amb} \langle \mu, \alpha \rangle \rightarrow \mu \; M_{\langle amb, beh \rangle} \langle \mu, \alpha \rangle$$
$$beh \rhd \langle amb, beh \rangle \; : \; \forall \alpha \mu. \, M_{beh} \langle \mu, \alpha \rangle \rightarrow \mu \; M_{\langle amb, beh \rangle} \langle \mu, \alpha \rangle$$

The above morphisms are internal Koka functions that will be used at the translation phase to appropriately lift the monadic computations.

General User-defined Morphisms. Figure 4 generalizes the previous concrete example to any morphism declaration. The judgment $\Gamma \vdash$ morphism $s\ t\ e\ :\ \Gamma'$. states that under a kind- and type- environment Γ, the morphism declaration from effect raws s to t results in a new type environment Γ' that is extended with the morphism from the source effect s to the target effect t, when the expression e has the appropriate morphism type. The first premise ensures that s is always a sub-effect of the target effect t.

3.3   Type-Directed Monadic Translation

Next, we define the type-directed monadic translation $e \rightsquigarrow_\epsilon e' \mid \upsilon$ that takes an effect expression e to the monadic expression e'.

Computed Effects. Our translation needs two effects ϵ and υ: the *maximum* (inferred) effect ϵ and the *minimum* (computed) effect υ. After type inference, every function body has one unified effect ϵ, that consists of the unification of all the effects in that function. Our translation computes bottom-up the minimal user-defined portion of each separate sub-expression, where υ should always be contained in ϵ. Specifically, we define *computed effects* υ as effect types ϵ that have the following grammar: $\upsilon ::= \mu \mid \langle l_1^\mu, \, ..., \, l_n^\mu \rangle \; (n \geq 0)$

Thus, computed effects can be a row of user-effect labels (including the empty row) or an effect variable. Note that because user effects are always constants, and according to the equivalence rules for rows [15], we consider computed effect rows equal up to reordering. For example $\langle l_2^\mu, l_1^\mu \rangle \equiv \langle l_1^\mu, l_2^\mu \rangle$.

The computed effects are syntactically restricted in that a row of monadic effects cannot end with a polymorphic tail μ. This limits the functions that a user can write: no user-defined effects can be in a row that has a polymorphic tail.

We convert a regular effect type ϵ to a computed effect $\overline{\epsilon}$, and dually, we apply $\tilde{\epsilon}$ to an effect ϵ to remove the user defined effects:

$$\begin{aligned}
\overline{\langle l^\mu \mid \epsilon \rangle} &= \langle l^\mu \mid \overline{\epsilon} \rangle \text{ if } \overline{\epsilon} \neq \mu & \langle l^\mu \mid \tilde{\epsilon} \rangle &= \tilde{\epsilon} \\
\overline{\langle l^\kappa \mid \epsilon \rangle} &= \overline{\epsilon} \quad\quad \text{ if } \kappa \neq u & \langle l^\kappa \mid \tilde{\epsilon} \rangle &= \langle l^\kappa \mid \tilde{\epsilon} \rangle \\
\overline{\langle \rangle} &= \langle \rangle & \tilde{\langle \rangle} &= \langle \rangle \\
\overline{\mu} &= \mu & \tilde{\mu} &= \mu
\end{aligned}$$

The above function is partial: when called with a type that combines a user-defined effect with a polymorphic tail it fails and the compiler raises an error.

$$\mathsf{bind}^v_{\langle\rangle}(\epsilon, e_x, x, e) = \mathsf{val}\ x\ =\ e_x;\ e$$
$$\mathsf{bind}^{\langle\rangle}_{v_x}(\epsilon, e_x, x, e) = dict_{v_x}.map\ \langle\sigma_x, \sigma, \epsilon\rangle(e_x, \lambda^{\langle\rangle}\ x\ :\ \sigma_x.\ e)$$
$$\qquad\qquad \mathsf{with} \vdash e_x : \mathsf{mon}\langle v_x, \epsilon, \sigma_x\rangle,\ \vdash e : \sigma$$
$$\mathsf{bind}^v_{v_x}(\epsilon, e_x, x, e) = dict_{v_x \oplus v}.bind\langle\sigma_x, \sigma, \epsilon\rangle(e'_x, e')$$
$$\qquad\qquad \mathsf{with} \vdash e_x : \mathsf{mon}\langle v_x, \epsilon, \sigma_x\rangle,\ \vdash e : \mathsf{mon}\langle v, \epsilon, \sigma\rangle$$
$$\qquad\qquad e'_x\ =\ \mathsf{lift}^{(v_x\ \oplus v)}_{v_x}(\epsilon, e_x),\ e'\ =\ \lambda^{\tilde{\epsilon}}\ x\ :\ \sigma_x.\,(\mathsf{lift}^{(v_x\ \oplus v)}_{v}(\epsilon, e))$$

$$\mathsf{lift}^v_v(\epsilon, e)\quad =\ e$$
$$\mathsf{lift}^v_{\langle\rangle}(\epsilon, e)\quad =\ dict_v.unit\langle\sigma,\ \epsilon\rangle(e)\ \text{where}\ v \neq \langle\rangle,\ \vdash e : \sigma$$
$$\mathsf{lift}^{v_t}_{v_s}(\epsilon, e)\quad =\ v_s \triangleright v_t\langle\sigma,\ \epsilon\rangle(e)\quad \text{where} \vdash e\ :\ \mathsf{mon}\langle v_s, \epsilon, \sigma\rangle$$

Fig. 5. Helper functions for binding and lifting.

To join computed effects we use the $\oplus$ operator:

$$\langle\rangle \oplus v_2 \qquad\qquad = v_2$$
$$\mu \oplus \mu \qquad\qquad = \mu$$
$$\langle l\,|\,v_1\rangle \oplus \langle l\,|\,v_2\rangle = \langle l\,|\,v_1 \oplus v_2\rangle$$
$$\langle l\,|\,v_1\rangle \oplus v_2 \quad = \langle l\,|\,v_1 \oplus v_2\rangle \quad \text{if}\ l \notin v_2$$

Again, this function is partial but we can show that the usage in the translation over a well-typed koka program never leads to an undefined case.

Type Translation. The type operator $[\![\cdot]\!]$ translates effectful- to monadic types.

$$[\![\alpha^\kappa]\!] \qquad\qquad = \alpha^\kappa$$
$$[\![\tau \to \epsilon\ \tau']\!] \qquad\quad = [\![\tau]\!] \to \tilde{\epsilon}\,\mathsf{mon}\langle\bar{\epsilon}, \epsilon, [\![\tau']\!]\rangle$$
$$[\![c^\kappa\langle\tau_1, \ldots, \tau_n\rangle]\!] = c^\kappa\langle[\![\tau_1]\!], \ldots, [\![\tau_n]\!]\rangle \qquad with\ c \neq \to$$
$$[\![\forall\alpha^\kappa.\sigma]\!] \qquad\quad = \forall\alpha^\kappa.\,[\![\sigma]\!] \qquad\qquad with\ \kappa \neq \mathsf{e}$$
$$[\![\forall\alpha^\mathsf{e}.\sigma]\!] \qquad\quad = \forall\alpha^\mathsf{e}.\,\mathsf{tdict}\langle\overline{\alpha^\mathsf{e}}\rangle \to \langle\rangle[\![\sigma]\!]$$

For function types $\tau \to \epsilon\ \tau'$ the effect ϵ is split to the build-in effect portion $\tilde{\epsilon}$ and the user-defined portion $\bar{\epsilon}$. The effect of the translated type is only the build-in portion $\tilde{\epsilon}$ while the result is monadically wrapped according to the user-defined portion $\bar{\epsilon}$ using the mon operator

$$\mathsf{mon}\langle\langle\rangle, \epsilon, \sigma\rangle \qquad\qquad = \sigma$$
$$\mathsf{mon}\langle\langle l^\mathsf{u}_1, \ldots, l^\mathsf{u}_n\rangle, \epsilon, \sigma\rangle = M_{\langle l^\mathsf{u}_1, \ldots, l^\mathsf{u}_n\rangle}\langle\epsilon, \sigma\rangle\ \text{where}\ n \geq 1$$
$$\mathsf{mon}\langle\mu, \epsilon, \sigma\rangle \qquad\qquad = (evaluated\ at\ instantiation)$$

The mon operation derives a monadic result type and effect. For polymorphic effect types, mon cannot be computed until instantiation. We therefore keep this type unevaluated until instantiation time. As such, it is really a *dependent type* (or a type parametrized over types). In our case, this is a benign extension to $\lambda^{\kappa u}$ since $\lambda^{\kappa u}$ is explicitly typed. After instantiation, the type argument is not polymorphic, thus mon will return a concrete type.

Translation $\boxed{e \rightsquigarrow_\epsilon e \mid v}$

$$(\textsc{Con}) \quad \frac{}{c^\sigma \rightsquigarrow_\epsilon c^{[\sigma]} \mid \langle\rangle} \qquad\qquad (\textsc{Var}) \quad \frac{}{x^\sigma \rightsquigarrow_\epsilon x^{[\sigma]} \mid \langle\rangle}$$

$$(\textsc{Lam}) \quad \frac{e \rightsquigarrow_\epsilon e' \mid v}{\lambda^\epsilon x : \tau.\, e \rightsquigarrow_{\epsilon_0} \lambda^\epsilon x : [\![\tau]\!].\,\mathsf{lift}_v^{\bar\epsilon}(\epsilon, e') \mid \langle\rangle}$$

$$(\textsc{TLam}) \quad \frac{e \rightsquigarrow_\epsilon e' \mid \langle\rangle \quad \kappa \neq \mathbf{e}}{\Lambda\alpha^\kappa.\, e \rightsquigarrow_\epsilon \Lambda\alpha^\kappa.\, e' \mid \langle\rangle} \qquad (\textsc{TLam-E}) \quad \frac{e \rightsquigarrow_\epsilon e' \mid \langle\rangle}{\Lambda\mu.\, e \rightsquigarrow_\epsilon \Lambda\mu.\lambda^{\langle\rangle}\, dict_\mu : \mathsf{tdict}\langle\overline\mu\rangle.\, e' \mid \langle\rangle}$$

$$(\textsc{TApp}) \quad \frac{e \rightsquigarrow_\epsilon e' \mid v \quad \kappa \neq \mathbf{e}}{e[\tau^\kappa] \rightsquigarrow_\epsilon e' [\![\tau^\kappa]\!] \mid v} \qquad (\textsc{TApp-E}) \quad \frac{e \rightsquigarrow_\epsilon e' \mid v}{e[\epsilon'] \rightsquigarrow_\epsilon e'[\![\epsilon']\!]\, dict_{\overline{[\![\epsilon']\!]}} \mid v}$$

$$(\textsc{App}) \quad \frac{\begin{array}{c} e_1 \rightsquigarrow_\epsilon e_1' \mid v_1 \quad e_2 \rightsquigarrow_\epsilon e_2' \mid v_2 \quad e_1 \downarrow v_3 \quad \vdash e_1 \,:\, \sigma_1 \rightarrow \epsilon\, \sigma_2 \\ v_3 = \bar\epsilon \quad v = v_1 \oplus v_2 \oplus v_3 \end{array}}{e_1\, e_2 \rightsquigarrow_\epsilon \mathsf{bind}_{v_1}^{v_2 \oplus v_3}(\epsilon, e_1', f, \mathsf{bind}_{v_2}^{v_3}(\epsilon, e_2', y, f\, y)) \mid v}$$

$$(\textsc{Val}) \quad \frac{e_1 \rightsquigarrow_\epsilon e_1' \mid v_1 \quad e_2 \rightsquigarrow_\epsilon e_2' \mid v_2}{\mathsf{val}\ x\ =\ e_1;\ e_2 \rightsquigarrow_\epsilon \mathsf{bind}_{v_1}^{v_2}(\epsilon, e_1', x, e_2') \mid v_1 \oplus v_2}$$

$$(\textsc{If}) \quad \frac{e_1 \rightsquigarrow_\epsilon e_1' \mid v_1 \quad e_2 \rightsquigarrow_\epsilon e_2' \mid v_2 \quad e_3 \rightsquigarrow_\epsilon e_3' \mid v_3 \quad v = v_1 \oplus v_2 \oplus v_3}{\mathsf{if}\ e_1\ \mathsf{then}\ e_2\ \mathsf{else}\ e_3 \rightsquigarrow_\epsilon \mathsf{bind}_{v_1}^{v_2 \oplus v_3}(\epsilon, e_1', b, \mathsf{if}\ b\ \mathsf{then}\ \mathsf{lift}_{v_2}^{v_2 \oplus v_3}(\epsilon, e_2')\ \mathsf{else}\ \mathsf{lift}_{v_3}^{v_2 \oplus v_3}(\epsilon, e_3')) \mid v}$$

Fig. 6. Basic translation rules. Any f and y are assumed fresh.

$\mathsf{tdict}\langle\rangle$ is a dependent type used to get the type of a polymorphic dictionary:

$$\begin{array}{ll} \mathsf{tdict}\langle\langle\rangle\rangle & = tdict\langle M_{uid}\rangle \\ \mathsf{tdict}\langle\langle l_1^\mu, \ldots, l_n^\mu\rangle\rangle & = tdict\langle M_{\langle l_1^\mu, \ldots, l_n^\mu\rangle}\rangle\ \text{where}\ n \geq 1 \\ \mathsf{tdict}\langle\mu\rangle & = \text{(evaluated at instantiation)} \end{array}$$

The type translation function $[\![\cdot]\!]$ reveals how the *to_eff* and *from_eff* are internally implemented. If we apply type translation to their signatures, we see that both become identity functions. The translation of *to_eff* is $[\![M_{eff}\langle\epsilon, \alpha\rangle \rightarrow \langle eff|\epsilon\rangle\, \alpha]\!]$ which is equivalent to $M_{eff}\langle\epsilon, \alpha\rangle \rightarrow \epsilon\, M_{eff}\langle\epsilon, \alpha\rangle$, i.e. *to_eff* is implemented simply as $\lambda x.\, x$. Similarly, *from_eff* is implemented as $\lambda f.\, f()$.

Monadic Abstractions. Figure 5 defines two syntactic abstractions $\mathsf{lift}_{v_s}^{v_t}(\epsilon, e)$ lifts the expression e from the source v_s to the target v_t computed effect. If the computed effects are the same e is returned. If effects are different $v_s \neq v_t$ and the source effect is empty, the lifting is performed via a call to the *unit* field of the dictionary of the target effect $dict_{v_t}$. Otherwise, the lifting is performed via the morphism $v_s \triangleright v_t$. Note that the monadic *unit* and the morphism operators are effect polymorphic thus *lift* is also parametric on an effect $\epsilon :: \mathbf{e}$ that is used to instantiate the effect variable of *unit* and $\triangleright$. Furthermore, *lift* fails if the morphism $v_s \triangleright v_t$ is not defined.

$\text{bind}^v_{v_x}(\epsilon, e_x, x, e)$ binds the expression e_x to the variable x that appears in e. The expression e_x (resp. e) has computed (*minimum*) effect v_x (resp. v) and ϵ is the combined (*maximum*) effect of the binding. If e_x does not have any computed effect binding is simply a val-binding, otherwise both expressions are lifted to the effect $v_x \oplus v$ and binding is performed via a call in the *bind* field of the dictionary of the target effect $dict_{v_x \oplus v}$.

As an optimization, if $v = \langle\rangle$ our system uses the monadic *map* instead of lifting ϵ to v_x and then using *bind*. As in *lift* the combined effect ϵ is used to instantiate the effect variable of the monadic operators. This optimization is similar to the ones used to avoid unnecessary "administrative" redexes, which customary CPS-transform algorithms go to great lengths to avoid [23].

3.3.1   Monadic Translation

Finally, we define the monadic translation relation $e \leadsto_\epsilon e' \mid v$ as shown in Fig. 6, where ϵ is inherited and v synthesized.

Values. Values have no effect, and compute $\langle\rangle$. Rules (CON) and (VAR) are simple: they only translate the type of the expression and leave the expression otherwise unchanged. Rule (LAM) states that when translating $\lambda^\epsilon x : \tau.\, e$ the type τ of the parameter is also translated. Moreover, the effect ϵ dictates the maximum effect in the translation of the body e. Finally, we *lift* the body of the function from the computed minimum effect to ϵ.

Type Operations. Type abstraction and application preserve the computed effect of the wrapped expression e, and the Koka type system guarantees that type abstraction only happens over total expressions. In (TLAM-E) we abstract over an effect variable μ, thus we add an extra value argument, namely, the dictionary of the effect that instantiates μ, i.e. $dict_\mu$: $\text{tdict}\langle\overline{\mu}\rangle$. Symmetrically, the rule (TAPP-E) that translates application of the effect ϵ' applies the dictionary $dict_{\overline{\epsilon'}}$: $\text{tdict}\langle\overline{\epsilon'}\rangle$ of the effect ϵ'. Note that if the computed effect $\overline{\epsilon'}$ is a set of user-defined effects, say $\langle\text{amb}\rangle$, then the rule directly applies the appropriate dictionary $dict_{amb}$, i.e. the dictionary value that Koka created from the amb effect definition. If the computed effect $\overline{\epsilon'}$ is an effect variable μ, then the rule applies the appropriate variable dictionary $dict_\mu$, i.e. the variable abstracted by a rule (TLAM-E) lower in the translation tree. By the way we defined computed effects, the final case is the computed effect $\overline{\epsilon'}$ to be the empty effect $\langle\rangle$, and then the identity dictionary $dict_{uid}$ is applied. This is because in the computed effects world the total effect $\langle\rangle$ *is* the identity effect uid. In our rules we used the $\langle\rangle$ effect as it is more intuitive.

Application. The rule (APP) translates the application $e_1\, e_2$. The minimal computed effect of the application is the union of the computed effects of the function e_1 (that is v_1), the argument e_2 (that is v_2) and the computed effect of the body of the the function. The maximum effect of the function is v_3.

Finally, the rule (VAL) translates val-binding `val` $x = e_1; e_2$ by binding e_1 to x in e_2. Similarly, the rule (IF) translates if e_1 then e_2 else e_3 by first binding e_1 to a fresh variable y, since e_1 may have user-defined effects and then lifting both branches to the computed effect v that is the union of the computed effects of the guard v_1 and the two branches v_2 and v_3.

3.4 Soundness

From previous work on type inference for Koka [15] we have that the resulting explicitly typed Koka is well-typed, i.e.

Lemma 1. (*Explicit Koka is well-typed*) If $\Gamma \vdash k : \sigma \,|\, \epsilon \rightsquigarrow e$ then $\vdash e : \sigma \,|\, \epsilon$.

Here, the relation $\Gamma \vdash k : \sigma \,|\, \epsilon \rightsquigarrow e$ is the type inference relation defined in [15] where the source term k gets type σ with effect ϵ and a corresponding explicitly typed term e. In this paper we show that our translation preserves types according to the $\llbracket \cdot \rrbracket$ type translation. The proof can be found in [28]

Theorem 1. (*Type Preservation*) If $\vdash e : \sigma$ and $e \rightsquigarrow_\epsilon e' \,|\, \langle\rangle$, then $\vdash f : \llbracket \sigma \rrbracket$.

4 Related Work

Many *effect typing* disciplines have been proposed that study how to delimit the scope of effects. Early work is by Gifford and Lucassen [9,16] which was later extended by Talpin [27] and others [18,26]. These systems are closely related since they describe polymorphic effect systems and use type constraints to give principal types. The system described by Nielson et al. [18] also requires the effects to form a complete lattice with meets and joins. Wadler and Thiemann [30] show the close connection between monads [17,29] and the effect typing disciplines.

Java contains a simple effect system where each method is labeled with the exceptions it might raise [11]. A system for finding uncaught exceptions was developed for ML by Pessaux et al. [19]. A more powerful system for tracking effects was developed by Benton [3] who also studies the semantics of such effect systems [4]. Recent work on effects in Scala [24] shows how restricted polymorphic effect types can be used to track effects for many programs in practice.

Our current work relies heavily on a *type directed* monadic translation. This was also described in the context of ML by Swamy et al. [25], where we also showed how to combine multiple monads using monad morphisms. However, Koka uses row-polymorphism to do the typing, while [25] uses subtyping. A problem with subtyping is that it leads to too complicated types.

A similar approach to [25] is used by Rompf et al. [23] to implement first-class delimited continuations in Scala which is essentially done by giving a monadic translation. Similar to our approach, this is also a *selective* transformation; i.e. only functions that need it get the monadic translation. Both of the previous works are a *typed* approach where the monad is apparent in the type. Early work by Filinski [6,7] showed how one can embed any monad in any strict language that has mutable state in combination with first-class continuations (i.e. *callcc*). This work is untyped in the sense that the monad or effect is not apparent in the type. In a later work Filinski [8] proposes a typed calculus where monads are used to give semantics to effects. This work does not include effect inference or polymorphism though.

Algebraic effect handlers described by Plotkin et al. [20] are not based on monads, but on an algebraic interpretation of effects. Even though monads are more general, algebraic effects compose more easily. Bauer and Pretnar describe a practical programming model with algebraic effects [2], and a type checking and inference system [1, 21]. Even though this approach is quite different than the monadic approach that we take, the end result is quite similar. In particular, the idea of handlers to *discharge* effects, appears in our work in the form of the *from* primitives induced by an *effect* declaration.

References

1. Bauer, A., Pretnar, M.: An effect system for algebraic effects and handlers. Logical Methods Comput. Sci. **10**(4), 1–29 (2014)
2. Bauer, A., Pretnar, M.: Programming with algebraic effects and handlers. J. Log. Algebr. Methods Program. **84**(1), 108–123 (2015). doi:10.1016/j.jlamp.2014.02.001
3. Benton, N., Buchlovsky, P.: Semantics of an effect analysis for exceptions. In: TLDI (2007). doi:10.1145/1190315.1190320
4. Benton, N., Kennedy, A., Beringer, L., Hofmann, M.: Relational semantics for effect-based program transformations with dynamic allocation. In: PPDP (2007). doi:10.1145/1273920.1273932
5. Elliott, C., Hudak, P.: Functional reactive animation. In: ICFP (1997)
6. Filinski, A.: Representing monads. In: POPL (1994)
7. Filinski, A.: Controlling effects. Technical report (1996)
8. Filinski, A.: Monads in action. ACM Sigplan Not. **45**, 483–494 (2010)
9. Gifford, D.K., Lucassen, J.M.: Integrating functional and imperative programming. In: LFP (1986). doi:10.1145/319838.319848
10. Girard, J.-Y.: The system F of variable types, fifteen years later. TCS **45**, 159–192 (1986)
11. Gosling, J., Joy, B., Steele, G.: The java language specification (1996)
12. Hicks, M., Bierman, G., Guts, N., Leijen, D., Swamy, N.: Polymonadic programming. In: MSFP (2014)
13. Kiselyov, O., Shan, C.: Embedded probabilistic programming. In: Taha, W.M. (ed.) DSL 2009. LNCS, vol. 5658, pp. 360–384. Springer, Heidelberg (2009). doi:10.1007/978-3-642-03034-5_17
14. Leijen, D.: Koka: programming with row-polymorphic effect types. Technical report MSR-TR-2013-79, Microsoft Research (2013)
15. Leijen, D.: Koka: programming with row polymorphic effect types. In: MSFP (2014). doi:10.4204/EPTCS.153.8
16. Lucassen, J.M., Gifford, D.K.: Polymorphic effect systems. In: POPL (1988)
17. Moggi, E.: Notions of computation and monads. Inf. Comput. **93**, 55–92 (1991)
18. Nielson, H.R., Nielson, F., Amtoft, T.: Polymorphic subtyping for effect analysis, the static semantics. In: LOMAPS (1997)
19. Pessaux, F., Leroy, X.: Type-based analysis of uncaught exceptions. In POPL (1999). doi:10.1145/292540.292565
20. Plotkin, G.D., Matija, P., Handling algebraic effects. **9** (2013). doi:10.2168/LMCS-9(4:23)2013

21. Pretnar, M.: Inferring algebraic effects. Logical Methods Comput. Sci. **10**(3) (2014). doi:10.2168/LMCS-10(3:21)2014
22. Reynolds, J.C.: Towards a theory of type structure. In: Programming Symposium (1974)
23. Rompf, T., Maier, I., Odersky, M.: Implementing first-class polymorphic delimited continuations by a type-directed selective cps-transform. In: ICFP (2009)
24. Rytz, L., Odersky, M., Haller, P.: Lightweight polymorphic effects. In: Noble, J. (ed.) ECOOP 2012. LNCS, vol. 7313, pp. 258–282. Springer, Heidelberg (2012). doi:10.1007/978-3-642-31057-7_13
25. Swamy, N., Guts, N., Leijen, D., Hicks, M.: Lightweight monadic programming in ML. In: ICFP (2011). doi:10.1145/2034773.2034778
26. Talpin, J.-P., Jouvelot, P.: The type and effect discipline. Inf. Comput. (1994). doi:10.1006/inco.1994.1046
27. Talpin, J.P.: Theoretical and practical aspects of type and effect inference. Ph.D. thesis, Ecole des Mines de Paris and University Paris VI, Paris, France (1993)
28. Vazou, N., Leijen, D.: From monads to effects and back - technical report. Technical report, July 2015. http://goto.ucsd.edu/~nvazou/padl16/techrep.pdf
29. Wadler, P.: The essence of functional programming. In: POPL (1992)
30. Wadler, P., Thiemann, P.: The marriage of effects and monads. In: TOLC (2003). doi:10.1145/601775.601776

Author Index

Antoy, Sergio   65

Barták, Roman   3

Carette, Jacques   135

Dasseville, Ingmar   13
Denecker, Marc   13
Dovier, Agostino   30

Formisano, Andrea   30

Gill, Andy   153
Grebe, Mark   153

Hage, Jurriaan   83
Hanus, Michael   65

Janssens, Gerda   13
Jelínek, Jan   3

Kjellerstrand, Håkan   48

Leijen, Daan   169

Pieter, Van Hertum   13
Pontelli, Enrico   30

Serrano, Alejandro   83
Shan, Chung-chieh   135

Tarau, Paul   99, 117

Vazou, Niki   169
Vella, Flavio   30

Zhou, Neng-Fa   48

Printed in the United States
By Bookmasters